SERVICE CONTRACTING

A LOCAL GOVERNMENT GUIDE

Second Edition

SERVICE CONTRACTING

A LOCAL GOVERNMENT GUIDE

Second Edition

Edited by Kelly LeRoux

Leaders at the Core of Better Communities

ICMA is the premier local government leadership and management organization. Its mission is to create excellence in local governance by developing and advocating professional management of local government worldwide. ICMA provides member support; publications, data, and information; peer and results-oriented assistance; and training and professional development to more than 8,200 city, town, and county experts and other individuals throughout the world.

icma.org/press

Library of Congress Cataloging-in-Publication Data

Service contracting : a local government guide / edited by Kelly LeRoux. — 2nd ed.
    p. cm.
  Rev. ed. of: Service contracting / Donald F. Harney. c1992.
  Includes bibliographical references and indexes.
  ISBN-13: 978-0-87326-718-2 (alk. paper)
  1. Municipal services—Contracting out—United States. 2. County services—Contracting out—United States. I. LeRoux, Kelly. II. Harney, Donald F., 1929- Service contracting.
  HD4605.S47 2007
  352.5'38214—dc22

                                        2007023869

Design: Charles Mountain

Printed in the United States of America
2014 2013 2012 2011 2010 2009 2008 2007 5 4 3 2 1

About the editor

K elly LeRoux is an assistant professor in the Department of Public Administration at the University of Kansas. She holds PhD, MPA, and MSW degrees from Wayne State University. Prior to beginning an academic career, she worked as an administrator for a nonprofit behavioral health organization based in the Detroit metropolitan area. Professor LeRoux conducts research in the areas of alternative service delivery, government-nonprofit relations, and metropolitan governance. Her recent work has appeared in the *Urban Affairs Review*, the *American Review of Public Administration*, *Public Works Management and Policy*, and the *International Journal of Organizational Theory and Behavior*.

Contents

Sidebars

Foreword

Even before a reader opens the cover of this book, there are two excellent reasons to take time with this new version of ICMA's *Service Contracting*. First, local governments are more engaged than ever before in contracting and service contracting has grown relative to standard purchases of goods. In fact, it is not too much to say that without a significant level of service contracting, many (if not most) local governments could not carry out their full range of responsibilities. Second, ICMA has long provided excellent tools for managers, but it has been a long time since the previous version of the *Service Contracting* volume was issued and much has changed in the field. In short, we need updated tools to manage these essential activities.

In keeping with the tradition and purposes of ICMA's publications, this book is a practical resource that provides tools for dealing with the well-known and long-standing difficulties of service contracting, but it also engages the changing opportunities and challenges in the field. For example, one of the themes that flows through the book is the increasing need to make wider use of more flexible contracting processes such as negotiated approaches to contracting and hybrid procedures. But the book also confronts the challenges that arise in using those tools and the types of constraints that may bar their application. Similarly, it recognizes the increasing trend toward contracting with a wider array of service providers, including nonprofit organizations and other local jurisdictions and the use of public/private competition. Along the way, Professor LeRoux provides a rich mixture of examples, model forms and procedures, and lists of warnings from lessons learned by others. She does so in a crisp and easily accessible format.

Finding the optimal combination of accountability and flexibility in the quest for the best deal for the public is at the heart of contemporary service contract work, and this volume provides a useful blend of traditional and contemporary suggestions for how to achieve that mix. It is a resource that local government managers will want to keep beside other important and frequently used resources on their bookshelves.

Phillip J. Cooper
Mark O. Hatfield School of Government
Portland State University

Preface

Local governments provide a wider array of public services today than at any other point in history. What is most remarkable is that they manage to do so in a climate of both limited resources and higher expectations from citizens. In the fifteen years that have elapsed since the first edition of *Service Contracting* was published, local governments have been inundated with pressures to reinvent, reengineer, and otherwise transform themselves into more efficient and effective providers of public services. Many local governments have turned to service contracting as a means to that end and have found it to be a useful tool for achieving cost savings and, in some instances, improving service quality. Local government managers who rely on service contracts in some form or another or are considering the possibility of service contracting should find this volume both timely and relevant.

While the ethics and basic principles of service contracting have not changed since the first edition of this book was published in 1992, many of the practices have been transformed by electronic and telecommunications technology. This new edition of *Service Contracting* has been updated to reflect these technological developments. It also addresses several recent developments in local government contracting including special considerations for contracting with the nonprofit sector, contracting through networks, new methods for monitoring contractor performance, and injecting competition into public service delivery through public-private competition.

The goal of this second edition remains the same as the first: to equip local governments, regardless of size, with the basic tools and guidance required for planning, developing, and administering an efficient and effective service contracting program. In taking readers through every phase of service contracting from start to finish, this volume remains the most comprehensive guide available to service contracting in local government. Chapters 1 and 2 lay the foundation for the rest of the book by describing the service contracting environment and providing practical advice on how to establish a structure for successful contract management. Chapters 3 and 4 detail the processes of planning the bid document and preparing the scope of work. Chapters 5 and 6 provide step-by-step instructions for incorporating legal logistics into the bid document and setting up a balanced and impartial bid evaluation committee. Chapters 7 and 8 describe how to develop the contract once an award is made and how to establish protocols for performance monitoring. Chapters 9 and 10 offer guidance on dealing with performance problems and managing transitions in service provision such as changing from one private contractor to another and bringing previously privatized services back in house.

The first edition of this book was written by Donald F. Harney, purchasing agent for Arlington County, Virginia, with editorial help from Sandra Chizinsky. Their work provided the bedrock, the structure, and much of the content for the current book.

Several people deserve thanks for their efforts and assistance in the completion of this project. A number of seasoned practitioners lent their technical expertise in the form of specific contributions to this book. William Hatley, attorney and former director of community planning and development, Lincoln Park, Michigan, provided the discussion of subcontracting federal grant funds in Chapter 1. Kim S. Eagle, evaluation manager, Charlotte, North Carolina, shared her detailed knowledge of public-private competition processes in Chapter 10. She provides a practical step-by-step guide for the growing number of local governments experimenting with this approach. James Davis, executive director of Blueprint 2000 and Beyond (an intergovernmental agency of Tallahassee and Leon County, Florida), contributed information on contracting for construction and major infrastructure projects in Chapter 3 and in each of the appendices. Jerry Schulz, consultant and former manager of information systems for Waukesha County, Wisconsin, provided information in the same places, speaking to the matter of contracting for computer and information technology services.

The content of this book was also improved through the recommendations of several professors and industry and local government practitioners. Deborah Auger, associate professor, University of Delaware; Dennis Daley, professor, North Carolina State University; Terry Raney, senior vice president, CACI International, Inc., and instructor, Florida Institute of Technology; and Ruth Shane, professor (retired), Florida State University, provided valuable suggestions for revising the first edition. John Bennett, city manager, Rome, Georgia; John Flint, city manager, Weston, Florida; John McDonough, city manager, Sandy Springs, Georgia; John Mahin, purchasing manager, Johnson County, Kansas; Cynthia Seelhammer, deputy city manager, Phoenix, Arizona; and Richard Warren, purchasing director, Arlington County, Virginia, all devoted time to reviewing various parts of the manuscript and deserve thanks for their feedback and practical insights. Professor Jonas Prager of New York University reviewed the manuscript in its entirety and provided many helpful comments and suggestions. Kate Babbitt provided careful copyediting and helped improve the readability of the book by clarifying wording and concepts in a number of places. Finally, Christine Ulrich, ICMA Press editorial director, was instrumental in every phase of this project, from helping plan changes for the revised edition, securing participation of the reviewers and contributors, and reviewing each draft to keeping everyone on track with deadlines.

We hope this book will serve as a useful reference for local government practitioners engaged in the service contracting process and those who are considering service contracting as an alternative to public service delivery. Moreover, those teaching courses in privatization, public procurement, and contract management should find this volume the perfect vehicle for imparting practical know-how on service contracting processes. Last, students of public management and administration who are planning to enter careers in local government should find this guide indispensable.

Kelly LeRoux
Department of Public Administration
University of Kansas

1

Management Issues in Service Contracting

Faced with the reality of limited resources and increasing citizen expectations, many local governments have turned to service contracting as a way of saving money or at least avoiding cost increases. Although service contracting is often proposed as a "quick-fix" remedy for budget problems, public officials must be cautioned that service contracts are not created overnight; some contracts take several months to a year or more from start to implementation. A service contracting program therefore requires planning, careful consideration of available options, and attention to the local government environment.

Local governments today have more alternative service delivery options than ever before. Today's contracting environment presents many opportunities for service contracting. As a result, public managers face a number of choices. With adequate planning and careful review of contracting options, each local government can create a service contracting program that reflects the specific needs of the community and its budget.

Before embarking on a contracting program, the local government should ask the following questions:

- What do we hope to accomplish through service contracting?
- Is cost savings the only objective, or are there other desired outcomes?
- If other goals are involved, can contracting goals be ranked?
- Do local procurement ordinances permit consideration criteria other than cost savings in the provider selection process?
- Might a particular type of organization (e.g., public, for-profit, or nonprofit) be best suited to fulfilling the contracting goals of a service that is to be contracted out?
- What steps can the local government take to ensure the best fit between service goals and contractor performance?

The local government professional may be called upon to address and resolve the issues discussed in this chapter even before the invitation to bid is made. This chapter addresses the issues of involving management in the contracting process;

surveying the legal, social, and political environment; determining whether there will be adequate competition among contractors; working with alternative contract partners, including nonprofits and other governments; assessing the viability of managed competition and partial contracting models, such as in-house bidding, phasing in, or pilot projects; planning for a fallback position; and understanding the ethical issues in service contracting. Though not all these issues will arise in every community, the local government manager must be aware of how they can affect a service contracting program.

Involving management

Management involvement will vary from one local government to another, depending on the size of the jurisdiction and the number and complexity of contracts. In medium to large local governments that have personnel dedicated to contract management, the manager's involvement may be required only at certain stages. In

---

What is privatization?

Purists insist that privatization refers only to the outright sale of a government-owned asset to the private sector, releasing the public sector from any responsibility for delivering the service. Examples include New York City's sale of the city-owned WNYC-TV television station to ITT Communications and Dow Jones in 1996 and the sale of the United Nations Plaza Hotel to an overseas hotel chain the following year.

However, financing of large public sector infrastructure projects has resulted in many more-complex relationships between the public and private sectors. Large infrastructure projects such as major road and bridge projects that were once exclusively the domain of government are now developed in partnership with private firms. The term "privatization" has expanded to include a range of alternative methods for providing public services, such as user fees, voucher systems, franchises, subsidies, service contracting, and reliance on volunteers. Given the range of forms privatization can take, these methods may also be generally referred to as public-private partnerships.

Sale of public enterprises   The outright sale of a public enterprise by a local government is rare. Local governments tend to enter into public-private partnerships with the private sector and seldom relinquish complete control of a service. Examples of public-private partnerships include publicly funded wastewater treatment plants or waste-to-energy installations that are constructed, operated, managed, and staffed by a private corporation;

long-term leases of public land to developers for hotels, office buildings, and retail space in exchange for the construction and leaseback of recreation and other public facilities on the site; private operation of publicly built prisons; and private design, construction, and operation of toll roads on public lands.

User fees   User fees are based on the premise that those who benefit directly from a service should pay for it. For example, the fees charged for the use of a golf course can fund all or part of the maintenance and operation of the facility. The trickle-down effect of impact fees a local government assesses often results in substantial user fees to those benefiting from housing or commercial development. Impact fees imposed on developers and other private users have financed all or part of capital improvements such as streets, water mains, sewer lines, airports, and highways. Impact fees are usually imposed when development projects require expansion of or adversely affect the existing infrastructure. User fees also provide funding for additional police patrol service, recreation facilities, and public transportation.

Voucher systems   As an alternative to providing the service directly, local governments can issue cash vouchers that may be presented in the open market for full or partial payment for services delivered by nonprofit or for-profit contractors. Vouchers permit citizens to purchase their publicly funded service from the provider of their choice. Examples include rent vouchers, food stamps, school choice vouchers,

smaller local governments and those that cannot afford staff to manage contracts, the manager may have to be extensively involved in all phases of the program. In any case, the manager must have a general understanding of the need for planning and the planning process in order to properly supervise the contracting program.

In large and mid-size local governments that contract for a number of goods and services, the manager's involvement is selective, tracking only those contracts that are the result of the initiative of a governing body, those with a considerable impact on citizens, or those that affect local government operations as a whole. Planning for individual service contracts does not usually require the involvement of the manager, and he or she is kept up to date on contract planning through reports or briefings by staff. Bidding is the phase of contracting in which the local government manager is most likely to be involved. During the administration of the contract, the manager should receive periodic reports about contracts that are particularly important, contracts that have potential problems, or contracts that may

daycare vouchers, and direct care services for persons with disabilities.

Franchises   Local governments establish franchises with private contractors who provide services to citizens at a set or regulated price. The citizens pay the contractor directly for the service, and the contractor is typically the only authorized deliverer of the service. Franchises include such varied services as cable television and Internet, waste collection, waste-to-energy plants, and ambulance services. If multiple franchises are granted for a given service, each franchisee pays the local government for the franchise privilege.

Subsidies   Subsidies are similar to vouchers in that all or part of the cost of a service provided by the private sector is funded by government grants. Subsidies commonly fund housing, health care, chore services for the elderly and disabled, transportation, and organizations that provide job training and legal aid.

Service contracting   Service contracting is the most common method of alternative service delivery used by local governments; it is also the most inclusive. A single service contract may incorporate one or more of the other approaches to privatization. For example, a service contract may provide for a contractor, or consortium, to perform any or all of the following for a major project: design, financing, construction, operation, and maintenance functions. A toll bridge, for example, could be designed, financed, constructed, operated, and maintained by

a contractor. The contractor in return receives the toll revenues or a portion of the toll revenues for a specified period of time. At the conclusion of the period, the bridge reverts back to public ownership. The time period of the contract is based on the contractor's recovery of his investment. As another example, a vehicle towing contract may be structured as a franchise. It may also include a provision for user fees in which vehicle owners are charged when the government disposes of vehicles abandoned on public streets in violation of ordinances. Contracts may be designed to purchase a single service or multiple services. Contractors can include private for-profit firms, nonprofit organizations, and other local governments.

Volunteers   Local governments can establish or strengthen volunteer programs to obtain assistance in providing public services. Volunteers can "adopt" and maintain landscaped traffic islands or median strips near their homes, provide support services to a public library, assist in health and social service programs, serve as sports coaches or playground personnel, staff summer camps, serve as professional advisors for local government programs, assist in cable television broadcasts, and provide assistance to elderly and disabled citizens. Jeffrey Brudney offers insight into the use of volunteers in local government in "The Effective Use of Volunteers: Best Practices for the Public Sector," *Law and Contemporary Problems* 62, no. 4 (1999): 219-255.

require corrective action. Managers should be notified in advance of any changes to contracts.

The service contracting environment

The service contracting environment is shaped and constrained by legal, political, and social factors. Different groups in the local landscape may weigh in on contracting matters with different opinions. For example, elected officials, department and middle managers, local government employees, labor organizations, and citizens view contracting from different perspectives. The local government professional must take this range of perspectives into account when implementing a service contracting program. A manager may enhance the likelihood that a contracting program will be successful by tuning into the legal environment as well as the attitudes and concerns of interested groups.

The legal environment

Legal restrictions imposed by city procurement ordinances can greatly constrain contracting options. The roots of many problems that develop in service contracting programs lie in the narrow range of options in public purchasing ordinances. Local governments relying on purchasing ordinances and regulations adopted many years ago may be working with antiquated documents that are too rigid to satisfy the requirements of service contracting today.

Before undertaking a service contracting program, review existing regulations. When possible, amend these regulations to include procedures that allow negotiation in the purchase of services.

Liability is another facet of the legal environment with which managers must contend. Legal action is not uncommon in service contracting, and the local government manager must be prepared to deal with it. The local government contracting staff and anyone involved in the procurement process must be on the alert for any act that conflicts with local or state statutes.

Personal liability of public employees varies from state to state, from locality to locality, and from case to case. This chapter does not address all the legal aspects of personal or governmental liability. Questions of the extent of liability of individuals involved in the contracting process, the governing body, the local government manager, or the local government should always be directed to the jurisdiction's legal department.

The political environment

Elected officials   Elected officials are well aware that although the responsibility for delivery of service that is contracted out shifts to the contractor, fiscal and political accountability for the service remains with the governing body and the local government manager. It is the responsibility of the local government manager to keep elected officials informed of the status of the service contracting program. Although it is important to report successes, it is equally important to report shortcomings: Elected officials may need to be reminded that service contracting is not a cure-all for past service problems, especially if an emergency appropriation is needed to avert or correct a problem.

Local government employees and public sector labor unions   It is not uncommon for service contracting plans to generate resentment within the local government work force. Even department or middle managers who support service contracting can damage the program's chances for success through inaction or lack of knowledge of service contracting procedures. Other managers may actively oppose service contracting if they think that it will diminish their power or alter the structure of a department that has been carefully built over the years.

This book does not address all the courses of action available when management and labor are on opposite sides of service contracting decisions. Because the issues service contracting raises are highly individual and depend on factors such as labor agreements and the policies of the governing body, there are few simple answers or broadly applicable guidelines. The best approach is the one that works in the individual local government. A good general guideline, however, is to keep local government employees and labor organizations informed of the status of the project and encourage their input. The sidebar "Overcoming barriers" highlights an example of contracting for fire services in which challenges from labor unions were successfully resolved.

Many local governments include a no-layoff policy in their service contracting plans. When a service contract is expected to have an impact on the work force, delaying the start of a contract for six months or a year can provide the time needed to train employees in other skills. While it lengthens the planning process, the additional time also allows attrition to reduce the number of in-house employees that are adversely affected when the contract begins.

Some local governments require the new contractor to hire displaced public employees and retain them for a minimum period. This may not always be feasible. Training public employees to meet the job requirements of their private sector counterparts may result in higher costs for the contract than for in-house service, and forcing a contractor to accept all employees can reduce the number of interested bidders. A better approach may be to require that the contractor give preference to qualified public employees when staffing the contract service. Through a competitive sourcing approach, a bid from an employee or labor organization could keep the service in house if the existing local government is able to successfully compete for the contract award. Chapter 10 discusses public-private competition in greater detail.

Overcoming barriers: Intergovernmental fire services in Plymouth, Michigan

The intergovernmental fire services agreement between the city of Plymouth and the charter township of Plymouth was initiated to save money, improve service to both communities, and reduce service duplication by consolidating fire departments. When the plan was first proposed, it met intense opposition from public sector labor units representing fire personnel from both departments. By planning carefully, introducing a "no-layoff" policy that allowed enough time for attrition, and agreeing to retain the best features of both units' contracts, the city and township managers negotiated a win-win outcome for both bargaining units.

While this arrangement has been largely successful since it began in 1994, the cost-sharing formula and the control of the fire department operations have been sources of contention between the two communities at times. Rather than abandon the effort, the two communities have modified their agreement to reflect changing needs. Over time, the intergovernmental consolidation has evolved into a purchase-of-services agreement between the city and township, and both communities continue to enjoy the benefits of cost savings.

Source: Southeastern Michigan Council of Governments, Joint Public Services Database, 2006.

The social environment

Citizens usually adopt a wait-and-see attitude toward service contracting. Whether the service deliverer wears a government or corporate uniform is secondary to the satisfactory delivery of the service at a reasonable price. In general, the services that generate the most citizen involvement are controversial or highly visible services such as those that provide direct services to residences (e.g., collection of waste and recyclable materials), services for maintaining or managing recreation facilities (e.g., golf courses, swimming pools), or services that fulfill a social need (e.g., services for the elderly, the homeless, or persons with disabilities). Expect extensive interaction with concerned citizen groups when planning for contracts in these areas. Whenever a planned contract may conflict with citizens' expectations, candid discussion and information-sharing can help reduce opposition.

The procurement process

Traditional **competitive sealed bidding**, a method originally designed for the purchase of goods, requires an award to the lowest responsive and responsible bidder.

Two bidding methods: Competitive negotiation and competitive sealed bidding

Competitive negotiation

While local governments should always strive to get the best value for their money, there may be times when the lowest bid is not necessarily the best deal for the public. In some cases, negotiation for the purchase of services may be in the local government's best interest. Negotiation is appropriate when the service specifications are imprecise or permit alternative delivery methods or when the qualifications of a contractor are more critical to the success of the program than the price. Competitive negotiation is also known as competitive sealed proposals.

The basic steps in competitive negotiation are as follows:

Prepare and issue a request for Proposals (RFP)   The local government prepares and solicits proposals through a request for proposals.

Provide public notice   The local government provides adequate public notice of the RFP a reasonable period of time before the date proposals will be opened.

Receive the proposals   Upon a set date, the local government receives and opens all the proposals, which avoids disclosing the contents of any one proposal to competing offerors during the process of negotiation. A register of proposals is prepared for public inspection after the contract award.

Clarify evaluation factors   The RFP states the relative importance of price and other factors and subfactors, if any, that are to be considered in the bid selection process.

Meet with responsible offerors and discuss revisions to proposals   As established in the RFP, discussions may be conducted with responsible offerors that submit proposals that are determined to be reasonably likely to be selected for award. Discussions are for the purpose of clarification and to assure full understanding of and responsiveness to the solicitation requirements. Offerors must be given fair and equal treatment with respect to opportunity for discussion and revision of proposals. Revisions may be permitted after submission and prior to award for the purpose of obtaining best and final offers. During these discussions there must be no disclosure of any information about proposals submitted by competing offerors.

Award the contract   The contract is awarded to the responsible offeror whose proposal conforms to the solicitation and is determined to be the most advantageous for the local government, taking into consideration price as well as the evaluation factors set forth in the RFP. No other factors or criteria may be used in the evaluation and contract award process.

(continued on page 7)

Competitive sealed bidding is the method used most often for purchasing services when the service can be described completely and accurately and the qualifications of the respondents can be easily identified. However, many areas of service contracting cannot be described completely and accurately in a **request for proposals (RFP)**, and there are times when the qualifications of the contractor may be more important than a price difference of a few dollars. Following competitive sealed bidding procedures for complex contracts or for new areas of service often results in a situation in which a much more qualified bidder whose bid is well within the projected budget for the service is rejected in favor of a marginally qualified but less expensive contractor whose bid may be only a few dollars lower.

To allow staff to give contractor qualifications more weight than the cost of the contract, many local governments expand or replace their purchasing regulations with provisions of the American Bar Association (ABA) Model Procurement Code[1] that permit an element of negotiation. Competitive sealed proposals are the code's primary example of negotiation in public contracting. The term is synonymous with the more commonly used term **competitive negotiation**. Under competitive negotiation procedures, the terms of the service contract, the price for the service,

---

(continued from page 6)

Debrief bidders   The local government may choose to furnish bidders with information about the selection decision and the basis for the contract award. Providing unsuccessful bidders with feedback may help to improve the quality of proposals in the future and helps to sustain the pool of competitive bidders.

Competitive sealed bidding

Competitive sealed bidding does not involve negotiation with bidders after the receipt and opening of bids. Contract awards are based strictly on price and responsiveness to the criteria set forth in the invitation for bids. Competitive sealed bidding remains the most appropriate procurement method when service delivery specifications are precise, there are qualified competitors, and quality control can be enforced adequately by the local government.

The basic steps in competitive sealed bidding are as follows:

Prepare and issue an invitation to bid   The local government issues an invitation to bid that includes a description of the service being purchased and all contractual terms and conditions applicable to the procurement of the service.

Provide public notice   The local government provides adequate public notice of the invitation for bids a reasonable period of time in advance of the date the bid will be opened.

Open the bids   The local government opens the bids publicly in the presence of one or more witnesses at the specific time and place designated in the invitation for bids. The amount of each bid, other relevant information that may be specified by state or local regulation, and the name of each bidder is recorded. The record and each bid should be open to public inspection.

Accept and evaluate the bids   Bids are unconditionally accepted without alteration or correction. Bids are evaluated based on the requirements established in the invitation to bid, which may include criteria to determine acceptability such as inspection, testing, quality, workmanship, delivery, and suitability for a particular purpose. Those criteria that will affect the bid price and will be considered in the evaluation for award should be objectively measurable (e.g., discounts, transportation costs, total or life-cycle costs). The invitation to bid must set forth the specific evaluation criteria to be used. Bid evaluation may not use criteria that are not set forth in the invitation to bid.

Award the contract   The contract is awarded with reasonable promptness by written notice to the lowest responsible and responsive bidder whose bid meets the requirements and criteria set forth in the invitation for bids.

Source: Adapted from *The Model Procurement Code for State and Local Government* (Chicago, Ill.: American Bar Association, 2000), Article 3, Part B.

the method of service delivery, and the conditions of performance are all negotiable. A negotiated contract is awarded to the contractor who best meets the needs of the local government at a reasonable price, not necessarily at the lowest price. For example, competitive negotiation allows award to a contractor who may not propose the lowest price but who offers a depth of experience not available from the other bidders.

A second method of procurement in the ABA code that includes the use of limited negotiation is multistep sealed bidding. Under this procedure, a bidder submits two sealed envelopes to the local government as its bid response. Each envelope represents a step in the multistep bidding process. The first envelope contains the bidder's credentials and technical proposal for the service without a price; the second envelope contains the price. This envelope remains sealed. After identifying the bidders who meet the criteria for award, the local government representative opens their price envelopes. The price envelopes of those who were eliminated are returned unopened. The award then is made to the lowest qualified bidder. The competitive negotiation and competitive sealed bidding procedures are summarized in the "Two bidding methods" sidebar and are discussed more fully, along with the multistep bidding method, in Chapter 3.

Competitive negotiation and multistep bidding are useful contracting tools when the quality of service delivery is considered to be more important than the cost. Quality is critical to the success of the contract when it deals with an aspect of social services and other programs that provide services directly to individual clients. Other examples in which quality is critical include the provision of technical or support services such as Web design and maintenance or software development.

Determining the extent of competition

While the contract is still in the planning stage, the local government must determine whether there are contractors in the local marketplace who are qualified to provide the service. Without adequate competition, there is no point in proceeding with contract planning. Proposed service contracts may have to be shelved indefinitely if there are not enough qualified competitors to support a request for bids.

The information needed to determine the level of competition can be obtained from the lists of potential bidders compiled by the purchasing department (the bidder list), by the department currently responsible for providing the service, and by the purchasing departments of other area local governments. Other sources that may include more current listings of contractors include the Internet, telephone yellow pages, Chamber of Commerce business listings, local government business license listings, and rosters of trade or business organizations.

Firms identified as a result of the search are sent letters asking whether they are interested in responding to a request for bids for the service, a process generally known as a **request for information (RFI)**. The letter should describe the proposed scope of work in enough detail for contractors to decide whether the service is within their capability. Prices, even general estimates of cost, should not be requested at this time. A review of the responses will indicate whether there is reasonable competition.

As part of the solicitation for a service, the local government manager should determine whether other nearby governments have contracted for the service. If so, obtain from each government a copy of its bid document, contract, bidder list, bid responses received, and prices paid for the service. Never overlook the opportunity to benefit from the experience of other local governments, especially experience within the same geographical region. Talk to the contract administration staff, department heads, and anyone else who can provide insight into any problems that may have occurred. This information can prove invaluable in the decision to support or reject a proposed service contract.

Alternative contract partners

Public managers today have many options for the production and delivery of services to the public. Local governments should weigh the costs and benefits of the different service delivery options available before pursuing any one option. Reliance upon other governmental and nongovernmental entities has become increasingly common. The discussion below focuses mainly on contracting with nonprofits and the local government's role in subcontracting federal grant funds. However, interlocal contracting is another common option for service delivery, and local governments should not rule out the possibility of contracting directly with a neighboring local government to provide a service.

Indeed, local governments are uniquely suited to provide some services such as police, fire, and corrections. If the local government hopes to achieve cost savings by contracting for any of these types of services, another local government would be the natural sector of choice as a contracting partner. The "Public sector service contracting options" sidebar highlights some of the ways local governments partner through intergovernmental agreements as an alternative or supplementary approach to contracting with the private sector.

Contracting with nonprofits

Many local governments contract with nonprofit organizations. While the vast majority of contracts local governments make with nonprofits are with social service agencies, they may also contract with other types of nonprofits such as mediation centers, neighborhood associations, or research firms. Unlike contracting for landscaping or street paving, where cost savings is the main objective and contractor performance is relatively easy to measure, contracting for social services often involves multiple goals, ambiguity in defining the services to be delivered, and difficulty in specifying performance expectations. Competitive negotiation is therefore the best method of source selection when contracting for social services. It is important that the local government have an opportunity to clarify objectives and to seek clarification on bidders' intentions as described in proposals before making a final contract award.

In many ways, contracting with nonprofits is no different than contracting with for-profit firms. The methods described throughout this book for bidding and awarding contracts to for-profit businesses are the same methods to be used with nonprofit businesses. Indeed, nonprofits often find themselves in competition with for-profit social service providers. When issuing the request for proposals for a social service contract, local governments should make every effort to ensure that the RFP will be noticed by all qualified bidders, nonprofits and for-profits alike.

Although they may compete to provide the same service, nonprofits are different from for-profit businesses. For-profit businesses have a clear incentive to keep operating costs low in order to make a profit; that is why they are in business. In contrast, nonprofits cannot disburse any profits to staff or board members, so they are less motivated by financial gain. The motives of nonprofit boards and staff for wanting to do business with government may stem from a desire to extend their services to more people.

On the other hand, it is not uncommon for nonprofits to underestimate the cost of doing business, particularly nonprofits fueled by enthusiasm for expanding their

Public sector service contracting options

Service contracting is not limited to contracting with the private sector. Intergovernmental agreements can provide another component to any service contracting program. Different types of intergovernmental agreements include intergovernmental service contracts, joint service agreements, intragovernmental consolidation, and intergovernmental service transfers.

Intergovernmental service contract   Intergovernmental service contracts are a common alternative to direct service delivery. When a local government has excess service capacity in a given area, it can sell the excess to another local government that cannot provide the service itself. Intergovernmental service contracts are legally binding agreements between two or more local governments in which one pays the other for the delivery of a particular service. Generally speaking, written agreements are preferable. Unwritten agreements could create confusion later on if the person who negotiated them leaves the organization. Any written agreement to pay another unit of government for services is a contract, even if the document is simply a memorandum of understanding.

Joint service agreement   Joint service agreements are drawn up between two or more units of government for the joint planning, financing, and delivery of a service. Joint service agreements are slightly different from intergovernmental contracts in that each party in the agreement plays some role in the production of the service, whereas in intergovernmental contracting arrangements, one unit produces the service and the other purchases it. Joint service agreements specify the division of labor, mutual responsibilities, and liabilities of various parties when multiple jurisdictions collaborate. When using joint agreements, it is important to establish up front who will control the operation and how costs will be split. Establishing an oversight committee with elected officials from both parties should help to ensure that

costs are distributed equitably and that both parties maintain satisfaction with the agreement.

Local governments sometimes make agreements for the joint purchase of equipment and supplies that both governments need, as in the case of piggyback contracts. When a medium- to large-sized local government has an existing private sector service contract or is planning one that also meets the needs of one or more neighboring local governments, this common need presents an opportunity for other local governments to piggyback on the first local government's contract. Piggybacking sometimes refers to a cooperatively bid service contract in which local governments combine their requirements into a regional service contract, enabling them to benefit from the economies of scale that may be available because of the higher contract volume.

Intragovernmental consolidation   Some local governments can save money by consolidating services currently decentralized within the local government instead of contracting a service to the private sector. For example, separate custodial service and building maintenance operations often exist independently within several departments. Vehicle and equipment maintenance for police, sheriff, public works, and parks might be splintered among the various departments. Whenever the same service is delivered to different departments, it should be considered a candidate for consolidation into a single centralized service organization that can provide the service to all departments. Intragovernmental consolidation yields savings by establishing a single management and supervisory organization for a given service and by making more efficient use of personnel.

Intergovernmental service transfer   Intergovernmental service transfers occur when total responsibility for the provision of a service is transferred from one governmental unit to another. Such transfers may be permanent or temporary.

Source: Adapted from Advisory Commission on Intergovernmental Relations, *Intergovernmental Service Arrangements for Delivering Local Public Services* (Washington, D.C.: Government Printing Office, 1985).

mission and bidding on a government contract for the first time. Nonprofits with no prior government experience are particularly susceptible to cost overruns. Generally speaking, be prepared for a steep learning curve when contracting with nonprofits that are first-time government providers. In regions where there are few social service suppliers to choose from, the local government should anticipate investing some time working with the nonprofit contractor to answer questions and help solve problems until the organization has a good handle on what it takes to meet the local government's expectations.

Even in more populated areas, competition for some types of social services may be limited. Only a small percentage of nonprofit social service agencies are equipped to fully comply with regulatory requirements. Many public mental health services, for example, are funded by the federal Medicaid program through funds contracted out to nonprofits by county governments. Providers are often required to submit claims electronically along with data on performance indicators. In the process, they must ensure the security of information systems in order to comply with federal Health Insurance Portability and Accountability Act (HIPAA) regulations to protect client privacy. Compliance with these regulations and requirements demands large investment costs and is beyond the capacity of most nonprofits. This makes it difficult for new providers to enter the market, which can limit competition. In these instances, local governments may find it to be in their best interest, as well as those of service recipients, to issue contracts for longer periods of time. Issuing a contract for multiple years with an option for renewal provides stability for service recipients and for both parties to the contract when there is no competitive market for the service.

Subcontracting federal grant funds

Many communities today receive funding through federal grant programs that finance a wide range of local services, including work force development, health care for the indigent, emergency management planning, public assistance, housing, and community development. One of the most visible examples is the Community Development Block Grant (CDBG). These grants are issued to state, county, and municipal government grantees by the federal Department of Housing and Urban Development (HUD) in order to provide affordable housing, economic development, social services, and public works at the local level.

This program and many other federal grants are flexible; they allow the local government grantee to provide the services itself or to contract with another entity to provide the services. If the local government opts to contract with a private provider (often a nonprofit) to provide the services, the contractor is known as a subrecipient of the grantee. Subrecipients have traditionally accounted for the bulk of public service spending and about 50 percent of the economic development activities undertaken using CDBG funds.

If the local government opts to use a subrecipient, it should be aware of the federal regulations and requirements that accompany federal funding. While the local government can contract out for the actual provision of services, it cannot contract away the ultimate responsibility for ensuring that services are provided to those for whom the service is intended. Moreover, the local government cannot delegate responsibility for ensuring that the money is properly expended and that both the local government and its subrecipient(s) are in compliance with applicable regulations.

After determining that a subrecipient will be used and that it has the capacity to do the job, the manager drafts and executes a subrecipient agreement. HUD requires signed contracts between the parties, and a well-drafted agreement is important to a successful relationship.[2] The agreement should spell out the amount of funding being provided, the types of services and amounts being delivered, and the federal regulations applicable to the arrangement. The agreement should be approved by the legal department, and it is always a good idea to run it by the federal granting agency (HUD, in the case of CDBG funds) for its review and input. The Web sites of federal agencies are good sources of information about subrecipient agreements and the ongoing monitoring responsibilities of the grantee.[3]

The local government must monitor the subrecipients' activities by reviewing the reports the subrecipient submits and by visiting the subrecipients' service location. A site visit at least once a year is recommended. HUD publications provide an excellent checklist that the contract manager can use during the annual monitoring visit. When the grantee is subsequently monitored by HUD, it is important that the grantee's files contain evidence that proper monitoring was conducted and that any problems discovered were followed up on and corrected.

Managed competition and partial contracting models

Public-private competition

The practice of in-house bidding, also known as **public-private competition** and managed competition, is becoming a common strategy among local governments for alternative service delivery. Before in-house competition with the private sector became viable, departments attempting to stave off contracting prepared extensive analyses explaining why their method of service delivery was either less expensive "in the long run" or more effective than that proposed by the lowest bidder. But the cost comparison was commonly made after the opening of bid responses, raising doubt among the bidding contractors about the reliability and objectivity of the department's figures.

Today, local governments use in-house bidding more often but in a significantly different form. When they compare their cost of service to that of the private sector, the comparison is made in writing and is sealed and submitted before the time set for receipt of bids. Private contractors are much more accepting of this approach, and most now view the local government's submission as just another bid.

The local government manager should review the option of in-house bidding during the early stages of planning to decide whether it is to be part of the program. Encouraging in-house bidding is an effective incentive for employees and their labor organizations to work cooperatively with management to prepare the local government's bid. Preparing an in-house bid is discussed in more detail in Chapter 10 of this book.

Pilot projects

A pilot project is an effective way to assess whether to include a particular service in a contracting program. Pilot projects involve short-term contracting out of part of a service on a pre-established geographic basis in order to test the possibility of contracting out the total service area. Pilot projects typically run from three months to a year, allowing short-term, low-risk experimentation in new contracting areas. A pilot project also provides an opportunity to observe the performance of the pilot project contractor and test and refine new service specifications. The pilot project

Why can the private sector deliver the same service at lower cost?

One would expect a public organization to deliver services at less cost than a for-profit organization, but the reverse is often the case. The reasons are not completely clear, but there are three possible contributing factors: employees, equipment, and management.

Employees Opponents of service contracting often claim that the private sector pays lower salaries and provides fewer fringe benefits than the public sector. Although this is sometimes true, it is not always the case: salary disparity alone cannot be clearly established as the principal reason for the lower cost of private sector service delivery.

A more likely cause is the difference in the way employees are used. Public employees and their supervisors tend to be generalists, working in an environment of ever-changing conditions and uncertain budget resources. A crew that collects solid waste may operate a collection vehicle or crane truck one day and be assigned to clean up a transfer station the next, depending on shifting priorities in the department and the size of that day's work force.

In contrast, a private contractor's employees are often assigned to a single task. Because they are not faced with daily changes in assignment, they have an opportunity to become specialists in their fields and to increase their productivity. This may explain why private employees sometimes perform tasks more quickly than public employees or why the same task may require fewer private employees.

Equipment The equipment of a private contractor is generally well-maintained, top-of-the-line, heavy-duty equipment purchased to meet the most severe requirements of the task to be performed. A vehicle is often assigned to a single driver or crew for a long period, which fosters a feeling of ownership.

Budget constraints make it impossible for many local government to purchase top-of-the-line equipment each year. When purchases have to be made within the limits of available funds, the equipment is sometimes not ideal for meeting the requirements of the task. When funds for replacing equipment are scarce, equipment may be overused.

Budget crunches and hiring freezes may permit local governments to provide only the barest preventive maintenance program. Less expensive, less durable equipment that is overused and undermaintained has to be repaired and overhauled more often. Equipment that breaks down frequently cannot be assigned to a single operator or crew for any length of time.

Local governments could write more stringent performance criteria or structural minimums into purchasing specifications and provide the funding necessary for specialized heavy-duty equipment. But budget priorities make this approach the exception rather than the rule.

Management A private contractor is likely to be in a better position to use task and cost management to improve profits and reduce costs. For example, a private contractor who wants to remain in business cannot tolerate employees wasting effort or material in their work. Though the private sector's expectations of employees may result in higher turnover, private firms face no restrictions on cash or other awards for good performance. Because of the "carrot" of reward and the "stick" of discharge for poor performance, private contractors can demand and expect a higher level of productivity than their public sector counterparts. Public agencies have a difficult time finding a motivator as powerful as profit. Also, private agencies are less constrained by rules than public agencies, so they have more flexibility to experiment and innovate.

Although effective supervision and training can make some local governments competitive with private contractors in the management of tasks, few local governments can compete in the management of costs. Managing an expenditure budget does not necessarily encourage effective management of costs. In local government, the reward for spending less than the budgeted amount is usually a pat on the back and a reduced budget allocation the following year. As a result, a department becomes more skilled at finding ways to spend its budget allocation than at identifying ways of reducing expenditures so that funds can be returned to the local government treasury.

also permits fine-tuning of contract monitoring and the administration techniques to be used in the full contracting program. Most important, the pilot project provides an opportunity for direct comparisons of cost and service quality between public and private employees.

Pilot projects are particularly useful for contracts in which service is delivered at more than one location. A pilot project in refuse collection could consist of one or two collection routes; a pilot in street sweeping could cover a representative district; a pilot in landscaping could cover a specific geographical area. Services restricted to a single operating area are usually not good candidates for pilot projects, since there is no basis for comparison.

Pilot projects require careful design. They can fail to produce a meaningful comparison if they are not monitored effectively and objectively or if the area selected has unusually difficult service conditions or otherwise does not fairly represent the total service area. But valid comparisons between public and private sector performance can help the local government manager decide whether contracting out should be abandoned or pursued.

The pilot project approach works as well for new services as for existing services being considered for conversion to contracting. With new services, the pilot project provides the data necessary to determine whether the cost of contracting is comparable to the cost of providing the service in house.

Phasing in

If the pilot project shows potential for successful contracting, the local government manager must then decide whether to phase in the service or contract for the entire service area at once. When a service is phased in, it is separated into its component parts and these components are contracted out separately about every six months over a one- or two-year period. For landscaping, refuse collection, or street sweeping, the parts could be geographical. For highway or street maintenance, the contract could be separated into elements of the construction trade: curb, gutter, and sidewalk maintenance; asphalt resurfacing; or slurry sealing. Grass mowing can be separated into geographical areas or into specialty areas such as flail mowing, reel mowing for fields and parks, and finish mowing for specially landscaped areas.

Administering a phased-in contract under which awards may be made to different contractors for each phase can be difficult, but the rewards can outweigh the disadvantages. The principal benefit is that the two or more contractors performing the service serve as backup to each other in the event that one contractor defaults or is otherwise unable to provide the service. (Another way some larger local governments ensure backup capacity is contracting with multiple providers for the same service.) Another advantage of phasing in is that the resultant smaller contracts encourage broader competition and create good opportunities for small, minority, and disadvantaged businesses. Phasing in also allows additional time for attrition to reduce the affected work force and for the local government to retrain remaining employees.

Contingency planning

An important part of planning for a service contract is having a backup plan in case the contractor defaults. The contingency plan may call for the local government to resume the function in the event of a contractor default, but this is not the only option for dealing with a default situation. Indeed, many local governments will find it impractical or not financially feasible to retain in-house service capacity and contract the service out at the same time.

One way to reduce the likelihood of default or at least provide early warning of problems is to require contractors to submit a contingency plan as part of their bid, outlining the actions they will take when they experience capacity issues. As an important adjunct to the contingency plan, local governments should require bidders to demonstrate their ability to obtain performance (performance bonds are discussed at greater length in Chapters 4 and 7). Another option is a pre-established agreement with one or more neighboring local governments to purchase services on a short-term basis until the contract can be bid again. Although the local government may have to pay a premium for the service, such an arrangement may be necessary to ensure that there is no lapse in the provision of an essential public service.

If the local government can afford to retain 20 or 25 percent of the service capability in house, employees in the retained service area will be available to respond to service interruptions caused by contractor default. These in-house crews also can observe—and test, where appropriate—work techniques or equipment the private contractor uses that may be different and perhaps more efficient than those the local government uses. However, it is unrealistic to rely on in-house backup capability alone, since the in-house crew will not be able to pick up a service two or three times its normal workload on short notice. The manager must insist that alternative fallback plans are prepared before the contract is let. Chapter 9 of this book provides more information on establishing contingency plans.

Ethics and conflicts of interest

Although seldom the cause of contractor claims, conflict of interest is of special concern to everyone involved in the service contracting program. Conflict of interest laws ensure that the decisions of public officials are not influenced by the desire for personal gain or favoritism toward a particular contractor. Most instances of conflict of interest are fairly straightforward. One would not, for example, accept season football tickets from a potential contractor. Since the appearance of impropriety can do as much damage to the reputation of a local government's contracting effort as an outright illegal act, it is always best to err on the side of caution.

Some local government regulations forbid employees involved in the contracting process to accept anything from a contractor of more than nominal value—often as low as one to five dollars. And to avoid even the appearance of impropriety, most purchasing professionals follow the guideline of accepting nothing from a contractor, no matter how insignificant the item or how low the value. Questions regarding possible conflict of interest must always be referred to the legal department for resolution.

Most local government purchasing regulations include a section on ethics in public contracting. Some of the more rigid regulations include immediate termination of employment as a penalty for willful violations. Typical provisions prohibit a public employee involved in a purchasing transaction from accepting a gift, payment, loan, money, services, or anything of more than nominal value from a contractor involved in that transaction. They place the same ethical requirements on contractors doing business with the local government, and they establish rules for the subsequent employment of a public official by a business with whom the official had dealings while in local government service.

Although it is not unusual for staff involved in the contracting program to be called upon to defend contract-related actions or decisions, either at an administrative hearing or in a court of law, public contracting laws generally uphold the decisions of public employees who act in good faith and honestly exercise their discretionary powers. The courts seldom overturn the decision of a public employee in a contracting matter unless it is demonstrated conclusively that the employee's decision was arbitrary, capricious, willfully negligent, or illegal. In most cases, the most severe action of a court ruling in favor of a protest sets aside the award.

Guidelines to the National Institute of Governmental Purchasing code of ethics

I. Responsibility to your employer

- Follow the lawful instructions or laws of the employer.
- Understand the authority granted by the employer.
- Avoid activities that would compromise or give the perception of compromising the best interest of the employer.
- Reduce the potential for charges of preferential treatment by actively promoting the concept of competition
- Obtain the maximum benefit for funds spent as agents for the employer.

II. Conflict of interest

- Avoid any private or professional activity that would create a conflict between personal interests and the interests of the employer.
- Avoid engaging in personal business with any company that is a supplier to the employer
- Avoid lending money to or borrowing money from any supplier.

III. Perception

- Avoid the appearance of unethical or compromising practices in relationships, actions, and communications.
- Avoid business relationships with personal friends. Request a reassignment if the situation arises.
- Avoid noticeable displays of affection that may give an impression of impropriety.
- Avoid holding business meetings with suppliers outside the office. When such meetings do occur, the meeting location should be carefully chosen so as not to be perceived as inappropriate by other persons in the business community or by peers.

IV. Gratuities

- Never solicit or accept money, loans, credits or prejudicial discounts, gifts, entertainment, favors, or services from present or potential suppliers that might influence or appear to influence purchasing decisions.
- Never solicit gratuities in any form for yourself or your employer.
- Items of nominal value offered by suppliers for public relations purposes are acceptable when the value of such items has been established by the employer and would not be perceived by the offeror, receiver, or others as posing an ethical breach.
- Gifts offered exceeding nominal value should be returned with an explanation. If such gifts are perishable, they should be returned or donated to a charity in the name of the supplier.
- In the case of any gift, care should be taken to evaluate the intent and perception of acceptance to ensure that it is legal, that it will not influence buying decisions, and that it will not be perceived by peers and others as unethical.

V. Business meals

- There are times when during the course of business it may be appropriate to conduct business during meals. In such instances, the meal should be for a specific business purpose.

(continued on page 17)

Most claims involve violations of procedures; the rest are likely to concern allegations of favoritism or discrimination. A contractor may claim, for example, that staff involved in the bidding, award, or administration process made procedural decisions that were arbitrary and capricious or, in the worst case, fraudulent or illegal. If a towing contract is divided into geographical areas that appear to favor some contractors over others, a contractor who feels at a disadvantage may claim antitrust violations. If the bid of a minority-owned firm is rejected for no apparent reason, the firm may file a discrimination claim.

Since procedural violations are the most common claim made in legal actions against local governments, it is essential that local governments enforce adherence to procedures consistently. Examples of inconsistency include accepting a late bid for one contract but rejecting a late bid for another; waiving a bid bond requirement

---

(continued from page 16)

- Avoid frequent meals with the same supplier.
- The purchasing professional should be able to pay for meals as frequently as the supplier. Budgeted funds should be available for such purposes.

VI. Confidential information

- Keep bidders' proprietary information confidential.
- Develop a formal policy on the handling of confidential information.

VII. Relationship with the supplier

- Maintain and practice, to the highest degree possible, business ethics, professional courtesy, and competence in all transactions.
- Association with suppliers at lunches, dinners, or business organization meetings is an acceptable professional practice that enables the buyer to establish better business relations provided that the buyer keeps free of obligation. Accordingly, it is strongly recommended that if a seller pays for an activity, the buyer reciprocates.
- Purchase without prejudice, striving to obtain the maximum value for each dollar of expenditure.
- Do not show favoritism or allow yourself to be influenced by suppliers through the acceptance of gifts, gratuities, loans, or favors. Gifts of a nominal value that display the name of a firm that are intended for advertisement may or may not be accepted in accordance with the recipient's own conscience or jurisdictional rules.

- Adhere to and protect the supplier's business and legal rights to confidentiality for trade secrets and other proprietary information.
- Refrain from publicly endorsing products.

VIII. Relationship with the employer

- Remain free of any and all interests and activities that are or could be detrimental or in conflict with the best interests of the employer.
- Refrain from engaging in activities where the buyer has a significant personal or indirect financial interest.
- Exercise discretionary authority on behalf of the employer.
- Avoid acquiring interest or incurring obligations that could conflict with the interests of the employer.

IX. Relationships with other agencies and organizations

- A buyer shall not use his position to exert leverage on individuals or firms for the purpose of creating a benefit for agencies or organizations that he or she may represent.
- All involvement and transactions shall be handled in a professional manner with the interest of the buyer's employer taking precedent.

X. Relationships with professional purchasing organizations and associations

- It is the obligation and responsibility of the buyer, through affiliation with a professional organization, to represent that organization in a professional and ethical manner.
- A buyer shall not use his or her position to persuade an individual or firm to provide a benefit to an organization.

Source: Adapted from National Institute of Governmental Purchasing, "Guidelines to the NIGP Code of Ethics," 2001. Available at www.nigp. org/genlinfo/2001CodeofEthics.pdf

for one bid but not for another; and giving information that could affect the bid response to one contractor but not to others.

Knowing the law and adhering to it are one way to protect the local government from legal action. Local government personnel involved in service contracting can also protect the local government and themselves from legal action by knowing and adhering to a code of ethics. The National Institute of Governmental Purchasing (NIGP), an international organization of public purchasing professionals, encourages every person employed by any public sector procurement organization to adhere to its code of ethics (see the sidebar on pages 16 and 17).[4]

Learning the details of service contracting

The expansion of service contracting into larger and more complex contract areas presents many attractive options for local governments. Local governments that may have approached service contracting hesitantly in the past are applying it successfully in more public service areas than ever before. Responding to diminishing public resources and an increase in the level of service demanded by citizens and elected officials is not a simple exercise in public administration. To meet these challenges, local government managers and staffs must learn the details of service contracting to ensure that each contract is the best they can develop and that it is managed professionally and effectively.

Though many local governments have ongoing incremental contracting programs and may have established major contracts in the past, expanding a service contracting program without thoughtful planning can create serious problems down the road. Through careful planning and attention to detail, each local government can design a service contracting program to fit the needs and spending/ service preferences of the local community. This book aims to equip managers with the tools needed to build a service contracting program that matches local needs.

The remainder of the book is divided into four parts that correspond to the phases of the service contracting process. Service contracting involves three general phases—planning, bidding, contract administration—and a fourth phase that is rarely needed but that managers must prepare for nevertheless: contract termination. Chapters 1 and 2 address planning for an effective contract management program. Chapters 3, 4, 5, 6, and 7 discuss in detail the process of bidding and awarding contracts and dealing with disputes. Chapters 8, 9, and 10 describe methods for monitoring contractors and dealing with performance problems. Finally, Chapter 10 outlines the process of contract termination and bringing public services back in house.

Endnotes

1 American Bar Association, *Model Procurement Code for State and Local Government* (Chicago, Ill: American Bar Association, 2000), Article 3, Part B.

2 An excellent source of information in this area is U.S. Department of Housing and Urban Development, *Playing by the Rules: A Handbook for CDBG Subrecipients on Administrative Systems*, HUD publication 2005-05-CPD (Washington, D.C.: U.S. Department of Housing and Urban Development, 2005). This publication can be downloaded free of charge at www.hud.gov/offices/cpd/communitydevelopment/library/subrecipient/playing/chapter1.doc.

3 The HUD Web site (www.hud.gov) offers sample subrecipient agreements. Many state, county, and municipal Web sites also have excellent examples of subrecipient agreements. A simple Internet search under the term "subrecipient agreements" will return numerous examples of agreements being used today by governments, educational institutions, and nonprofits.

4 The National Institute of Governmental Purchasing has published "The NIGP Code of Ethics" at www.nigp.org/genlinfo/2001CodeofEthics.pdf.

2

Organizing for Service Contracting

A successful contracting program requires a certain skill set within the local government staff and ongoing capacity to monitor contractors. Defining an organizational structure for procuring and administering a contract is one of first tasks in establishing an effective service contracting program. Whether the local government has contracts for multiple services with multiple firms or has only a few small contracts and one person to manage them, establishing roles and assigning responsibilities at the outset can go a long way toward ensuring that selection and monitoring of contractors goes smoothly.

This chapter discusses several organizational models: centralized structure, decentralized structure, the combination model, and the network model. In a completely centralized model, the service contracting program operates outside the influence of affected departments. In the decentralized model, each department is fully responsible for its own service contracting program. The combination model uses variations between these two extremes to create a model that meets the needs of each local government. The network model integrates the functions of several contractors through either the government agency (department) or through a third-party principal contractor. Network models are especially common in organizations that manage health and human services.

These four organizational models may be most relevant for medium to large local governments that intend to contract or already do contract on a fairly large scale. If the scale of the contracting program is relatively small, a simpler and less structured approach may be warranted. The number of staff involved in contract operations should be proportionate to the size and number of contracts. It is important for the local government to create an organizational structure appropriate to the available staff and funding, the degree of expertise and commitment of department personnel, and the size of the contracting program. This structure should be created early in the planning stage.

Staffing the chosen model can be a greater challenge than deciding how to structure the management process. Many local governments do not have employees on staff with the skills necessary to create and implement a service contracting program. This chapter describes the basic skills required of staff members who will manage service contracts, suggests some ways to obtain training, and recommends training topics for staff who will administer contracts.

Centralized model

The centralized model provides more control of contract administration than the decentralized model. Centralization brings the program under the leadership of a single administrator. In this model, a single individual functions as the central source of authority in contract management. This person may be the local government manager or someone appointed by the manager to serve as the chief officer or director of contracts. The centralized model standardizes the monitoring and enforcement of contracts for all affected departments. The chief contracts officer receives objective information about the status of each contract and the total program.

Centralization is recommended when a given department lacks personnel with expertise in contract management and when the local government is venturing into new contract areas or establishing a pilot program. Centralization is also effective as an interim structure while department staff who will eventually assume responsibility for the contracted service are being trained in contract administration.

When the centralized model is first introduced, department managers may feel unfairly denied the right to manage a program that was once under their department's control, and their resentment may affect their work and their relationships with contract administration staff and the contractor. On the other hand, poor management may result when a contract is administered by a contract manager who is unfamiliar with the history of in-house delivery of the service. Both problems can be minimized through a combination of centralized and decentralized approaches.

A typical centralized model is shown in Exhibit 2-1. In this example, a project manager reports to the local government manager but still has considerable discretion in decisions affecting the program. The project manager directly supervises the contract manager, delegating enough authority that he or she can manage the program effectively. In larger organizations, the principal purpose of the project manager position is to provide the program with strong management. In smaller organizations, the duties of the project manager may be performed by the local government manager, the purchasing agent, or a senior member of one of the departments with the largest contracting program. The larger the organization is, the greater the need for either a project manager or a contract manager with adequate management authority.

The contract manager in Exhibit 2-1 would be responsible for managing contract administration for all service contracts and for providing guidance to contract administrators and field managers. The contract manager keeps the department informed about potential problems related to the unit's service contracts. In this example, the contract administrator serves as the administrative liaison for each contract, reporting directly to the contract manager and providing administrative assistance to one or more field managers. The contract administrator is the contract manager's link to the field manager. In a small service contracting program, the contract administrator's duties might be performed by the field manager. The field manager is responsible for most of the direct observation and monitoring of the contractors' performance. Depending on the scope and scale of the contracting program, the field manager's duties might not constitute a full-time job.

Exhibit 2-1 Centralized model for contract administration.

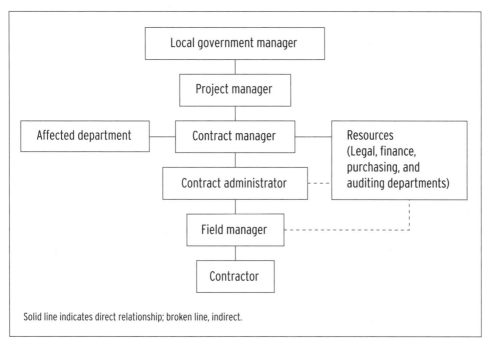

Staff members of the legal, purchasing, finance, or auditing departments who serve as resources provide an informal rather than a formal part of the service contracting program. They are included in Exhibit 2-1 to indicate their interaction with the contract manager or project manager, to whom they provide technical assistance and guidance when needed. Other departments may also serve as resources during the contract term, providing advice as required.

Decentralized model

Eliminating the role of the project manager is one option in the decentralized model. In this model, department program staff may frequently turn to the local government manager or contracts officer to resolve minor contract issues. An oversight committee made up of members of the purchasing, legal, finance, or auditing departments can provide guidance and fill some of the gaps created when the project manager position is eliminated.

Exhibit 2-2 provides an example of how a decentralized model might be set up. In decentralized models, the position of central contract manager is often eliminated and the functions are transferred to a department contract manager. The department contract manager reports to the department head and receives guidance on contract matters from the members of the resource team. Assigning the contract manager's duties to the contracts section of the purchasing department is an option for departments that cannot afford their own full-time contract manager.

Department contract administrators report to their department contract manager and perform the same functions as contract administrators in the centralized model. Department field managers are responsible for day-to-day observation and monitoring of contractor performance.

In the decentralized model, the resources (primarily legal and purchasing departments) provide guidance directly to the department and, when possible, assist with in-house training for department contract administrators and field managers. The

Exhibit 2-2   Decentralized model for contract administration.

Solid line indicates direct relationship; broken line, indirect.

extent of direction provided usually depends on the strength of the contract administration staff within the affected departments. Finance, auditing, and other departments are also available as resources.

Combination model

Many local governments adopt a flexible model (Exhibit 2-3) that includes features of both the centralized and decentralized models. In the flexible model, depart-

Single-handed contract administration

In local governments with small or medium-sized contracting programs, the contract managers, contract administrators, and field managers often are employees who take on contract administration in addition to their regularly assigned duties. As the contracting program expands or as the contracts become more complex, part-time duties gradually become full-time responsibilities. However, if the local government can afford a full-time employee to act as contract manager, an alternative approach can be used. In this model, the contract manager is responsible for all facets of the service contracting program, from program planning and administration to performing the duties of a field manager. A trained and experienced full-time contract manager can single-handedly administer twenty or more contracts depending on how complex they are and the amount of support provided by the departments involved.

This approach can be used as the first phase of a service contracting program or as a long-term model if contract administration funds or staff are limited. As the service contracting program expands, the contract manager can train department employees to assume part- or full-time duties as department contract managers, contract administrators, and field managers.

Exhibit 2-3 Combination model for contract administration.

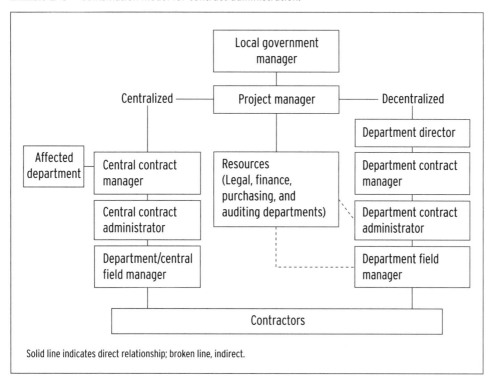

Solid line indicates direct relationship; broken line, indirect.

ments that are qualified to operate their own contract administration programs are granted independence and departments that are not qualified are assigned to the central contract manager. The contract manager functions as a resource for the decentralized departments and helps them as required but is not responsible for the outcome of their individual programs. The contract manager also serves as a resource for management, reporting periodically on the effectiveness of the total service contracting program, including the decentralized components.

Whatever the structure of a contract administration organization is, it must satisfy the local government manager's need for program control, suit the expertise of the departments involved, and meet the local government manager's goals for effective and objective program management.

Network model

Another way to organize for contract management is service contracting through network structures. In some ways, managing networks is more challenging than managing conventional contracts; it entails ensuring that several different contractors are performing well enough *together* to achieve a particular outcome that none could achieve on their own. This is the essence of effective network management. Securing cooperation and synthesizing the activities of private contractors who may be competitors in other contexts is no small task. However, with time, experience, and the right skill set, the project manager (or procurement officer) can lead the team in managing a service contracting network.

The network model has become increasingly common in recent years, particularly for organizations that provide social services. Networks are often the organizational structure of choice in contracting for mental health, child welfare, public health, transportation, and workforce development services. Generally, the government agency (department) functions as the network broker. It convenes network participants through a competitive negotiation process, then works to integrate the roles of network members (contractors) after contract awards are made. Each contractor provides a unique contribution to the final outcome of the service.

In many ways, contracting through networks is different from the traditional contracting relationship between the public agency and its service delivery agent in the private sector. One difference is that often the local government department delegates some of the management and oversight to a principal contractor. Networks involve complex linkages among contractors instead of the top-down, one-to-one relationships that characterize traditional contracting. Outcomes are measured not only on an individual contractor basis but on a network-wide basis, and contract administrators are ultimately concerned with performance of the network as a whole.

Exhibit 2-4 illustrates a common network management model in which a single local government department contracts exclusively with a principal contractor (using federal funds in part), who then serves as the network broker, facilitating interactions among a set of **contractors** and **subcontractors** who carry out the network's mission. In this illustration, top-level management staff of the principal contracting agency are directly accountable to and report to the local government agency. The local government's contract administrators directly monitor only the activities of the principal contractor, delegating responsibility for managing subcontractors to the principal contractor. In this model, the contract administration team can focus on monitoring, directing policy, and providing overall guidance for the delivery of the public service.

Exhibit 2-5 shows a variation of the network management model in which the local government department contracts with several core providers who in turn rely on a host of subcontractors. In this illustration, the local government contract administration team must directly monitor four contractors. The contract administration team must assess not only the individual performance of these organizations but also how well they are conforming to the rules of interaction and working

Exhibit 2-4 Network model for contract administration.

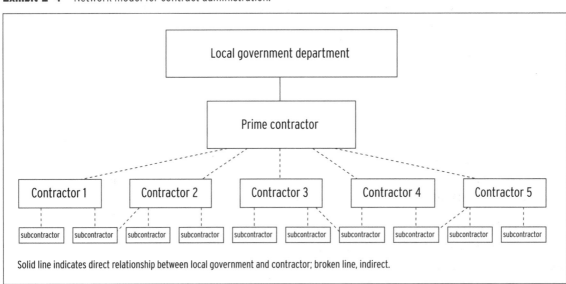

Solid line indicates direct relationship between local government and contractor; broken line, indirect.

Exhibit 2-5   Another variation of the network management model.

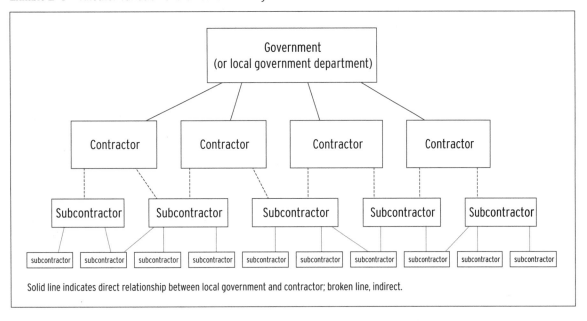

Solid line indicates direct relationship between local government and contractor; broken line, indirect.

together to achieve network goals. In networks of this size, the local government agency commonly monitors contractors by technical area; the local government's information technology staff monitors contractors' electronic billing, data capture, and reporting systems; the local government finance director monitors providers' budgeting and finance practices; the human resources director monitors providers' compliance with contractual requirements regarding staff qualifications, credentials, and training; and so forth.

Networks are often preferred when the service being contracted is complex and/ or covers a relatively large geographic area. For example, a county that contracts out for public mental health services might opt to divide the service area (county) into quadrants and contract with four core provider mental health firms to provide comprehensive screening, evaluation, and treatment in those four geographic areas. Those four agencies might serve as central intake points and determine client eligibility and the level of care to be provided (based on state and federal Medicaid guidelines) but then subcontract out for some client services, such as residential treatment or job training.

Alternatively, the services to be contracted might be divided up among core providers based on their areas of service specialty. In the mental health example, the local government mental health agency would contract with one organization to serve adults with mental illness, another organization that specializes in child and adolescent mental health, another that provides developmental disability services, and yet another that specializes in substance abuse treatment for the mentally ill. These four organizations might rely on subcontractors to provide some services to clients, but they might also contract with one another when client needs require the specialized services of another provider.

Because of the complexity of networks, managing them requires skills and expertise beyond those necessary for traditional contracting. The accompanying sidebar provides a list of skills relevant for managing service contracting networks.

Elements of network management

Service contracting networks are different from traditional principal-agent contract relationships in many ways, and managing them requires a specific set of skills:

- Big-picture thinking
- Coaching
- Mediation
- Negotiation
- Risk analysis
- Contract management
- Ability to tackle large-scale and unconventional problems
- Strategic thinking
- Interpersonal communications
- Project and business management
- Team-building

Source: Steven Goldsmith and William D. Eggers, *Governing by Network: The New Shape of the Public Sector* (Washington, D.C.: Brookings Institution Press, 2004).

Staffing

Most contract administration positions can be filled from department ranks, but even candidates proficient in their current specialties require training in the basics of contract administration. This section provides a brief description of typical functions performed by local government contract staff. They are general descriptions only; many of the duties associated with the positions described below will vary depending on the size of the local government, the budget, and extent of contracting. However a local government chooses to staff its contract management program, it is important bear in mind that job titles are less important than the technical ability and experience of staff assigned to perform the tasks.

Project manager

The project manager is often drawn from the staff of the local government manager. As the link between the service contracting program and the local government manager, the project manager should have the authority to act independently on most contracting issues, obtaining program direction as necessary from the local government manager. The duties of the project manager relate primarily to overseeing the program as a whole and do not normally require an extensive knowledge of the finer details of the contracted service.

Contract manager

Whether local governments use the centralized, decentralized, combination, or network model, many will have a contract manager or some variation of this position. The contract manager's responsibilities include prioritizing service requests from citizens or local government departments; reviewing and resolving contract disputes; negotiating contract amendments; evaluating contractors' performance; approving contractors' requests for payment; preparing performance records from information from field managers, clients, personal observation, and other sources; and training field managers in administering contracts and techniques for monitoring contracts. In addition, the contract manager plans for future contracts by updating the original contract and scope of work to reflect innovations in service delivery and identifying new areas where contracting might be used.

These duties require the contract manager to thoroughly understand public procurement, local government contract law, and the principles involved in the development of a contract. As mediator of contract disputes, the contract manager must also be able to view contract problems from the perspective of both the contractor and the local government. Finally, the contract manager must have a demonstrated ability to work effectively with public personnel at all levels and with all contractors, ranging from small entrepreneurs to national corporations.

Recruiting a contract manager   The most difficult task in recruiting a contract manager is developing a job description. The importance of interpersonal skills in contract management cannot be overemphasized. Although technical experience is important, a choice between a candidate with strong technical experience and a candidate with strong communication skills and somewhat less technical experience should favor the communicator.

Successful contract managers are recruited from almost every area of public service. Many come from the field of public procurement, while others come from the ranks of budget or management analysts. Still others are recruited from departments and assume contract administration duties when the service they were originally responsible for is contracted to the private sector. Searching within the ranks of local government may reveal an appropriate candidate for the position, but it is likely that training will still be necessary for effective performance.

The purchasing department as contract manager   In a combination model, if a department does not have a staff member who is qualified to perform the duties of the contract manager, the department contract administrator can take guidance from a nondepartment source such as the contracts section of the purchasing department. The purchasing department has experience contracting for goods and services, is accustomed to mediating disputes between departments and their sources of service and supply, and has a close working relationship with staff in every department. Local governments with purchasing departments should consider establishing the purchasing department as the contract manager for the local government. This can be an effective and much less expensive option than hiring professional contract managers for several different departments.

The consultant as contract manager   Some consulting firms offer contract management services. If funds are available, some local governments might hire a consultant to perform contract management duties. A consultant can be used as full-time manager and trainer in the beginning of the program and can be phased out as in-house employees are trained to do the job or are retained to manage the program on an ongoing basis. Local governments should weigh the financial cost of hiring a consultant against the alternatives of adding new permanent staff to the payroll or reassigning existing in-house staff whose time may be better spent on other duties.

The circuit-riding contract manager   Circuit-riding city managers have been part of local government management for years, and the same model can be applied to the field of contract administration. A local government that cannot afford a full-time contract manager may be able to join with nearby local governments to hire one contract manager to manage the contract programs for all of them. This approach is particularly useful when several local governments have service contracts that require a higher level of contract management expertise than any one of them can afford, when the sponsoring local governments have the same or a similar mix of general service contracts, and when none of the local governments has professional purchasing staff.

Contract administrators

If a local government has contract administrators, they are usually located within the department responsible for the service under contract. These contract administrators generally do not have full-time duties, and staff members who have other administrative functions, such as managing procurement, budget, or payment processes within a department, may serve as contract administrators. Brief training in the theory and practice of contract administration is usually all that current administrative employees need in order to perform contract administration duties.

Contract administrators provide administrative and program support to field managers by maintaining contract files and reviewing and approving contractors' payment requests. They report to their department heads on contract performance but receive guidance on contract matters from the central contract manager, departmental contract manager, or resource group assigned general responsibility for contract management.

Field managers

The field manager for each contract is the local government's first and most important contact with the contractor. Field managers are responsible for observing and objectively evaluating contractors' performance and addressing minor problems before they become major issues. A field manager may oversee multiple contracts, depending on their complexity and size, and may have additional duties within the department.

Because hands-on service experience is invaluable in performing their assigned duties, field managers are usually recruited from among line supervisors who have had experience with the service. Field managers monitor and evaluate on a one-to-one, day-to-day basis, reporting their interpretations of what they see to their supervisors. If the department has a contract manager, that person usually monitors and evaluates from a broader perspective than the field manager, using information from various sources—including field managers—and weighing the objectivity and level of competence of the sources. If the department does not have a separate contract manager, the field manager may be asked to do more monitoring.

New field managers, though they may have been excellent service supervisors, need specialized training in contract monitoring and administration to be effective in their roles. Reports to management and the governing body draw heavily from data compiled by field managers, so it is essential that they understand how their observations will be used by management to assess the performance and effectiveness of contractors.

Training

There are no guarantees of success, but effective service contracting programs have one thing in common: the members of the contract administration team have the skills and abilities to perform their assigned tasks. Training enables project managers, contract managers, contract administrators, field managers, and other contract management staff to obtain or refine the skills necessary to provide effective contract administration. It also enables them to function effectively as a team. In addition to a thorough understanding of their own jobs, each member of the contract administration team needs at least some familiarity with every other team member's job so that they can fill in for each other when needed. Backup knowledge of all team members' duties and interactions with contractor also preserves the department's capacity in the event of the sudden departure of a team member.

A consultant or in-house trainers or both can provide training in contract administration. A nearby local government with a successful contracting program may also have trainers available. Hiring a consulting firm to deliver part or all of the training may cost more than an in-house program, but it enables the local government to obtain an unbiased view of its training and management needs and gives it the benefit of the consultant's experience with other local governments.

A contract with a training consultant should require that firm not only to deliver training lectures but also to provide a lasting resource that will benefit the contract administration program after the consulting firm completes its initial assignment. For example, require the consultant to permit the local government to retain the firm's course outlines or training manuals for future use or to develop training outlines and operation manuals tailored to the local government's program. Include a provision that the consultant train the best of the local government's students or in-house trainers to use the firm's materials for future in-house training.

A local government that cannot afford outside training assistance can phase in the required training, hiring instructors as the budget permits. Low-cost training opportunities may also be available through trade and professional associations.

Subjects typically covered in a training program for a contract administration team are listed in the accompanying sidebar. Other topics can be added, depending on funds available and training needs.

Topics for a training program in contract administration

- Introduction to contract administration, including how service contracting developed and how it works
- Duties and responsibilities of team members, including how team members interact and techniques for building teams
- Techniques for monitoring contracts
- Evaluating contractors' performance
- Basics of government contract and procurement law, including the rights of the contracting parties, the legal nature of a contract, and principles of public purchasing
- Ethics in contract administration, including ethical standards and dealing with conflict of interest
- Developing specifications and interpreting contracts
- Documenting performance
- Negotiation

3

Planning the Bid Document

The bid document is the basis for the contract. It defines the responsibilities of the contractor as well as those of the local government. It also describes the details of performance, which become the yardstick against which the contractor's performance is measured. A well-written bid document cannot guarantee exceptional or even acceptable performance, but a poorly prepared one creates opportunities for substandard performance. Although contracts cannot address every contingency that may arise in the contract partnership, a good contract leaves little to interpretation or assumption. The local government must communicate very clearly to prospective bidders what is to be included in the bid or proposal. Exhibit 3-1 at the end of this chapter offers a sample set of response requirements that may be included in the bid document.

This chapter describes the planning and research required before the bid document can be written. It covers issues such as preparing the scope of work, timing the publication of the bid document, selecting a bidding method, selecting a contract type, and determining the minimum qualifications for bidders. This chapter also offers guidelines on how to prepare a request for qualifications, a document used to prequalify contractors before the bid document is published.

Preparing the scope of work

The bid document includes the scope of work, general terms and conditions, instructions to bidders, exhibits and attachments, and the bid form. The **scope of work** is prepared by a scope-of-work team. Because preparation of the scope of work requires expertise in the service being contracted out, the team is usually ad hoc. Often a simple scope of work is prepared by just one member of the purchasing staff working with a member of the department requesting the service contract.

For more complex service contracts, the scope-of-work team may consist of the field manager, a member of the purchasing staff, and the contract manager, who is in charge of administering the contract. Other team members may be added, but they function primarily as resources, providing assistance as required. They may be drawn from the legal department, from the department currently providing the service, or from any other part of the local government, depending on the technical assistance needed.

The scope of work should be simple, straightforward, and designed to ensure a realistic and acceptable level of service. All scopes of work should contain general terms and conditions. When there are special terms and conditions, some local governments opt to break them out into a separate section of the bid document. Those preparing the scope of work must resist the temptation to demand an ideal version of the service that expands beyond the service currently being delivered. For example, an in-house custodial supervisor may want the floor of every administration building to be polished and buffed daily. It might be tempting to include this in the scope of work, even though that level of service has never been provided in house. A scope of work that includes unrealistic or unreasonable requirements invites higher prices from contractors and may offset the savings anticipated from contracting the service.

Department representatives are the only members of the team likely to have firsthand knowledge of field conditions, so they play a critical role in developing the scope of work. For example, public works staff might provide information about poor soil conditions for the scope of work for a landscape service contract that will warn contractors that their maintenance costs may be higher than expected. Information that solid waste currently being hauled on a particular route is not typical for a neighborhood can alert a refuse collection contractor to examine the route closely before submitting a bid response. Providing data up front about unusual field conditions can prevent contract disputes and costly amendments to the final contract. A knowledgeable department representative can also help by familiarizing the team with terminology typical of the trade or service industry that should be used in writing the contract.

Working with consultants

For a major or complex service contract that is beyond the expertise of in-house staff, it is advisable to hire a consultant to prepare or help prepare the scope of work. A consultant serves as a resource for the team, not as its decision-maker. A consultant who writes the complete scope of work must be required to submit a draft for review at designated intervals to protect the local government from expensive and time-consuming rewrites of an unacceptable final product. At a minimum, the draft should be reviewed when it is 50 percent completed and again when it is 75 percent completed. Most consulting firms can write an acceptable scope of work for a contract, but the service contract team still must oversee the consultant's work to ensure that the final product is tailored to the needs of the local government. A consultant who develops a scope of work is generally prohibited from bidding on or being part of a team for the project for which he or she developed the scope of work.

However, a local government may decide to select contractors for a certain service based on their qualifications, and in this case, the contractors may help develop the scope of work for their service contracts.

Risk management

The risk/insurance manager or legal consultant must be informed whenever private contractors provide services on local government property or deliver services on behalf of the local government to employees, citizens, or clients of public programs. The risk or insurance manager must review the risks associated with the service to be provided, assess the types of losses that could occur, and specify appropriate insurance coverage. This also applies to subcontractors of award recipients. If it is anticipated that subcontractors will be used, ask the risk manager or legal advisor

---

Selecting qualified consultants

Following a decision by the city council, the Wentzville, Missouri (population 7,000), public works department now selects engineers, architects, and other consultants for city projects on the basis of the bidder's qualifications (including experience and cost history), not the lowest price. This change in the department's selection process has resulted in improved designs and savings of tens of thousands of dollars in capital costs, operations, and maintenance. Staff no longer develop the scope of work on their own; instead, the consultant is selected at the very beginning of the project and participates in developing the scope of the project. This usually produces a more accurate scope of work, dramatically reduces change orders to the initial contract as well as other administrative problems, and makes budgets more predictable and easier to manage. Because the consultants are selected for their expertise, many bring innovative ideas and knowledge of state-of-the art technology to their work.

Source: Bill Bensing, Public Works Director, City of Wentzville. Published in *Ideas in Action* 10, no. 3 (Fall 2004).

---

to delineate the appropriate insurance to be carried by the principal contractor and their subcontractor(s) and include this information in the scope of work.

When specifying insurance coverage, local governments must avoid using the same insurance requirements for all service contracts. If too much insurance is required for the risks associated with a specific contract, the higher insurance premiums will result in a higher contract price; if too little is required, the local government may pay less for the contract because of lower premiums but will be exposed to additional liability. The bid document should contain indemnification language that favors the local government. The form and extent of indemnification will vary depending on the type of contract and state laws.

Other resources

The designated scope-of-work team prepares the scope and (for less complex bids) may develop the entire bid document. However, other staff may assist as needed. The local government's legal department typically is responsible for final review of the bid document to protect the local government's interests in any future bidding or contract dispute. A fringe benefit of this review is that local government attorneys tend to read the entire bid document for sense and clarity as well as for legal defensibility. In the process, they often identify ambiguities and contradictions.

The auditing and finance departments review the portions of the bid document that affect their areas of operation. A clause that requires that the contractor provide evidence of a certain level of financial stability and clauses that define payments to the contractor, escrow requirements, the local government's right to audit the contractor, disposition of cash receipts, and provisions for discounts all require review.

Timing

Timing of bids is critical. Publishing and awarding contracts during the wrong season of the year may elicit bid responses with inflated prices or no bid responses at all. Careful timing permits the local government to enter the marketplace when the potential for competition and lower prices is greatest. Allow enough time for submission of bids, evaluation of responses, negotiation, and preparation of the contract. Time must be allowed between the award of the contract and performance of the contract to permit the contractor to mobilize the personnel and equipment needed. A milestone schedule beginning with the date the service is required and moving backward to a project start date can be a helpful management tool.

Seasonal demand

A sellers' market occurs when the demand for a service is greater than the number of qualified firms available to provide the service. When demand is high, the more-qualified contractors may restrict their bidding to the more profitable contracts of larger local governments or bid only at premium prices for smaller ones. As a result, smaller local governments may receive bid responses only from smaller or less-qualified contractors. Attempting to establish a snow removal contract in December or an air conditioning service contract in August usually elicits responses with premium prices, responses from marginally qualified contractors, or no responses at all. Contracts for road maintenance, landscaping, or any service for which demand peaks during a particular time of the year are subject to fluctuations in demand. To avoid a seasonal sellers' market, time the bidding and award process to fall between the end of the busiest season for the service and the midpoint of its off-season. Bidding for the service should occur when the demand for it is low.

The fiscal year

To simplify year-end closing and the budget process, local governments often schedule the termination of service contracts to coincide with the end of the fiscal year. Although this may make good sense to financial planners, it can work against attempts to obtain better bid responses from qualified contractors, particularly for smaller local governments. A month or two before the end of the fiscal year, several medium-sized or large local governments in the same geographical area may be bidding simultaneously for identical services. When few qualified contractors are available, a sellers' market is created that makes it difficult for smaller local governments in the same contract cycle to attract the more-qualified contractors. Few contractors bother with small contracts when the larger ones in the region are let for bidding simultaneously. To avoid being at a disadvantage, smaller local governments should schedule their critical service contracts to expire three or four months or more before the end of a fiscal year and should try to combine their needs with those of other local governments in order to create a larger and more desirable contract package.

Attrition

Timing is critical when a service contract is expected to displace public employees. The local government should permit as much time as possible for attrition to reduce the number of employees affected before the effective starting date of the contract. When many public employees are affected, it is not unusual for a local government to begin the contract a year after the award date. Delaying the start of the contract also provides time to train affected employees for other assignments.

The bidding process

The goal of the scope-of-work team is to prepare a bid document that will attract competitive bid responses from qualified contractors. That goal may be jeopardized if time is too short to permit responsible bidders to prepare a well-researched response. Consider the response time from the bidder's point of view and allow adequate time for bidders to participate in the process.

Before submitting a bid, the contractor must have the bid document analyzed by its operations and legal staff, prepare questions for the pre-bid conference, calculate preliminary cost estimates, and select key staff and schedule them to attend the conference. The contractor may also need to inspect the work site. After the pre-bid conference (or after receipt of any amendments resulting from the conference), the contractor has more work to do. Contract costs must be determined, prices must be established, personnel and equipment needs must be forecast, and the response must be prepared. Time must also be allowed before the bid opening for the contractor to prepare the response to the pre-bid conference.

If a meeting is to be held with prospective bidders before the bid opening to discuss the bid document, no less than two weeks should elapse from the publication date of the bid document to the date scheduled for the meeting. (This meeting, the pre-bid conference, is discussed in more detail in Chapter 5.) To ensure that timing does not affect the quality of bid responses, a discussion of whether the original date that has been set to open the bid document is acceptable to all bidders should be on the agenda of every pre-bid conference. At least two weeks should elapse between the conference and the bid opening, but the local government may add a week or more to the original schedule as a result of questions or comments received at the conference. The date after which no more questions will be accepted, typically three to four days after the pre-bid conference, should be announced or issued in writing at the time of the pre-bid conference. Responses to all questions must be provided to all bidders.

All parties must exercise caution to ensure that once the procurement documents have been issued, no discussions with potential bidders are conducted except through the purchasing office. Individual discussions after the issuing of the bid document may be perceived as providing a competitive advantage and can be grounds for a successful protest.

To obtain maximum market exposure, basic support services that do not need a pre-bid conference require at least four weeks from the date the bid document is first distributed to potential bidders to the date set for receipt of bids (**bid opening**). Service contracts for major or complex service areas that are expected to attract larger contractors or for which prospective contractors must plan to acquire personnel or equipment may need a bidding period of six to eight weeks.

Lead time for service delivery

Simple contracts for basic support services can be in place and operating effectively three or four months after the decision is made to contract for a service. However, contracts that cover a complex service, affect public employees, or require a substantial capital outlay take much more time, and more than a year can elapse between the awarding of the contract and the start of service under the contract.

Contractors seldom have idle staff and equipment that can be diverted immediately to a new effort; they keep their organizations just large enough to handle current work. When they win a new contract, they need adequate time to hire new employees and purchase additional equipment. Some equipment may require lead times of several months or more for delivery. An early award also allows the contractor to use the awarded contract as collateral against loans that may be necessary to purchase equipment required for the contract. Sufficient time between the award and the start date of the contract enables contractors to plan effectively and may attract contractors who would otherwise not respond.

Bidding methods

The scope-of-work team must determine the bidding method to be used to select a contractor. The purchasing regulations of some local governments allow only competitive sealed bidding. Others allow both competitive sealed bidding and competitive negotiation. Still others authorize a third method called multistep bidding. Whichever process is used, a clear description of the method must be included in the bid document so that the rules are known to all bidders.

If the contract is funded in whole or in part by a state or federal agency, the bidding method may be mandated by the granting agency. The local government must carefully review underlying legislation or grant documents to identify what restrictions or requirements may pertain when the service is paid for with state, federal, or private funds.

Competitive sealed bidding

Competitive sealed bidding is the most common method used for purchasing services when the local government has the experience and skills necessary to define exactly the service to be provided. The local government prepares and mails a detailed specification to interested contractors. A pre-bid conference may or may not be held, and the award is made to the lowest **responsible and responsive bidder**.

First among the advantages of this method is that the risk of increased costs during the contract term lies solely with the contractor. The local government has no responsibility or liability if the contractor underestimates the cost of providing the service or if changing market conditions increase the contractor's costs during the contract term. Second, competition among bidders is based on price. The award is made to the lowest responsive and responsible bidder. Third, the award process typically is clear-cut and uncomplicated. Under competitive sealed bidding, only the lowest responsive and responsible bidder can be considered for award, regardless of the qualifications of the remaining bidders or how close their prices may be to that of the lowest responsive and responsible bidder.

One disadvantage of competitive sealed bidding is that the local government must define its service requirements exactly. The requirements cannot be changed or negotiated after the bids are opened. Another is that the prices received may not be the best available in a limited market where only one or two firms are qualified to respond. Local governments in a limited market may be better off choosing a bidding method that includes negotiation in order to obtain better prices.

Competitive negotiation

Competitive negotiation works best when highly technical services such as computer networking or software development are involved or when the contract requires highly specialized or professional staff, as in the case of health care and social services contracts. Competitive negotiation is often used also for contracting with architects, engineers, and similar providers of professional services. The procedure allows an award to the contractor with the best combination of price, experience, and quality of service delivery; award is not restricted to the lowest dollar offer.

The rules for applying competitive negotiation vary considerably among local governments. However, local procurement regulations generally specify the following conditions for using competitive negotiation:

1. The scope of work for the contract cannot be accurately and completely defined by the local government.
2. The service can be provided in several different ways, any of which could be acceptable.
3. The qualifications of the contractor and the quality of the service to be delivered can be considered more important than the price of the contract.
4. The expected responses may contain a different level of service than that requested, requiring negotiation to reduce or increase the price to match available contract funds.

In the competitive negotiation process, **offerors** generally respond to an RFP by submitting a sealed proposal that includes a statement of qualifications, a technical proposal describing how the service will be delivered, and an estimated price (if requested) for the service. Everything in the response, including price, is negotiable during the evaluation process.

Regulations authorizing competitive negotiation occasionally identify two subcategories of service: professional services (such as architecture, engineering, management consulting, law, and medicine) and nonprofessional services. Slightly different procedures are used for each.

Professional services   The RFP typically requests only the offeror's statement of qualifications. Many state and local governments prohibit firms that offer professional services (the professional specialties are usually defined by statute) from submitting and prohibit the local government from requesting a price for services. In jurisdictions where it is not legally prohibited, the local government should consider requesting pricing when soliciting bids for professional services. The most-qualified respondents are selected as finalists. They are then interviewed by an evaluation panel and ranked in order of their qualifications. After they are ranked, the price and the scope of work are negotiated with the first-ranked offeror until an acceptable contract price is established. If negotiations fail with the first-ranked offeror, they are officially terminated and negotiations begin with the second-ranked offeror, and so forth, until an acceptable contract is agreed to by all parties. Once negotiations are terminated with an offeror, the local government cannot reopen them.

Nonprofessional services   The qualifications of the offeror are requested in the original RFP. Price also can be requested, usually identified as a "nonbinding estimate of cost." After the evaluation of responses, the offerors most likely to be considered for award are selected and interviewed. Two or more of the finalists are then selected for simultaneous negotiations covering both the price and the content of the proposal. A best and final price is requested from each finalist and the award is made to the offeror with the best combination of proposal, qualifications, and price. Regulations also may permit simple ranking of offerors of nonprofessional services. Negotiation proceeds with the highest-ranked offeror first and so on with the others if negotiations fail with the highest-ranked offeror.

Advantages   There are several advantages to competitive negotiation. First, the scoring, interview, and negotiation processes permit in-depth analysis of every offeror's qualifications and capabilities, not just those of the one with the lowest bid.

Second, the service specifications and price may be negotiated to meet the local government's needs. If the original prices are too high, negotiation helps bring them within budget. The scope of work also may be negotiated, whereas with competitive sealed bidding, when original bids are unacceptably high, the remedy usually involves canceling the solicitation and starting the process all over again under revised specifications.

Third, the ability to negotiate a price is an effective technique in a market in which offerors may have little or no competition. Under competitive sealed bidding, when only one or two firms deliver a service, there is little incentive to reduce prices and bidders tend to price the service higher than when the market includes many firms.

Disadvantages Although there are few disadvantages to competitive negotiation, they are significant. First, the evaluation and award process can be lengthy. It is not unusual for the period between receipt of offers and award to be between thirty and sixty days. Second, it requires considerable record-keeping and scoring methods that are sometimes complex. If protests are received, the local government may have to defend subjective decisions it has made during the selection process. Third, the entire process must be managed carefully to make sure that evaluations and the final award are as objective as possible and that every offeror receives fair and equal treatment. Fourth, local government staff without experience in negotiation can be at a disadvantage dealing with experienced private sector bidders who have trained negotiators on staff.

Multistep bidding

Multistep bidding is not used as frequently as competitive sealed bidding or competitive negotiation, possibly because the process tends to generate more bidder protests than the other methods. However, if a local government does not have the expertise or time to define the required service accurately and is prohibited from using competitive negotiation, it should consider multistep bidding. This bidding process provides more flexibility than competitive sealed bidding because it permits an element of negotiation within the framework of competitive sealed bidding. During the first steps of the process, negotiation of the content of unpriced proposals is permitted; in the last step, the method requires award to the lowest responsive and responsible bidder. A principal advantage of multistep bidding is that the first steps of the process also serve as a method for prequalifying the respondents. Those with unacceptable qualifications can be eliminated.

Multistep bidding usually requires that the following conditions be met:

1. The scope of work cannot be accurately and completely defined by the local government.
2. The service can be provided in several different ways, most of which could be made acceptable through negotiation.
3. The expected responses may contain a different level of service than that requested, requiring negotiation to match the proposal with the needs of the local government.

The process has two or more steps. In the first step, the offerors submit a statement of qualifications and an unpriced technical proposal describing the proposed service delivery method in a sealed envelope marked "Technical Proposal." Price may be submitted at this time in a separate sealed envelope marked "Price." Price also can be submitted later, usually as the last step in the process. The evaluation panel opens the technical proposals and decides which bidders are qualified and could be considered for award. The panel rejects unacceptable technical proposals or technical proposals from unqualified bidders at this time. Affected bidders are notified of the rejection, and their price envelopes, if they have been submitted, are returned to them unopened.

If necessary, negotiations are conducted with the remaining qualified bidders to amend their technical proposals to make them generally equivalent. If one technical proposal requires more staff and equipment to implement than another, they should not be considered equivalent. When the technical proposals of all the finalists are deemed generally equivalent and acceptable for award, the evaluation panel opens the sealed price envelopes of all the finalists. The award, based on price alone, is then made to the lowest responsive and responsible bidder.

Multistep bidding can be used for service contracts in which the contents of the acceptable technical proposals are not expected to vary significantly among bidders and the need for negotiation is expected to be slight. The competitive negotiation method is recommended for complex service areas or when the local government wants to obtain as much information as possible about service delivery options before making an award.

Advantages Multistep bidding has several advantages. First, it combines the elements of competitive bidding and negotiation into a single method, permitting establishment of a contract tailored to the local government's needs that is still awarded to the lowest responsive and responsible bidder. Second, the procedure permits comparative evaluation of different methods of performing a service without initial price comparisons. Third, the negotiation process allows local governments to obtain better insight into each bidder's knowledge and ability to provide the service than competitive sealed bidding does. Fourth, this method of procurement is effective when competition is limited, price negotiation may be advisable, and competitive negotiation is not allowed.

Disadvantages The multistep process can be lengthy. Also, there are several steps at which a bidder can be disqualified, creating more opportunities for protests.

Two-step method

Similar to the multistep method, a two-step method is frequently used for larger, more complex projects. It also contains similarities with the professional services contracting method. Many contractors prefer this method because step one is inexpensive, reducing the cost of the initial bid preparation.

Step one is the **prequalification** of bidders and the development of a short list of not less than three firms that will be issued the RFP. The local government releases a **request for qualifications (RFQ)** or **letter of interest** (see the sections on bidder qualification method, qualification criteria, and preparing an RFQ later in this chapter). The RFQ contains a summary of the project and requests specific information from those who respond. Responses should be limited in length, ten pages or less in a prescribed format, to facilitate evaluation. The goal of step one is to identify the most qualified firms who respond.

In step two, the local government releases the RFP only to the most qualified bidders as identified in step one. Once proposals are received, selection can be based on competitive negotiations or competitive sealed bid. A price proposal can be required with the technical proposals or separately after technical proposals are evaluated.

A/B is a variation of the multistep or two-step process that reflects innovation in the selection of a contractor. The local government divides the cost (A) by the technical score (B) to get a cost per technical point. The lowest cost per technical point is the low bid. This methodology allows a contractor with a higher price but a higher technical score to win. This is just one example of how contract evaluation methodology can be tailored to reflect a desire for high quality or technical expertise and not just low cost.

The advantages of the two-step method are:

1. Prequalification of contractors provides a level of confidence that the ultimate winner is fully qualified to satisfy the scope of work.

2. Contractors tend to prepare better proposals when their chance of winning has been increased by the elimination of all but two or three of the best-qualified contractors.

3. Step one is relatively inexpensive for contractors.

The disadvantages are similar to those of multistep contracting.

Bidding methods for construction contracting

Two bidding methods apply particularly to construction jobs: design-build and construction management at risk.

Design-build   In design-build, contractors form teams to deliver the product. This method is widely used in vertical construction and is becoming very common in the transportation sector. Many local governments hire a project manager to lead the RFP process for design and construction management. If a project manager is hired, the bid evaluation team must still include staff of the local government.

The contractor team will consist of a design firm and a construction entity and can include a quality assurance/inspection firm as well. The scope of work for these contracts is referred to as a design criteria package. This package provides a description of the product to be acquired and may range from partial plans to artists' renderings with physical dimensions to a narrative of the product. Bidding contractors satisfy those items in the design criteria package at their discretion, and the owner relinquishes control over the project design. This places a great emphasis on the completeness of the design criteria package to ensure that the goals and expectations of the issuing agency are met.

Design-build proposals are very detailed and very expensive for the bidders to prepare. Because of the expense of preparing the proposal, a stipend may be paid to the unsuccessful bidders to defray some of the bid cost. The stipend is not intended to repay the entire bid preparation cost but only a small percentage, generally less than 25 percent. This offers several advantages. First, it may increase competition, since smaller firms may not be able to compete without the stipend. Second, the RFP can provide language to ensure that the bidder's proposal becomes the property of the issuing agency as a result of payment of the stipend. This allows the issuing agency to incorporate innovative aspects of unsuccessful proposals in negotiations with the winning firm.

Bidders for design-build projects develop design proposals that optimize their own construction abilities. The proposals are evaluated based on published criteria that are contained in the RFP and may include such items as management, design quality, innovation, schedule, quality control, and environmental sensitivity.

The advantages of this methodology are:

1. Disputes between the designer and the contractor are eliminated because they are on a single team.

2. Constructability reviews occur on an ongoing basis with the designer.

3. There is potential for time savings because the contractor may be able to begin the initial phases of the project before the final design is completed. In a road project, for example, the clearing of the right of way could begin with the finalization of the plans.

4. There is some potential for cost saving, generally associated with time savings.

The primary disadvantage is that the issuing authority releases a large amount of control to the contractor for the details of the design.

Selection of the successful bidder in a design build is flexible and is based on the needs of the issuing authority. The lowest bid may be used, which minimizes cost, but that strategy may fail to capitalize on imagination or innovation.

Construction management at risk Construction management at risk, or CM-at-risk, has grown in popularity for larger projects and is well suited for projects of a longer duration or where a project may have multiple phases that require continuity of management. This methodology allows the CM-at-risk contractor to participate in the early planning and design of projects. It also allows the contractor to provide continuous reviews and allows the CM-at-risk to fast-track key components of the project, such as items that require a long lead time to acquire. The issuing agency selects a CM-at-risk contractor based on qualifications (see bidder qualifications method later in this chapter). Once the selection is made, the contractor becomes part of the project team.

The CM-at-risk contractor assumes the responsibility to deliver the project at a "guaranteed maximum price" that is negotiated between the firm and the issuing agency. The CM-at-risk acts as the general contractor during construction, assuming the risk of subcontracting, cost, and schedule.

The advantages of this methodology are:

1. The CM-at-risk provides preconstruction services such as reviews of schedule, budget, and constructability.

2. The CM-at-risk prepares bid documents, manages all pre-bid activities, and selects subcontractors.

3. During construction, the CM-at-risk performs quality control and project management.

4. As compared to the design-build method, the issuing agency retains more control until the guaranteed maximum price is negotiated. After this point, the CM-at-risk must be compensated for changes that negatively impact the cost.

The disadvantage is additional cost and some loss of control.

Multistep, two-step, design-build, and CM-at-risk are but a few of the delivery methods that may be used for large projects. Each project must be evaluated based on its individual circumstances and the best delivery method must be selected based on its merits. The goal is to tailor the contract methodology to best satisfy the goals and expectations of the issuing agency.

When bidding fails

A solicitation may not generate any responses. The reasons could be that the scope of work was too restrictive, too comprehensive, or too large for available contractors or that not all possible bidders were aware of the solicitation. Contact all potential bidders on the bidder list to find out why they did not respond. If they considered the scope of work too restrictive, revise the bid document to eliminate as many restrictive sections as possible and then re-bid. If the scope of work was too large, consider dividing it geographically or into its component tasks. Research the market to identify additional potential bidders. Advertise for bidders in different newspapers or regional trade association publications. If additional potential bidders are found or the bid document can be revised, make the necessary changes and reissue the bid.

Sole-source contracting

The American Bar Association's Model Procurement Code for State and Local Governments defines **sole source** as "only one source for the required supply, service, or construction item" and recommends that separate regulations be promulgated to "establish standards applicable to procurement needs that may warrant award on a sole source basis."[1] Most local regulations permit sole-source purchasing of goods and services only upon a written finding that only one qualified source is available. Most also require a written statement that a search for alternative sources has been made and a justification showing that the only service method acceptable to the local government is that provided by the identified source. After the decision to contract on a sole-source basis has been made and approval has been obtained (if necessary), the following steps are taken:

1. To the extent possible, the local government identifies the fair market value of the service to be procured. It can determine an estimated value by contacting other users of the contractor's service or by identifying the costs paid by area local governments for similar services.

2. The local government prepares a draft contract that specifies its needs.

3. The local government negotiates the extent of the service to be delivered and the price with the contractor.

4. When an agreement is reached, the local government submits the final contract for any required approvals.

Often there are valid reasons for contracting on a sole-source basis, but identifying a provider as a sole source without searching for additional providers by going through the bidding process should be considered only as a last resort, even when it is likely that only one bid response will be received. An award to a single respondent is generally much easier to defend than an award to a sole source.

When a competitive sealed bid for a service results in only one response and no other bidders can be located to support a re-bid, sole-source contracting is usually the only course to follow. A single response to a competitive sealed bid should not be accepted unless the price is fair and reasonable or it is not likely that negotiation will reduce the price. In a single-bid marketplace, it is probable that the single bidder is aware of the lack of competition and will submit a price based on the exclusivity of the service, not on fair market value. If the single bidder's price is higher than expected, it is best to reject the bid, cancel the competitive sealed bidding procedure, and immediately negotiate with the single bidder on a sole-source basis to obtain a better price. Local regulations might not permit negotiations while the original competitive sealed bid remains in effect; rejection and cancellation clear the path for sole-source negotiations. If the original solicitation was let under competitive negotiation and the local government decides to award on the basis of the single bid response, negotiations can commence immediately.

Contract types

Many types of contracts are based on the method used to price a service. The most common are the firm fixed price, fixed price with escalator (also known as firm fixed price with economic price adjustment), fixed price with incentive, fixed price combined, cost plus fixed fee, percentage of revenue, and time and material contracts. The types are not mutually exclusive; aspects of each may be incorporated into a hybrid type when appropriate. The accompanying sidebar lists several contract types discussed in this section.

Fixed price contract

The **fixed price contract** is commonly used for terms of one year or less for personal, professional, or training services or for any service whose price is not expected to vary significantly because of market fluctuations during the contract term. This contract type is also used for services based on a unit price such as a per diem rate for residential, medical, or social services; unit prices for support or repair services; and hourly rates for professional consultations. The price cannot be adjusted during the contract term. The contractor bears the risk of unforeseen costs and makes a profit only if costs are controlled. If the contractor submits a price that is subsequently discovered to be too low, cost-control measures the contractor may initiate to minimize expected losses could affect the quality of service provided. Local governments that select this contract type must therefore monitor service quality closely to prevent or minimize decline in the quality of the contractor's performance.

Common types of contracts

Firm fixed price   Contracts that usually last for one year or less and contracts that are not affected by market fluctuations.

Fixed price with escalator   Primarily multiyear contracts with pricing factors subject to market fluctuation.

Fixed price with incentive   Single or multiyear contracts in which savings could result through increased productivity or cost reduction without affecting the quality of the service. Both the contractor and the local government can benefit from savings the contractor achieves.

Cost plus fixed fee   Single or multiyear contracts primarily in the fields of architecture, engineering, and other professional and consulting services.

Time and materials   Contracts for trades services and other areas in which the time of completion cannot be determined or the agreed-to price is based on hourly rates and material provided.

Percentage of revenue   Contracts in which the local government receives a portion of the revenue generated by the contract. Examples are contracts for concessions and for adult education.

Fixed price with escalator contract

The **fixed price with escalator contract** allows the contract price to be adjusted periodically. This option is useful for contracts that will be in effect for more than one year and for those with costs for material or labor that are subject to rapid market fluctuations. The contract as well as the bid document must specify the escalator factors used for price adjustment and the times during the contract term when the adjustments will occur (usually annually). Because the contract price follows market prices, contractors are less likely to inflate future-year unit prices to protect themselves against possible increases in operating costs.

The most commonly used indexes upon which to base an escalator are the U.S. Department of Labor Consumer Price Index for All Urban Consumers (CPI-U) and the Consumer Price Index for Urban Wage Earners and Clerical Workers (CPI-W). Using the data in these indexes requires the establishment of two points of reference. The first is the expenditure category within the CPI-U that most nearly applies to the content of the contract, as there are more than 100 expenditure categories to select from. The second point of reference is the month used to calculate the annual price change. Annual price adjustments are based on the percentage of change, up or down, in the index for the twelve months preceding the specified month. The CPI calculates the percentage of change for the preceding twelve-month period, so the appropriate percentage is easy to find.

When establishing the month to be used to calculate the annual price change, it is important to account for the delay in the publication of the CPI. Because of this delay, the month used to calculate price adjustments should be at least four or five months before the expiration date of the current contract. For example, a March CPI would be used to calculate prices in effect for the contract year starting in August. The extra lead time permits the local government to re-bid if the increase in the CPI is so high that it chooses not to offer a renewal option to the contractor or if the contractor exercises the option to decline a renewal because it considers the price increase too low.

The CPI is available in bimonthly regional editions covering twenty-six of the nation's larger metropolitan areas.[2] These editions, based on regional data, track local market conditions much more closely than the edition based on national data.

Any periodical that publishes market-change indicators can be used as an index for a fixed price with escalator contract. Remember that the index used must be identified exactly in the bid document along with the day, week, or month that will

---

The flexible index

If an index is applied to a long-term contract of four or five years, the movement of the index may not reflect local conditions over the multiyear period and may result in unrealistic increases or decreases in the price of a contract. If the percentage of increase in a national index is less than that of the local market, the quality of service may suffer if the contractor cuts costs to offset added expenses of operation. The contract should therefore include a provision that the percentage of change in the index is the maximum increase or decrease allowed on each contract anniversary date. The actual price can then be negotiated from the current (pre-escalator) price up to the maximum percentage of change in the escalator. The variations that can be used to calculate future prices against a base index are limited only by the imagination of the team drafting the scope of work.

Multiple indexes

For contracts in which costs can be affected by more than one area of market fluctuation, two or more indexes can be used to adjust annual contract prices. For example, a refuse collection contract can be affected by changes in tipping fees at the disposal facility and by changes in the economy affecting labor and equipment costs. To permit the use of both market indexes, specify that the contract unit price per household be submitted in two components, the first representing the amount of the unit price allocated by the contractor for collection and the second the amount allocated for disposal. The collection component is tied to the CPI, and the disposal component is tied to the percentage of change in tipping fees at the disposal facility. Any contract that has a unit price with a cost component that is subject to frequent change is a candidate for the use of dual indexes. Examples include hauling contracts in which unit prices are split into motor fuel and "other" costs and contracts to manage residential facilities in which prices are split into food and other costs. When a unit price is split into its component parts, each having its own index, annual adjustments reflect actual market conditions more accurately.

be used to calculate the price change (e.g., "every Thursday," "annually in June," "the third Tuesday of each month").

Fixed price with incentive contract

Local governments may also use fixed price with incentive contracts. Although these contracts allow the contractor to make additional profit, the extra dollars paid to the contractor may increase productivity and quality of service and can even lower the net contract price.

The fixed price with incentive contract can be used effectively for a variety of services, from fleet maintenance to social services. Methods for applying incentives to obtain optimum performance can be devised to cover a broad range of activities. In tying the incentive to productivity, the contractor and the local government together set goals—for example, an ideal number of clients contacted or potholes repaired or a maximum number of complaints received or contract units rejected. The contractor earns a bonus—usually a cash payment—by exceeding the ideal. If the number of complaints exceeds the maximum, cash can be deducted from the next payment due the contractor. Bonuses can also be linked to a percentage of revenues received (e.g., from paid attendance at a recreational facility) in excess of specified goals.

It is not uncommon to use fixed price with incentive contracts to purchase health and human services. However, in purchasing services that involve complex decision making by the contractor with outcomes that are difficult to measure, local governments must structure contract incentives very carefully so as to not jeopardize the health and well-being of service recipients. For example, a local government contracting with a nonprofit organization for child welfare services may provide a financial incentive for each child successfully transitioned out of foster care or residential placement and returned to its natural family. This arrangement creates an incentive for the contractor to return children to their families earlier, but early return may not be in the best interest of every child.

When incentives are tied to costs, the contractor and local government together set a target cost for the contract. If less than the targeted amount is spent without affecting service quality, the contractor earns a bonus, usually half of the cost savings below target. The contract usually identifies the maximum cost savings allowed to prevent the contractor from cutting costs so drastically that service is affected. The local government and the contractor share equally any costs that exceed the initial target up to a preset maximum of usually 10 or 15 percent. The contractor assumes responsibility for all costs beyond this level.

Cost plus fixed fee contract

The **cost plus fixed fee contract** is a **cost reimbursement contract** used primarily for architectural, engineering, or consulting services. Under this method, the contractor is reimbursed for actual costs and paid a negotiated fixed fee (the contractor's profit) that does not change, even if costs escalate beyond the original estimation. If the contractor's duties increase or decrease in relation to the original scope of work, the fixed fee can be increased or decreased by contract amendment.

A major disadvantage of this pricing structure is that the contractor has no incentive to control costs because the fee is unaffected by increases in the original reimbursable costs. The reimbursable costs include the actual hourly charges of the contractor's personnel; payroll taxes, and benefits; other contract-related expenses such as travel, printing, telephone, and computer time; and hourly charges of approved subcontractors— all of which are reimbursed at the contractor's cost. In a cost reimbursement contract, no profit to the contractor or surcharge should be part of the reimbursable expenses, and requests for payment should be scrutinized to ensure that all costs are reasonable and can be allocated to the contract. Because the cost reimbursement contract seldom offers incentives for cost savings, cost control depends on effective monitoring of the contract. For example, should the local government feel that the number of labor hours is excessive, it may audit the contractor's employee time charges.

A common variation of this contract type that can help control unwarranted charges and the total contract cost is the cost plus fixed fee contract that includes a not-to-exceed limit on the contract cost. The contractor is held to a pre-established limit for all expense and labor reimbursements and is required to complete the scope of work at no additional cost to the local government if the not-to-exceed limit is reached, regardless of how much the contractor must spend to complete the originally assigned work.

The fee is not always a single payment to the contractor at the end of the project. It can be allocated proportionately when specific tasks are completed or when the local government receives deliverables required under the contract. For example, 10 percent of the fee can be paid for the submission and acceptance of preliminary design drawings, 20 percent for an acceptable final design, 20 percent for construction drawings that are 50 percent complete, and 20 percent for complete construction drawings. The balance can be retained by the local government until completion of the contract. The contract can include liquidated damages if the contractor fails to meet specific delivery dates. For example, if the contractor does not meet a deadline, the local government reduces the fee for that deliverable by one-thirtieth (more or less, as appropriate) for every day that the contractor fails to meet the deadline, up to a maximum of thirty days. This can be a strong incentive for a contractor to adhere to a preset contract schedule.

Time and materials contract

Time and materials contracts are used primarily with electrical, air conditioning, carpentry, painting, and other trade contractors whose services are provided on an as-needed basis or when the amount of labor or material required for the work cannot be forecast. The contractor is paid for the number of hours worked and the cost of the material. The hourly labor cost (time) is established in the original price, and the cost of material used (materials) is submitted as either a discount from a published price list or at contractor cost. Avoid time and materials contracts that allow a markup on the contractor's cost for material; in such arrangements, the contractor's profit increases in direct proportion to the amount of material used. This provides a built-in incentive to use more material than may be necessary, to use higher-priced material that may exceed quality standards, or to recommend replacement of parts or equipment that are still serviceable.

Percentage of revenue contract

Typically, percentage of revenue contracts are established for services provided to a third party for which the contractor receives revenues, such as food concessions, class instruction, and recreation camps. They are also called percentage of gross contracts.

Although the term "gross" usually refers to the total receipts of the contractor, gross must be defined carefully in the contract. It is not unusual for contractors to define gross revenue as gross receipts after taxes or after expenses. When establishing a percentage of revenue contract, the basis for calculating local government revenues should be gross receipts. The simpler the definition of gross, the simpler contract monitoring and auditing will be. Avoid writing a concession contract using net sales as the payment reference. The administration of a net sales contract is time consuming and expensive because every expense must be periodically audited. Contracts based on gross receipts can be monitored by requiring the contractor to use sealed tape-issuing cash registers or, for stadium or arena concessions where cash registers may not be practical, by establishing and monitoring a simple inventory control system for the product used (number of cups used by size to calculate soft drink sales, number of rolls used to calculate hot dog or hamburger sales, etc.).

There are two principal variations of the percentage of revenue contract. The first is called a fixed percentage of revenue contract, and it is usually applied when

Incentives in fleet maintenance contracts

Fleet maintenance and similar contracts often contain incentive provisions that are typically structured so that at year's end, if total expenditures are below the budget agreed upon during the prior year by the local government and the contractor, the contractor receives a portion of the savings as a bonus or incentive payment—payable only if the savings did not affect contract performance during the year. Similarly, if the contractor exceeds the budget agreed upon, the contractor is responsible for payment of all or part of the excess. The percentages applicable to such incentives and disincentives are negotiated annually. The following table depicts the key payment elements of a typical incentive contract.

Incentive		Disincentive
Under budget	Up to 10% over budget	In excess of 10% over budget
Savings shared 50-50 (or a negotiated percentage) by local government and contractor	Overruns of up to 10% shared 50-50 (or a negotiated percentage) by local government and contractor	Overruns in excess of 10% paid by the contractor

Table 3-1 Sliding-scale formula for a percentage of revenue contract.

Gross receipts	Percentage of revenue to local government
$0-$50,000[a]	0
$50,001-$75,000	3
$75,001-$100,000	6
More than $100,001	12

[a]Gross receipts of $50,000 are the contractor's break-even point.

past revenue figures are available. The existence of revenue data permits bidders to forecast revenue with reasonable accuracy. The local government may receive a fixed percentage of gross revenue as a bid—for example, 14 percent. The percentage remains the same throughout the contract term.

The second variation is the sliding-scale percentage of revenue contract, used when revenue forecasts are unreliable, a new concession is being established, or a concession has not realized its potential because of past poor management. With the sliding-scale percentage of revenue contract, which is summarized in Table 3-1, the payment to the local government increases as the contractor's revenue increases. Ordinarily, no payments to the local government are made until the break-even point is reached—the point at which the contractor's revenue equals the cost of obtaining that revenue. After the break-even point has been reached, the calculations of percentage start, increasing with each revenue increment. If gross revenue stabilizes in one or two years, the sliding-scale percentage of revenue contract can be converted to a fixed percentage of revenue contract or can remain in place throughout the contract term.

Cost plus a percentage of cost contract

No discussion of cost reimbursement contracts would be complete without a warning against the **cost plus a percentage of cost (cost-plus) contract,** which is specifically prohibited in state and local governments except in emergency contracting. This method allows the contractor to receive a percentage of all costs incurred in the performance of the contract as a fee to cover profit and overhead. Never use this type of contract except in an emergency when no other choice is available. The contractor has no reason to control costs; the more labor or material used, the higher the contractor's profit.

If the local government is not attentive to detail, the cost plus a percentage of cost contract can be worked into other types of contracts. If a contractor charges for the cost of material used in the performance of a contract plus a percentage of that cost as a handling charge, the material portion of the contract then becomes a cost plus a percentage of cost contract. Again, the greater the quantity or the more expensive the material used, the higher the contractor's profits.

An example of this type of contract-within-another-contract is found in architecture, engineering, and consulting contracts that contain a provision that allows the contractor to hire subcontractors and be reimbursed at the subcontractor's cost plus a percentage of that cost. This encourages the contractor to hire a more expensive subcontractor, even if qualified in-house staff are available. The more the subcontractor is paid, the higher the contractor's profit.

Whenever a percentage is proposed in any contract document, legal counsel must review the request to decide whether the provisions of state or local law are being violated.

Bidder qualification method

The scope-of-work team must decide early in the process how to establish the responsibility of the bidders and what criteria they must meet to be eligible for award. There are two ways to determine responsibility: postqualification and prequalification.

The most commonly used method in local governments is postqualification, in which any bidder may respond to a solicitation. The bid document includes minimum qualifications that bidders must meet. After the bidders are ranked by price, the lowest responsive bidder's qualifications are reviewed against the qualification criteria in the bid document. If they meet the criteria of the bid document, the response is accepted, and if all other requirements are met, that bidder receives the award. If the qualification criteria are not met, the bid response is rejected and the next lowest bidder is subjected to the same scrutiny.

The most common problem occurs when a low bidder who is rejected because of failure to meet specific qualification criteria protests the award, challenging the reasonableness of the qualification criteria. Management or the governing body may call for cancellation and a re-bid if convinced that the original solicitation was unfair. At the least, the award and the start of the contract are delayed while the protest is being resolved.

The second method of establishing bidder responsibility is prequalification, which is authorized by most local governments. Prequalification is used primarily for major construction projects, but it can be very effective in service contracting. Under this method, the local government issues a separate RFQ. The responses to this solicitation address only pre-established qualification criteria. The responses are examined, and only bidders who meet the qualification criteria are permitted to respond to the bid document.

The incidence of protest is about the same as that for postqualification, but the protests are often simpler to resolve because the issue of price is not involved. Moreover, because prequalification occurs before the bid document is published, more time is available to resolve protests.

Prequalification is used primarily under the competitive sealed bidding method. Both competitive negotiation and multistep bidding methods already include a form of prequalification. In competitive negotiation, the initial evaluation of the responses determines whether the contractor meets the qualification criteria of the RFP. The multistep bidding process also assesses each bidder's qualifications in the first step.

Qualification criteria

Whatever the method used, it is essential that the scope-of-work team exercise care and objectivity in creating the qualification criteria by which the responsibility of potential bidders or offerors is judged. The success of the entire service contracting program hinges on how well the local government matches qualified contractors to the service to be contracted.

It is very important to establish qualification criteria that comply with the requirements of the service contract but that can be met by enough contractors to ensure adequate competition. The first step in defining the minimum qualifications for bidders is to assess the level of expertise of available contractors. If their expertise is minimal, the scope of work may have to be modified to suit their capabilities. The scope-of-work team can assess the contractors' abilities by informally interviewing them or sending them a preliminary questionnaire on experience, existing contracts, and so forth or by contacting nearby local governments who have contracted for the same service and reviewing their bid responses. The same contractors probably will have submitted bids previously in most areas of the region.

Avoid using qualification criteria that do not affect a contractor's ability to provide the service or that limit competition. For example, in bidding out a social services contract, the local government might avoid establishing "tax exempt entity" as a qualification criterion because it may limit competition and preclude qualified for-profit businesses from competing. Qualification criteria must relate directly to the contractor's ability to provide the service and be broad enough to permit more than one contractor to qualify. The following are examples of criteria that may be used in both postqualification and prequalification procedures.

Experience

Complexity of the service does not justify requiring a great deal of experience nor does simplicity justify accepting very little. Contracts for low- or semiskilled labor-intensive services such as mowing, beach cleaning, or litter control may require that the contractor have as many years of experience in the field as a contractor that provides consulting or other semiprofessional or professional services. A contractor in the semiskilled labor field must have the experience and expertise to attract and retain a work force stable enough to carry out contractual obligations. This is not an easy task in the high-turnover environment in which this contractor must survive. An inexperienced contractor that submits a low bid for semiskilled or low-skilled labor contracts may not be able to produce the crews when needed.

The scope-of-work team must assess not only corporate experience but also the experience of the contractor's principals and staff responsible for service delivery. A firm may have only one or two years' experience in a service area, but one or two key employees may have more than twenty years' experience. This can be more than enough to qualify the firm as a responsible bidder.

References

The scope-of-work team should require that the contractors submit references for current and previous contracts. Specify that their experience must be in contracts that are similar to the proposed contract in type and scope. Avoid establishing a minimum number of references; one contractor with ten marginally acceptable references may not be as well qualified as another with one or two excellent references.

Financial stability

Requests for financial information typically are reserved for contracts with an extended term or a requirement for substantial capital outlay. It is advantageous to create a standard financial statement form for all bidders; this can be developed in house or commercial forms may be used. The finance or auditing departments can help by providing current industry standards for interpreting the statements and by selecting pertinent ratios as indicators of important financial characteristics.

Other qualification criteria

Requests for other information—such as availability of personnel and the condition and availability of equipment—should be included in the RFQ to help the local government assess the capabilities of the contractor.

Preparing an RFQ

When using the prequalification method, the scope-of-work team must issue an RFQ. The format should be kept as simple as possible. A description of the steps for preparing and issuing an RFQ follows.

The RFQ format

In the introduction, briefly explain the purpose of the RFQ and in general terms describe the services to be purchased and the approximate size of the contract (e.g., list the number of buildings to be cleaned, acres to be mowed, annual hours of service required).

List the requirements for experience, evidence of financial stability, and references and other pertinent criteria. Request copies of any required licenses or certifications.

Describe the method the local government will use to qualify respondents. Use qualification criteria that clearly establish a pass/fail standard. For example, a pass/fail standard for basic experience could state: "The supervisory personnel of the bidder (or the bidding firm) must have successfully completed two contracts of the same size and scope within the past five years." The pass/fail standard is expressed in the words "of the same size and scope." This eliminates inexperienced contractors and those experienced only in smaller contracts who may want to expand into larger contracts; in such a situation the contractor would be learning how to operate them at the local government's expense.

Include the general terms and conditions and the insurance requirements of the final contract. Require that any exceptions to them be identified in the response.

The process

The local government sends the RFQ to all potential bidders. To ensure the widest possible distribution to qualified contractors, send the RFQ to those on the **bidder lists** of area local governments, on trade association member lists, and in the listings in the yellow pages; post the RFQ on public bulletin boards; and advertise it in a local or regional newspaper or trade magazine. Anyone can respond to an RFQ. Avoid selective invitations to potential bidders, which violate the requirement that public procurement be conducted in open competition and may be specifically prohibited by state or local government regulations.

The scope-of-work team reviews all responses and selects those that meet the requirements. If only one or two responses are received when more were expected, conduct a telephone survey of all contractors who received the RFQ to determine why they did not respond. If the number of responding bidders does not offer adequate competition, adjust the qualifications to attract more bidders and reissue the

RFQ. It is better to reissue an RFQ than to have a limited bidder list. When reviewing bidder responses, do not use any criteria that were not identified in the original RFQ. A disqualified respondent is likely to succeed in protesting the use of undisclosed criteria.

Respondents who have been disqualified must receive written notice of the disqualification and the reasons for it. Because they have the right to protest a disqualification, the reasons for establishing the specific qualification criteria and a justification for each disqualification must be put in writing and made part of the RFQ files.

Endnotes

1 American Bar Association, *Model Procurement Code for State and Local Governments* (Chicago, Ill.: American Bar Association, 2000), Article 3, Part B, Section 3-205.

2 Information on obtaining the Consumer Price Index can be obtained from the Bureau of Labor Statistics Web site at www.bls.gov/cpi. To receive the Consumer Price Index news release by e-mail, one can subscribe to the BLS news service free of charge at http://www.bls.gov/bls/list.htm.

Exhibit 3-1 Sample set of response requirements.

RFP NUMBER _____

TITLE _____

The written response shall include the following information:

Restatement of the proposed work in your own words to allow the evaluation panel to determine whether your perception of the scope of the contract conforms with that of [local government].

Proposed staffing, with an estimate of time to be devoted by each principal of the firm, staff member, consultant, or subcontractor; include resumes of each if not previously submitted.

Proposed budget for the project, by phase if applicable. The budget proposed will help determine whether [local government] and your firm have similar and realistic expectations of the scope of the contract.

Names of contracts of a similar scope performed by the individuals to be assigned to the project.

Sample of work products such as reports generated for similar assignments by the individuals to be assigned to the project.

Detailed response to the following questions: [List any questions generated by the panel for the offeror].

Please note: The [local government] will use all the criteria described or referred to in the original solicitation and in this letter to evaluate the written response.

4

The Scope of Work

The scope of work is the heart of the bid document. A well-written scope of work can do more for the success of a contract than any other part of the contracting process.

The goals of a scope of work are clarity, completeness, and logical development. The first section of this chapter offers guidelines to help ensure that the scope of work will be understood by its two principal audiences: the contractor and the local government contract administration team. Subsequent sections address the logical development of the scope of work. Sample formats are provided for the scope of work for competitive sealed bidding, competitive negotiation, and multistep bidding. These sample formats can help to ensure that the scope of work includes all the necessary components presented in a logical order.

Terminology and word choice

The scope of work must be clear, specific, and appropriate to the audience because the terms and conditions of service delivery specified within it are the point of reference for resolving problems throughout the contract term. Questions to ask while writing the scope of work include "Will it make sense to the contractor?" and "Will it make sense to the contract manager?" For example, when the public and private sectors use different terms for a function, process, or task, use the terminology the private sector uses. If it is possible to misunderstand a term, include a definition so that all parties have the same frame of reference. Terms that are unique to the public sector also must be defined. Many private firms are not familiar with local government terms such as "fiscal year," "encumbered," "appropriated," and "full-time equivalent." Whenever there is a possibility that a word or term can be misinterpreted, change it to its common equivalent, define it, or delete it.

The terms "should" and "may" have no place in a scope of work unless there is a clear need to advise the contractor that the action requested is purely optional. These words do not refer to mandatory action. Instead, they give a contractor the choice of complying or not complying. The words "either," "any," and "and/or" also offer choice. When action is mandatory, use the word "shall" or "must."

When referring to actions or events that will occur after the contract begins, refer to the contractor and not to the bidder, the successful bidder, the consultant, the vendor, or the provider. Use the word "bidder" and its variations only when referring to activities or requirements that pertain before contract performance begins. When referring to the local government in bid and contract documents, use the local government's full name (city of Anywhere).

A bid form is the pricing form completed by bidders in response to an **invitation for bids (IFB)**, or **solicitation**. A proposal is the form completed by offerors as part of their response to an RFP. Although the term "**proposal**" is often used when referring to the response to a competitive bid, the correct term is "**bid**" or "bid form." The terms "bid" and "proposal" have different meanings. "Bid" indicates that the contract will be awarded to the lowest responsive and responsible bidder; "proposal" indicates a negotiated award. Mixing terms in the bid or contract documents can cause problems in resolving protests or contract disputes in a court of law.

Avoid using phrases or clauses in the scope of work whose meaning is arguable or ambiguous. If work is to be done to a professional standard, identify and describe the standard. The phrase "to the satisfaction of the project officer" establishes no standard and can be challenged as unenforceable. Because the phrases "acceptable quality" and "high quality of workmanship" and similar generalizations cannot be clearly defined or quantified, they pose problems if a contract dispute arises. Replace them with language that describes measurable levels of quality or workmanship. The accompanying sidebar lists terms that should not be used in a scope of work or in a bid document.

The first time an abbreviation, acronym, or short form of a name is used, use the full spelling of name first and place the abbreviation, acronym, or short form in parenthesis immediately after it. Subsequently, only the abbreviation, acronym, or short form needs to be used.

Scope of work types

There are three general types of scope of work: performance specification, technical scope of work, and hybrid scope of work. These types provide general descriptions

---

Ambiguous phrases

When a phrase is ambiguous, the intent of the contract will generally be interpreted in favor of the party that did not write the contract; this rule disadvantages the local government as the author of the contract.

- accurate workmanship
- as determined by/as directed by
- as soon as possible
- best commercial practices/carefully performed/clean and orderly/good materials/good working order/highest grade/highest quality/neatly finished
- in accordance with applicable published specifications
- in accordance with industry standards/in accordance with instructions/in strict accordance with/in the judgment of/in the opinion of
- of a standard type/of an approved type
- to be furnished if requested/to the satisfaction of/unless otherwise directed/workmanlike manner

Source: Adapted from Edward R. Fisk, *Construction Project Administration*, 7th ed. (Upper Saddle River, N.J.: Prentice Hall, 2003).

for the scope of work and may be used whether the service is being bid through competitive sealed bidding, competitive negotiation, or multistep bidding.

A performance specification scope of work prescribes the end product and functions that must be performed or a standard that must be met. It is well suited for technical projects such as software development or mechanical design and other services in which the end result can be defined. Performance specifications should include an established method for evaluating the product to ensure that it conforms to the scope of work.

A technical scope of work mandates the specific details of the final product. A contract that contains technical drawings is a technical specification. It is the responsibility of the contractor to provide the product exactly as prescribed in the drawings. The risk is assumed by the issuing authority; if the contractor satisfies the technical specification, then he or she has satisfied the contract requirements.

Hybrid scopes of work combine technical and performance requirements. Risk is shared, however; the more technical the scope of work, the more risk is assumed by the issuing agency and vice versa.

The scope of work for competitive sealed bidding

This section provides a model format that can be used to structure the scope of work for competitive sealed bidding. The accompanying sidebar provides a summary of this model. Each subsection corresponds to an element in the scope of work. The model format can be used for virtually any service contract. Although most scopes of work

---

Suggested outline for the scope of work

Introduction and general information   Purpose or objective, history and background, contact persons, bidding method, pre-bid conference, contractor qualifications, calendar of events

Task description   Work to be done by the contractor

Constraints on the contractor   Worksite conditions, ordinances, security control

Contractor personnel requirements   Qualifications of key personnel, employee identification, additional personnel responsibilities

Contractor responsibilities   Quality control program, service complaints, emergency assistance, work schedule

Local government responsibilities   What the local government must do for or provide to the contractor

Evaluation of contractor performance   Performance standards, evaluation forms, incentives, liquidated damages

Reporting requirements and procedures   Contractor's reporting schedule and responsibilities

Special conditions   Payment procedures, insurance, bonds, alternative surety, contract extension and renewal

Special instructions   Evaluation of responses

Price ranking of bidders   The method for ranking bidders by price

Exhibits   Technical reports, maps, drawings, schedules, photographs, letters of recommendation, letters of intent to collaborate (if services are to be delivered through a network or if the primary contractor intends to use sub-contractors)

will contain the elements listed in the format, the order of entries can be changed to suit local preferences or conventions. The section also contains references to clauses given in full in Appendix A that can be used in developing the scope of work.

Just as there are no strict rules for format, there are none for the length of the scope of work; it can be one page for a simple service or fifty pages for a complex one. The best guideline is that the scope of work should contain enough information to encourage bids at a price and of a quality that are acceptable to the local government. How much information is enough? Knowing when to stop adding details is not easy, but when a member of the scope-of-work team asks "Why is this in the spec?" it is probably time to stop writing.

Introduction and general information

The introduction states the purpose of the scope of work—what the local government expects to accomplish with the contract—and it may include a history or background of the service. It gives a brief overview of the work required and defines the extent of the service to be provided and the contract term. The time and place of any pre-bid conference and a general statement of the minimum experience and qualifications required of the contractor are also usually included in the introduction.

Purpose or objective   The statement of purpose or objective of the scope of work expands the brief overview of the service included in the introduction by identifying the bidding method to be used, the rules that apply to its use, and the local government department whose service is being contracted out. It also states whether the contract will be monitored by the affected department or by a central contract monitoring and administration team. In addition, the introduction gives a statement of the goals and objectives of the service that may include the relationship of the service to the total local government operation; the frequency of service; the size of the contract and an indication of the level of effort expected of the contractor; and any other information that would help the bidder understand the local government's needs.

The introduction also gives an indication of the amount of work to be done in an estimate of the size of the contract, expressed in terms of annual expenditure by the local government or number of units of service required (e.g., the number of clients to be served, pieces of equipment to be maintained, acres to be mowed, or curb miles to be swept). It also gives the start and end dates of the contract and the location where the work is to be performed.

History and background   A history and background section is included if it will help the bidder better understand the service to be provided. A simple service contract may not require a history and background section, but one is always included when a service is contracted out for the first time. It gives the bidder a better understanding of how the service was delivered by the local government, and it can explain why the service is now being offered for delivery by a private contractor.

Contact persons   During the bidding process, many local governments prohibit bidders from making direct contact with any public employees except the purchasing staff. This policy can be effective when applied to the purchase of goods, but when it is applied to the purchase of services, it can generate unnecessary problems by denying bidders the opportunity to obtain firsthand information on the service delivery procedures currently in place. No matter how well written, a scope of work or a response to an inquiry cannot provide a bidder with the same grasp of service delivery as one-to-one contact with a knowledgeable department representative.

It is possible to control contacts with public employees while still providing the bidder with access to the information necessary to be fully responsive. Bidder contacts can be limited to a technical contact (a department representative who is completely familiar with the service area) who is responsible for responding to service delivery questions and a contract contact (a purchasing staff representative) who is responsible for responding to questions on the bid document and bidding procedures. Bidders must be cautioned that statements of contacts that appear to materially change the scope of work or any part of the bid document cannot be relied on unless they are covered in a formal amendment to the bid document. See "Additional information" in Appendix A.

Any contact between bidders and local government staff should be prohibited for the last week or ten days before the date set for opening the bid responses. If contact is not cut off at a specific time, bidders may continue to call to ask questions about the work or the specifications up to the day set for receipt of bids, possibly delaying the bid opening if an amendment is required in order to respond to a bidder's question. If the bidders' questions and comments up to the specific cutoff date are substantive and indicate that clarification of the bid document is necessary or that pertinent information was omitted, issue an amendment.

Pre-bid conference Whenever a pre-bid conference is scheduled, whether attendance is mandatory or optional, include the time, date, and location in the bid advertisement and on the cover page of the bid document. This information should also be included in the introduction to the scope of work, particularly if attendance is mandatory. Complete details of the conference are given in the instructions to bidders section of the bid document.

The pre-bid conference provides bidders with an opportunity to ask questions about the service and the bid document in a public setting. Whenever possible, it is held at the service delivery site. Bidders can then inspect the site and note apparent service constraints or visible problem areas. Some conferences are held in two parts: a guided tour of the site followed by a conference with those who attended the tour. If attendance at the pre-bid conference is mandatory, the bid document must state that bidders must attend both the tour and the conference to qualify for participation in the bid. When the service encompasses a large geographic area, the local government should arrange a transportation vehicle large enough to accommodate all the bidders. No more than one tour and one pre-bid conference should be held because bidders must have the opportunity to hear all questions from all other attendees. See "Pre-bid conference (mandatory)" and "Pre-bid conference (optional)" in Appendix A. Additional information on structuring and managing a pre-bid conference is included in Chapter 5.

Contractor qualifications The experience, qualifications, and evidence of financial stability required of each bidder must be completely described in the qualifications section. The description of experience may include, for example, the number of years of experience, level of technical knowledge, and the degrees, certifications, and organizational accreditations required. Financial stability may be determined by requesting the bidder's most recent financial statements, evidence of bonding capability, and evidence of ability to obtain necessary insurance. Require recent references as evidence that the firm has performed satisfactorily for others in contracts of similar size and scope. Ask for the name and telephone number of a responsible contact for each reference.

If any special trade, professional, or business licenses are required of employees by local law, they also must be listed in the bid document, as well as any other special experience or qualification deemed necessary by the local government. If the service requires only that the firm be in the business of providing the service, a broad qualification clause can be used. (See "Qualifications of bidders" in Appendix A.)

Calendar of events It is useful to include a calendar of key events in either the introduction to the scope of work or the instructions to bidders section (discussed in Chapter 5). A calendar of key events should include dates for the bidding and award processes and should list the estimated date of completion for each. Identify the estimates as target dates that may be changed if required. The events usually included in a calendar of events are the distribution of the bid document, the pre-bid conference and site tour, the bid opening, bidder interviews, identification of the successful bidder, the contract award date, and the start of contract performance.

Task description

The task description section of the scope of work sets forth the duties of the contractor. The professional literature on service contracting describes methods for preparing task descriptions ranging from measurement and analysis of inputs and outputs to the creation of complex models delineating tasks and subtasks. These methods may be appropriate for academics, but they cannot be applied with confidence by the average local government employee without specialized training.

In an ideal scenario, the staff of the department currently providing the service prepares a task description independent of the scope-of-work team. After the two groups reconcile conflicts between the two documents, they merge them. However, most local governments will find this approach an impractical use of staff and time. In most cases, the scope-of-work team will take responsibility for preparing the task description, which should include input from department staff if feasible.

The task description details the local government's expectations of the service based either on available professional literature or the department's knowledge of the service as it has been delivered in other local governments.

The scope-of-work team also identifies aspects of the service that can be evaluated to determine whether the service is being delivered effectively. The evaluation includes a quantity-oriented assessment that specifies how many units of work should be delivered in a given day or week (how many curb miles swept, clients served, acres mowed, etc.) and a quality-oriented assessment describing how it will be determined whether the units of work meet contract requirements (height of grass, degree of cleanliness, client satisfaction levels, complaints received, etc.). This information, although it is not directly related to the task description, is used to develop the performance requirements section of the scope of work.

While carrying out these tasks, the scope-of-work team may contact area local governments and professional organizations and research public procurement Web sites to obtain sample scopes of work. The team should also gather as much information as possible on how the private sector delivers the service. In addition, contractors identified as potential bidders can be asked for copies of bid documents or contracts they have received. It is important to collect more than one sample scope of work to obtain a broad picture of the different descriptions of the service,

Finding the right level of service

Only the minimum service requirements should be included in the task description. Including unnecessary service enhancements can result in responses that are priced higher than the present cost of service delivery. On the other hand, exceptionally low service requirements may yield savings but produce an unacceptable level of service. To protect against service requirements that are too low, identify tasks indirectly related to the service that were formerly performed by public employees and ensure that they are included in the task description. If a street-cleaning crew also removed drifting sand or debris from a parking lot or if refuse collection included picking up newspapers from various drop-off points, cleaning up sidewalk trash spills, or collecting discarded appliances or furniture, include those tasks in the description unless they will continue to be performed by public employees or will be purchased under a separate contract.

the evaluation methods used, and the problems others have encountered. The team then prepares its own draft of a task description on the basis of the experiences of other public and private purchasers of the same service. Because of the variety of sources used, this draft represents a composite view of the service and may well include more details and address more problems associated with the service than the draft prepared by the department.

The task description that emerges from this process should reflect the department's service needs and incorporate the best features of the task descriptions collected from other sources. In addition, it should translate this information into the clear language and understandable format that a useful and complete bid document requires.

If time permits, set the task description aside when it is finished. After a few days, review it for details and completeness, remembering that the contractor will have no responsibility for performing any duty that is not described. The level of completeness also largely determines the appropriate bidding method. A clear and detailed task description usually permits competitive sealed bidding. However, if the description is not precise or complete, competitive negotiation may be more appropriate.

Constraints on the contractor

Any conditions that could affect efficient service delivery, hamper effective performance, or increase costs to the contractor must be disclosed to the bidders. Typical constraints are associated with worksite conditions, unusual ordinances, or security control systems of the local government.

Worksite conditions   All known conditions at the work site that can adversely affect the contractor must be identified to avoid disputes about added costs and liability after the award. If unusual conditions exist at a work site, describe them. For example, defective floor coverings can affect maintenance costs. Limited or extended hours of operation of a public facility can affect the cost of custodial or other services delivered at the site.

Ordinances   Local laws, regulations, or policies that may affect the contractor's level of service, the workweek, or the time of day performance occurs must be identified in the scope of work. Local ordinances may require collection and disposal methods that are more complex than standard refuse collection practices of the industry. The use of heavy equipment or other machinery may be restricted by noise ordinances, limiting the hours such equipment can be operated. For example, if the contractor's workday is from 6:00 a.m. to 3:00 p.m. and the local government's noise ordinances are in effect until 8:00 a.m., the contractor must schedule employees for a later workday because of the restriction. This situation may arise around noisy services such as refuse collection and mowing. This could bring the hourly wages paid to employees into premium time, resulting in higher contract costs. Contract costs may also increase if contractors must schedule work on weekends and holidays, as they often do during peak seasons.

Security controls The local government's building and facility security regulations must be described clearly if the contractor will require access to public property for operations or for storage. Access to some facilities may require that contract employees obtain security clearances, possibly adding expense for the contractor. Accountability is always required for keys to park gates, buildings, or parking meters. For example, parking meter collection contractors are commonly held responsible for rekeying every affected parking meter if an employee loses a set of keys. Whenever security can be compromised by the contractor, appropriate **liquidated damages** (monetary damages assessed for failure to perform all or part of the contract) should be incorporated into the scope of work. The section of the scope of work pertaining to contractor constraints must address all such issues.

Contractor personnel requirements

Few things affect the quality of a service as much as the use of unqualified contractor personnel. The contractor must be given detailed information on the experience and qualifications required of personnel assigned to the contract.

Qualifications of key personnel Require the contractor to submit the résumés of his or her field supervisor, team leader, or project manager with the bid response. Include minimum experience requirements and qualifications for these positions in the scope of work. It may also be necessary to require proof of professional licensure or certification of the contractor's personnel if appropriate to the service being contracting; nursing services and counseling are two examples. Do not expect that because of the stature of the contractor in the industry they will provide only qualified personnel; impeccable references are no guarantee that every field supervisor, team leader, and project manager is well qualified. In addition, require that the local government have the right of approval of replacement staff if the originally assigned field or project supervisor changes during the term of the contract. Indeed, some local governments have opted to include a clause establishing the right of dismissal in the event that the contract manager becomes dissatisfied with the performance of a contractor's employee. (See "Contractor personnel" in Appendix A.)

Contractor employee identification For some contracts—such as day custodial work, refuse collection, food concessions, or any other service area in which the contractor's employees are in contact with the public—it may be desirable to require that the contractor provide a full work uniform to employees. Uniforms are advisable for any service for which public employees performing a similar service wear uniforms. By requiring uniforms, the local government forces the contractor to place its image and reputation on the line if complaints are received about discourtesy or poor performance.

Although many contractors in service areas such as refuse collection, landscaping, and custodial services routinely provide employee uniforms without a contract requirement, it is best not to take this for granted. Include in the scope of work a specific description of any required uniforms: the minimum uniform may be a T-shirt, jacket, coveralls, or smock with the contractor's name prominently displayed. Also include a means of enforcing uniform requirements—perhaps through a deduction from the contractor's payment for each day that an employee is observed out of uniform.

Additional personnel responsibilities   Additional personnel-related requirements for contractors that should be included in the scope of work and monitored and enforced throughout the contract term include the following:

- A policy of employing only those who possess the required skills and experience for the job classification.
- Maintenance of a work force of sufficient size to handle the contract, including reserve personnel to fill vacancies during absences due to illness, vacations, and holidays.
- Written personnel policies governing behavior, substance abuse, and relations with customers and the public.
- Regular filing of updated charts with the contract administration team showing the number of personnel assigned to the contract, current vacancies, and weekly work schedules.

Contractor responsibilities

As the scope of work is developed, other responsibilities and requirements that may not relate directly to the actual provision of the service may be added as they are identified. Other contractor responsibilities may include the implementation of a quality-control program, the development of policies to respond to service complaints, or the provision of assistance to the local government during emergencies or natural disasters. While it is often appropriate to require the contractor to have protocols for responding to service complaints, the contractor should not be the only recourse available to citizens making complaints. The local government should publicize available avenues for citizen feedback, including hotline numbers (see Chapter 8), and require contractors to publicize this information. This provides the local government with a check against unresponsive private service providers.

Quality control program   Contractors providing complex or highly visible services should be required to have a quality control program in place to ensure that the service is provided as specified. Bidders can be required to submit an outline of their existing quality-control program with their bid response; if such a program does not exist, they may submit a draft of one for review. Once a contract is awarded, reports, files, and inspection data related to the program must be made available on demand to the contract manager throughout the contract term. The quality control program of the contractor must include at least the following three components: an inspection system covering all the performance requirements in the scope of work that specifies the areas to be inspected on either a scheduled or unscheduled basis and the individuals who are responsible for the inspection, a method of identifying unacceptable service quality, and a description of the type of corrective action to be taken if service quality is unacceptable.

Service complaints   Describe how the contractor must respond to service complaints. Use the scope of work to communicate early to the bidders the local government's expectations regarding response time to service requests, the resolution of complaints, and payment for the costs of correcting a complaint when the fault is that of the contractor. If the contractor is charged with responding directly to service complaints, specify which records are to be maintained, how they are to be kept, and the frequency with which the local government will review the records.

Emergency assistance   If the service contract includes the use of specialized equipment, the contractor can be required to rent the equipment to the local government for emergency needs such as snow removal, flood control, storm recovery, or rescue operations. Include space in the bid response form for the bidder to enter the unit prices for emergency rental of the equipment, including operators.

Trade references and standards   When federal or state statutes, trade standards, or other materials are used to establish requirements in the bid document, a copy of these references must be available on demand for review and inspection by bidders. If the local government cannot produce a copy of a specified citation, standard, or method within a reasonable time after a bidder's request, the bidder may be successful in challenging its inclusion in the bid document.

Work schedule   For many contracts involving outdoor activities, knowing where the contractor's crews are at all times is essential to effective contract administration. The scope of work must require that the contractor provide a weekly or biweekly work schedule indicating when and where crews will be working. Include a requirement that the schedules are to be approved in advance by the field manager or contract manager.

Local government responsibilities

In service contracting, the local government assumes its own set of contractual duties and obligations. Its principal obligation is, of course, to pay for satisfactory service. Other obligations may include the provision of support services to the contractor such as space for storage of equipment or supplies, parking for employees of the contractor, prepaid utility services, or the use or lease of local government equipment or facilities.

The scope-of-work team must assess the financial impact of each additional contractual responsibility that the local government may choose to assume. If the contractor provides support services, expect the cost for these services to be inflated by an amount set aside for overhead (profit), resulting in a higher contract price. If the local government provides the services, the cost may be more easily controlled, but the price paid to the contractor does not represent the contract's true cost. However, when the local government can provide existing facilities and equipment or other amenities to the contractor without any unusual expense, the provision of support services can contribute to overall contract savings.

The local government may choose to assume certain obligations in order to maintain control in areas perceived to be performed better or more securely in house. The local government often retains control of functions such as making the deposit of daily revenues received by the concessionaire, retaining custody of facility keys, providing repairs and maintenance to a public building used by the contractor, or making determinations about eligibility for social services. The local government may also want to purchase and retain ownership of equipment and lease it to the contractor for the contract term. It is not necessary for a local government to relinquish control of every facet of a service when contracting.

Evaluating contractor performance

When it prepares its draft of the scope of work, the department identifies the areas of performance to be evaluated and the quantity and quality requirements for each area that can be used to establish performance standards in the contract. This is a required part of the scope of work, especially if liquidated damages can be assessed against the contractor for unacceptable performance.

The description of the evaluation method should not be lengthy. It must be detailed enough to identify the areas to be evaluated, define deficient performance by the contractor, and specify the liquidated damages that can be assessed for deficient performance. Methods can range from a simple pass/fail evaluation of the contractor's product against an established standard to an evaluation of the impact of the contractor's service on customers or clients. This section should also specify the intervals at which the contractor's performance will be assessed (weekly, monthly, annually, etc.).

Whether simple or complex, every evaluation system should encourage cooperation with the contractor so that an acceptable level of service can be maintained throughout the contract term. In addition, evaluation systems must be structured so that they do not interfere with service delivery. A more complete discussion of performance monitoring is included in Chapter 8.

Performance standards   Establishing a zero-fault performance standard is unrealistic. Establishing a single point where acceptable performance stops and unacceptable performance begins is equally unrealistic; gray areas must be considered. To incorporate these gray areas into an evaluation system, establish several levels below the perfect level of performance. The first level defines a specific range—for example, up to three faults within a month as acceptable performance or anywhere within that range. A second level—from four to seven faults within a month—represents marginal performance. A third level—more than seven faults within a month—defines unacceptable performance. Performance at the second level generates a warning notice.

Performance at the third level suggests serious problems with service delivery, requiring possible enforcement of any liquidated damages provisions of the contract and, if warranted, notice of default. Exhibit 4-1 at the end of this chapter shows a typical multilevel performance evaluation model.

Liquidated damages   The scope of work must describe the liquidated damages that can be assessed against the contractor for unacceptable performance. Approach the use of liquidated damages provisions cautiously. Contractors might not submit a bid response if they feel that the provisions are too harsh or unreasonable; expect those that do respond to increase the contract price to help offset any possible assessment of liquidated damages during the contract term.

The term "penalty clause" is often used incorrectly to refer to liquidated damages. Never refer to liquidated damages as a penalty against the contractor. A liquidated damages provision is included in a contract when the local government may reasonably expect to suffer a loss or damage if the contractor's performance does not meet contract requirements. Because the local government is paying for acceptable performance, whenever performance is unacceptable, the government is actually overpaying for the service. Liquidated damages provisions help quantify this overpayment. The local government can then deduct a specified amount or percentage as liquidated damages from the next payment made to the contractor. The exact amount of damage is usually difficult or impossible to ascertain or prove. The only condition that local governments must meet in establishing the amount of liquidated damages is that the amount must not be excessive or out of proportion to the extent of the poor performance and must represent reasonable compensation for the damage done.

There is always the temptation to assess high amounts for liquidated damages of $1,000 or more per day or a 20 percent or more deduction from a contractor's payment, but if a protest that the damage amount is unreasonable goes to court and the local government does not have a good justification for the amount, the court will probably set the clause aside, leaving the contract with no liquidated damages clause at all. The key to establishing liquidated damages amounts is reasonableness.

There are many ways to assess liquidated damages for poor performance; most are variations of a few basic systems. Whichever system is used, it must be included and described in the performance evaluation section of the scope of work. In the system illustrated in the accompanying sidebar, points are assigned for failure to meet required standards and a percentage of the contractor's fee is deducted from the payment depending on the number of points.[1] The number of points and the percentage deducted can be increased or decreased according to the number of tasks being evaluated.

If one job, such as custodial services, has twenty areas of performance to be evaluated and another, such as mowing, has only a few areas, the same evaluation scale may not work for both. More latitude (a higher number of points allowed before liquidated damages are enforced) should be given in a contract with twenty or more areas in which things can go wrong; less latitude (fewer points allowed before enforcement of damages) should be given in a contract with only a few areas. For example, building-cleaning contracts contain many tasks, and many poor performance points can accumulate in a week. A mowing contract with fewer tasks to evaluate would have considerably fewer. Exhibit 4-2 at the end of this chapter illustrates a performance evaluation system for towing contracts.

Incentives   Whenever liquidated damages are part of a contract, consider including incentives for exceptional performance. Cash or other rewards can help balance any negative effect of liquidated damages provisions on a contractor. An incentive provision tells the contractor that the local government is just as eager to reward good performance as it is to assess damages for poor performance. The format used is the same as that used for assigning liquidated damages. The scope-of-work team defines superior performance and develops incentives or bonuses that can be issued on a percentage or lump-sum basis. In the previous sidebar, for example, if zero points were assessed against the contractor, a percentage bonus of 2 percent or 5 percent of the month's invoice could be awarded. In Exhibit 4-2, the towing contractor could be awarded a lump-sum bonus of $100 or more for any month in which the contractor always arrived at the accident scene on time.

Evaluation of nonquantitative service areas   Quantitative measures can be used to evaluate aspects of services to which they may not seem to apply. For example, the

A point system for assessing liquidated damages

Assign one or more points for each basic task inadequately done for each day that the fault is not corrected. Total all points received by the contractor in one month. Establish a number of points below which no liquidated damages will be assessed; for example, five points or fewer per month. This represents acceptable performance. Each level of performance is assigned progressively higher percentage values for assessment of liquidated damages. The total deduction is cumulative; calculate the amount to be deducted from the contractor's compensation for that month by adding the percentages deducted for each level.

Level	Number of points	Percentage deducted
1	1-5	0.0
2	6-10	0.1
3	11-15	0.4
4	16-25	0.8
5	26+	2.0

If more than 25 points are accumulated in any one week or more than 75 in any consecutive four-week period, the contract is subject to termination.

Scoring Example 1: Under this formula, if a contractor receives 26 points, the deduction is 12.5 percent (the total of the percentages assessed at each level) of the monthly invoice and the contract is considered a candidate for termination.

1-5	=	5 points x 0.0%	=	0.0%
6-10	=	5 points x 0.1%	=	0.5%
11-15	=	5 points x 0.4%	=	2.0%
16-25	=	10 points x 0.8%	=	8.0%
26+	=	1 point x 2.0%	=	2.0%

Total deduction (26 points) = 12.5%

Scoring Example 2: Under this formula, if a contractor receives 17 points, the deduction is 4.1 percent (the total of the percentages assessed at each level) of the monthly invoice.

1-5	=	5 points x 0.0%	=	0.0%
6-10	=	5 points x 0.1%	=	0.5%
11-15	=	5 points x 0.4%	=	2.0%
16-25	=	2 points x 0.8%	=	1.6%
26+	=	0 points x 2.0%	=	0.0%

Total deduction (17 points) = 4.1%

cleanliness of a street or facility, the impact of a service on a client, and the effectiveness of a training program can be measured quantitatively. First, the deliverables of the service must be analyzed. If the evaluation is to be based on cleanliness, assign a scale of point values to a written or photographic description of cleanliness. To assess client satisfaction, list the most likely types of complaints and the number of complaints that represent unacceptable performance. To evaluate quality of workmanship, use photographs or published trade standards to establish standards of workmanship, then assign point values for varying levels of workmanship.

Another approach is to use questionnaires to obtain evaluations of service quality directly from clients. Although a subjective evaluation made by a client may not be ideal for all service contracts, it can be an effective performance indicator if it is interpreted carefully. It also may be the only reasonable or cost-effective method for measuring the qualitative aspects of performance. Chapter 8 expands on the area of subjective evaluation, or outcome measurement.[2]

Reporting requirements and procedures

The scope of work must define all deliverables to be submitted by the contractor during the contract term, the dates that the deliverables are due, and the format to be used if a special format is required for a deliverable such as a report. Deliverables include reports containing details of contract activities, the numbers of clients served and units of service delivered, progress to date toward predetermined contract goals, and tangible products such as specifications or drawings. If the contractor is required to submit billing or data electronically, as is federally mandated for some services covered by Medicaid, the local government should explicitly define the procedure in the scope of work.

Special conditions

The special conditions of the scope of work are similar to the general terms and conditions of the contract, as discussed in Chapter 5. Whereas general terms and conditions apply to almost any contract, special conditions are usually specific to a contract. The special conditions discussed in this section are payment procedures, insurance, bonds, alternative surety, and contract extension and renewal. Other special conditions include provisions that allow local governments to buy the contractor's vehicles if the contractor defaults (see "Vehicle and equipment buyback" in Appendix A), procedures for the recovery of money the contractor owes the local government (see "Recovery of money" in Appendix A), and the terms and conditions of a sale or lease of local government vehicles to the contractor.

Payment procedures   Include instructions or special conditions that apply to payments or invoices the contractor submits. These may include procedures for separate billing to different departments receiving the services, special invoice formats, and required invoice attachments. The time needed by the local government to process payment must be clearly identified in the special conditions (twenty days, thirty days, etc.). The finance department must decide what time frame can be met regularly by the accounts payable staff. Short payment terms may attract more bidders, but use them only if the finance department can guarantee payment on the short deadline. Payment terms of twenty days are usually too short for the internal reviews, approvals, and computer processing required before checks can be issued.

On the other hand, small contractors, the foundation of most local government service contracting programs, have difficulty waiting more than twenty or thirty days for payment, especially if labor costs are a major portion of the contract. If the payment term is more than thirty days after invoice acceptance, small contractors may not be able to afford to participate or may be forced to respond with higher prices to offset the cost of possible bank loans taken out to cover slow payments by the local government. See "Payment terms and discounts (net 20- or 30-day)" and "Payment terms and discounts (2 percent 20- or 30-day)" in Appendix A.

Insurance   Establishing appropriate insurance coverage is the function of the risk or insurance manager or the legal department, not the scope-of-work team. Every service contract should require the contractor to obtain insurance sufficient to protect the local government. The insurance verifies that the contractor has the financial capability to compensate the public and the local government for injuries or damages arising from the contractor's negligence and to protect the assets of the local government from damage claims resulting from such negligence.

As important as the need for adequate insurance is, many local governments use the same insurance clauses or inserts for all types of services rather than tailoring the insurance coverage to meet the risk factors inherent in each service. To avoid exposing the local government to risks caused by inadequate or inappropriate insurance coverage, the risk manager or legal department should establish written guidelines for scope-of-work teams or purchasing departments to use to help them determine which services require special types of insurance or higher dollar limits than usual. A $500,000 limit on comprehensive general liability insurance may be reasonable for low-risk repair services, but it is inadequate for services in which equipment or machinery is used (mowing contracts, street maintenance, refuse collection, etc.). Too little coverage may lower the cost of a contract because of lower premiums, but it can create dangerous risks for the local government. Too much coverage may limit the number of bid responses, and the added premiums the contractor pays will surely be passed on to the local government in the contract price.

A critical reason for requiring a contractor to have adequate insurance is to create an insurance buffer between those damaged by the contract's actions and the local government. The contractor should always name the local government as an additional insured party in its policies. Then if the local government is sued with the contractor, the contractor's insurance carrier protects both the contractor and the local government as the additional insured party under the contractor's policy.

To develop the correct insurance requirements, all risks inherent in a specific service must be analyzed. If the service includes the temporary or semi-permanent garaging of local government vehicles at a contractor's facility, the garage keeper must be required to have insurance to recover damages from fire or explosion. If a contractor's employees handle cash, valuable documents, or materials, the contractor must provide coverage against employee dishonesty. Contracts dealing with the transport of fuel or hazardous materials and contracts under which the contractor must excavate also require special coverages to protect the local government.

Bonds   A requirement that a contractor provide bid, performance, or payment bonds is the most commonly used method of transferring the risk of contractor default to a third party. Although the prospect of transferring risk to a third party may seem appealing, the scope-of-work team must think carefully about whether to require bonds. The team must understand that payment against a bond may take many months. First, the local government has to declare the contractor in default. Then the bonding company has to agree with the local government's claim. Even when the local government has a good case, surety firms are generally slow to respond to a claim against a bond. Litigation is often the only way to collect.

One argument often advanced in support of bonds is that a contractor's bonding capacity is a good indicator of financial stability. However, this is not always the case; a surety firm's investigation of a bidder's financial stability may have occurred years earlier. Relying on an insurance company to establish the financial responsibility of a bidder is a poor substitute for independent investigation by the local government.

In many instances, bonds are not necessary if a contractor has been selected after a thorough review of references, qualifications, and financial stability. A formal guarantee of performance is little consolation to a local government faced with a floundering—but not defaulting—contractor, and even if a contractor does default, it may be months before any money can be collected. Finally, bonds and other guarantees can eliminate many small or minority-owned business enterprises from competing successfully for local government business.

The three types of bonds most used in service contracting are the bid bond, which guarantees that the bidder will enter into a contract; the performance bond, which guarantees that the contractor will perform the duties assumed by entering the contract; and the payment bond, which guarantees that the contractor will pay all suppliers and subcontractors who assist in the performance of the work. In each case, the guarantee is issued by a surety firm—an insurance company—to the local government. A fourth type of bond—the fidelity bond—is an insurance policy that guarantees the reimbursement of the local government for losses resulting from proven acts of dishonesty by contract employees who handle cash, including concessions or other revenues, or are exposed to opportunities for theft, such as custodial or clerical services.

The bid bond guarantees the local government that the bidder will enter into the contract if it is awarded; if the bidder does not accept the award, the bond is forfeited in whole or in part. A bid bond is issued most often in an amount equal to 5 percent of the total bid price, the amount commonly required by regulations or statute. In the event of default, the amount collected can range from the difference between the price of the bidder who declined the award and the price of the next higher bidder to the actual administrative costs for bidding the contract again. The entire amount of the bid bond is seldom collectable.

Surety companies investigate all claims to determine whether they agree that the fault lies with the contractor; they are not likely to pay a claim immediately. They may rule, for example, that some action of the local government forced their client's default. If the local government imposes conditions after award of the contract that were not in the original contract, thereby forcing the contractor to withdraw, the insurer may not agree to pay against the bid bond. In similar fashion, the insurer may deny payment if uncontrollable natural events such as fires or floods destroy part or all of the contractor's ability to comply with the contract. When a bid bond is required, the local government almost always rejects bid responses that are received without the bond attached at the time of bid opening.

A performance bond is issued to the local government by a surety company at the contractor's request after the contractor has received notice of award; the contract is usually not signed until the local government receives the performance bond. Bonding requirements vary considerably. Some local governments require a performance bond for every award for goods or services; others obtain performance and payment bonds only for construction contracts over a certain dollar value, usually $100,000. The amount of the performance bond is usually 100 percent of the contract price. Some local government regulations specify the minimum amount of the bond; others use considerable leeway to determine the amount and whether it will be issued as a percentage of the contract price or for a specific sum. Contracts awarded on an as-needed basis that do not have a fixed contract price (contracts for computer programming staff, for boarding up abandoned buildings, etc.) often call for performance bonds in amounts that may vary from $5,000 to more than $100,000. The amount depends on the estimated contract value, the importance of the service, and whether disruption of the service would result in a crisis. Collection of a performance bond can take months or even years if the bonding firm does not agree with the default claim of the local government; litigation is often required to collect.

A payment bond, which is issued in the same manner as a performance bond, is a surety company's guarantee that the contractor will pay its subcontractors and suppliers. Payment bonds are used primarily in construction contracts but are applicable to service contracts under which the contractor contracts all or part of the work to one or more subcontractors. The usual amount of a payment bond is 100 percent of the contract price.

By requiring the contractor to provide a payment bond to be held by the local government during the contract term, the local government ensures that suppliers and subcontractors will be paid for their services. The payment bond also protects the local government from suppliers' and subcontractors' claims of nonpayment by the contractor. They file their claims to obtain any money the contractor owes them with the surety company, not the local government. Without a payment bond, a supplier or subcontractor could sue the contractor directly for payment, sue the local government to reduce the contractor's payment by the amount owed to the subcontractor or supplier, or sue both at the same time.

The local government should not become involved with the collection efforts of claimants against the contractor. The claimants are responsible for taking any necessary legal action against the contractor or the bonding company.

Alternative surety   Many contractors who are otherwise qualified to perform a service may not be able to obtain bonding from a surety company because of the size of their firm or their financial condition. Others may choose not to obtain bonds because they consider the practice expensive or unnecessary. If the scope-of-work team decides that a performance bond or other guarantee of performance is essential and does not want to eliminate firms that cannot or choose not to obtain a performance bond, the team can consider accepting alternative guarantees.

Alternatives include the contractor's provision of a certified or cashier's check, personal bond, property bond, cash escrow deposit, or an irrevocable letter of credit from a bank or savings and loan institution. For low-risk service contracts, these guarantees may be more appropriate and easier to enforce than a performance bond. Moreover, when a default causes disruption in a critical service and rapid response is imperative, alternative guarantees can provide immediate cash that can be used to replace the defaulting contractor. When considering the use of alternative surety, always seek legal advice first. Some state laws prohibit its use. (See "Surety required" in Appendix A.)

Certified or cashier's checks   Contractors may purchase certified or cashier's checks from a bank or savings and loan association. There is commonly a small handling fee for the service. These checks are as accessible as cash; they differ from a contractor's business check in that the contractor cannot stop payment on them. Certified or cashier's checks are used primarily as an alternative to bid bonds. Because they require cash collateral equal to the face amount of the check, they are rarely used for the higher-value performance or payment bonds. Collection of any forfeiture is immediate; the local government has only to cash the check. However, it is wise to deposit such checks immediately after bid opening into a separate account to ensure that the cash is available when needed. Although payment against these types of check cannot be stopped by the contractor, a bank can stop payment when it is in financial crisis.

Personal bond   A personal bond is a guarantee against the assets of a contractor that the contractor will pay any claims regarding failure to accept award of a contract, failure to perform, or failure to pay debts. It is supported by an agreement in which the contractor pledges some or all assets to pay the claims. This agreement must be approved by the legal department of the local government. A personal bond cannot be approved until the finance or auditing department has certified that the contractor has the assets pledged. Collection against personal bonds may be time consuming and complex, depending on the conditions in the original agreement and the time required to convert pledged assets to cash. Litigation may be required to collect against this type of bond.

Property bond   The property bond is similar to the personal bond except that the assets the contractor pledges consist of real property. Collection against property bonds also depends largely on the conditions in the original agreement. Litigation may be required to collect against this type of bond.

Cash escrow deposit   Because the cash escrow deposit requires the contractor to tie up an amount of cash equal to the contract amount, it is seldom offered as an alternative performance or payment guarantee. It consists of a cash deposit by the contractor into an escrow account with the local government in an amount equal to the contract price. The ease of collection in the event of contractor default depends on the conditions in the original escrow agreement. Interest usually is considered the property of the contractor. The agreement may permit the contractor to collect the interest periodically or let it accrue until the escrow agreement is terminated.

Irrevocable letter of credit   An irrevocable letter of credit issued by a bank or savings and loan association can be used to guarantee performance or payment. The financial institution will release the face amount of the letter of credit, usually equivalent to the contract price, to the local government upon receipt of a written claim that the contractor has defaulted; payment is immediate. When obtaining this type of guarantee, be certain that the instrument is an irrevocable letter of credit; if it is not identified as irrevocable, it can be canceled by the contractor. Moreover, if a financial institution goes bankrupt or is taken over by a federal agency, its letters of credit can be among the first instruments to be voided. Before accepting a letter of credit, have the finance department review the financial statement or credit rating of the institution backing it. Do not accept letters of credit drawn on a financial institution with a poor credit rating.

The letter of credit, like the cash escrow deposit, is not used very often to guarantee performance because the contractor may have to deposit cash, bonds, or real estate with the issuing bank as collateral. These sources of cash would then be unavailable during the contract term.

Payments as a guarantee   Consider using the monthly payments made to the contractor as a guarantee. When payments are made to the contractor after the work is completed, the possibility that the local government will make deductions for poor service give it considerable financial clout with the contractor. Identify the criteria by which deductions will be made in the liquidated damages section of the bid and contract documents. Interruption of a contractor's cash flow is often more effective than a notice to declare the contractor in default and enforce the performance bond.

Contract extension and renewal A contract extension differs from a contract renewal. An extension generally is unplanned and seldom is forecast in the award or contract document; a renewal is a planned event that must be covered by a clause in the contract. If a contract calls for the contractor to provide and install a computer system, complete an architectural design, or complete a construction project on or before a specific date and the work is not done on time, the local government may grant an extension of the contract. The term "renewal" refers to a planned additional period of contract performance after the expiration of the original period, whether the original period was for one year or for five years or more. Even with this distinct difference in definitions, the term "extension" is still more commonly, but incorrectly, used by public purchasers and contract administrators to refer to a renewal. In this text, the term "renewal" is used when referring to a planned additional period of contract performance and "extension" when referring to an unplanned additional period.

Legal, fiscal, pricing, and timing considerations are associated with any contract renewal.

Legal considerations Failure to identify a specific renewal period in the original bid document may prevent the local government from being legally empowered to grant a renewal, even if the renewal is in its best interest. The terms of renewal must be part of both the original bid document and the contract. If no renewal provisions are included, any renewal that occurs after the original contract term could be legally viewed as a new contract, not a renewal. If it is classified as a new contract, re-bidding is required. When preparing the bid, award, or contract documents, include the method of determining the prices, terms, and conditions of the renewal period and note whether the contractor has the right to decline an option to renew.

A contract renewal provision in a bid document or an award often stipulates that the renewal is offered at the discretion of the local government. This provision usually states that the local government is not required to offer the option to renew to the contractor, and the contractor may accept or decline any offer made. If the contract includes a condition that the local government has the unilateral right to renew the contract automatically under the same terms as those in the original agreement, the contractor must accept a renewal if the local government offers one.

Fiscal considerations The local government must include a nonappropriation clause in the bid document to ensure that it has the authority to cancel the contract if the budget appropriation for a service is depleted. This clause affirms the right of the local government to cancel the contract if funds for its completion are not appropriated by the governing body. The clause must be reviewed by the legal department and adapted to meet local law; it should be included in every contract with a term that begins in one fiscal year and ends in another. (See "Nonappropriation" in Appendix A.)

Pricing considerations Local governments have a number of options for pricing contracts; one is to request a firm price for the second or third year of the contract at the time of the original bid. This approach can be costly because a cautious contractor may propose highly inflated prices for subsequent years to be on the safe side. Conversely, modest cost projections can easily lead to performance problems if the actual cost increases during subsequent years are higher than those projected. When faced with a potential loss, a contractor may first cut back on the quantity or the quality of the service.

A safer approach is to obtain a firm price for the first year and to link contract unit prices for succeeding years to a recognized index or escalator, as discussed in Chapter 3. The language of the **escalator clause** can be adjusted to apply to whatever indexes are most appropriate for use. Contract prices can be adjusted annually, quarterly, or monthly depending on the frequency of publication of the index and the volatility of the cost of the service. (See "Price adjustments based on the Consumer Price Index" in Appendix A.)

A third option allows renewal of the contract at the same prices, terms, and conditions upon mutual agreement by the local government and the contractor. This option assumes that the conditions of performance will not change substantially for one year or more. It is especially appropriate when the contractor is being paid a percentage of revenues for food or other concessions or for day-care services, for example, or when the contractor is being paid a fixed fee plus reimbursement for costs for professional and similar services. This option is also used when the local government is not sure at the time of contract execution that it wants to renew for an additional year. Mutual agreement permits the government or the contractor to withdraw without penalty. (See "Renewal of contract" in Appendix A.)

Timing considerations When establishing the number of days before contract expiration in which a decision to renew must be made, allow enough time to re-bid the contract if the incumbent contractor declines to renew. The time should be equal to the number of days between publication of the bid document and bid opening plus the number of days necessary to evaluate the documents and award a new contract plus the number of days necessary for the new contractor to start work.

Because renewals usually are incorporated into contracts that do not require extensive lead times for establishment, the total time needed between the anniversary date and the date to decide whether to renew is about three months and seldom more than four. Timing considerations would usually not apply to contracts that take an unusual amount of time to reestablish, as they normally run for a specified number of years without periodic renewals. Many types of social services fit this description, such as contracting with a children's residential treatment facility. If the provider demonstrates irreconcilable performance problems over a period of time and the local government chooses not to renew the provider's contract, local government staff need to start planning a year or more in advance to avoid a disruption in service and to ensure a smooth transition.

Renewal clauses apply after the base contract term. If a five-year period is considered a valid base contract term, include a renewal option of one or more years after that five-year term under the original terms and conditions. If an advertised five-year contract carries a provision to renew at the local government's option on each anniversary date, a contractor cannot consider it a firm five-year commitment. The possibility of cancellation by the local government on each anniversary date establishes five one-year contracts and not one five-year contract. If a bidder must make a capital investment for equipment, this procedure means that the bidder cannot rely on amortizing the investment over the advertised five years of the contract term, since the bidder could be terminated after one or two years with an inventory of nonproductive equipment.

Special instructions

The special instructions section of the bid document contains information that may not be pertinent to the scope of work but that is important to the local government and the bidder. This section may also include the method the local government will use to evaluate bid responses, the formula for ranking the bidders by price in a bid response containing multiple unit prices, special instructions on how to format the response (applicable primarily to responses under the competitive negotiation method), and the procedures for protesting the rejection of a bid. A number of these topics are discussed in the next section.

Price ranking of bidders   The price ranking method, which is included when a single price is being bid, consists solely of a statement that the award will be made to the lowest responsive and responsible bidder. However, many service contract bids require bidders to submit several unit prices. It is evident that the lowest responsive and responsible bidder is not easily discerned in such a situation. For example, a bid for removal of graffiti from public structures may include a price per square foot for removing the graffiti, a price per square foot for applying a protective coating to the surface just cleaned, unit prices for rental of steam cleaning machines or special aerial bucket trucks, and the cost of the various chemicals used. A method or formula is required to convert the various unit prices of each bidder into single comparable figures or into a single estimated annual contract price. Forecasting contract activity (units to be purchased and dollars to be spent), identifying the percentage of the total contract price of each item in the bid form, and comparing the unit prices bid to a sample job are all methods used in the comparative analysis of bids.

Whenever multiple unit prices are included in a bid document, include a method or formula to apply to the bid responses so that the local government and the bidders can easily calculate their ranking by price; everyone then knows who the lowest bidder is. In negotiated procurements, if the price estimates are public record, including a price ranking formula allows offerors the opportunity to compare the proposals received by the local government and gives them an idea of how to be more competitive if they are selected for contract negotiations.

If bidders do not agree with the method or formula proposed, they have the right to challenge it during the bidding process; it is usually too late to challenge it after the bid responses are opened.

Price ranking by forecasted contract activity   Many service contracts require contractors to submit labor rates for different categories of workers, unit prices for repairs or materials, or discounts for materials. For example, a contract for plumbing services may include a wage per hour for both a journeyman plumber and an apprentice plumber and unit prices for common repairs or for replacement of high-value items such as water fountains (unless the contract stipulates that these items will be replaced at the contractor's cost). In a contract for replacing lamps in lighting fixtures in sports fields, there will be separate prices for installing different types and wattages of lamps, realigning the lights, making minor electrical circuit repairs, and laying new electrical cable. But totaling the unit price for each task would not be a fair estimate of the contract cost because some tasks are performed more frequently than others.

To ensure that bidders' prices are compared fairly, the bid document must list the estimated number of times each task will be performed and the estimated number of units of material to be used during the contract term. These estimates allow the unit prices to be extended; the extensions can then be totaled to arrive at an accurate overall forecast of contract activity. This method assumes that the scope-of-work team can reasonably forecast the number of times certain tasks should be done and the amount of material that should be needed to do these tasks during a typical contract year. Exhibit 4-3 provides an example of a contract activity forecast used in a bid form for a relamping contract. (See "Requirements contract" in Appendix A to help avoid contract disputes over inaccurate estimates).

Without estimates of anticipated use for each price entry in the bid document, determining the lowest bid is at best a guess that may not withstand a bidder protest. Estimates of anticipated use must be included for each specific item or task identified in the activity forecast. Remember that the forecast must always be included in the bid documents: estimates or forecasts created after the bid opening are likely to be successfully protested.

Price ranking by percentage of contract budget Percentages are used to rank contractors' prices when the scope-of-work team cannot predict how many units of service will be purchased but can specify how much money is budgeted for the

Releasing budget information

Although many local governments do not advise prospective bidders of the amount of funds available for a contract service, disclosing the budget, maximum acceptable cost, or maximum unit price for client or other services in the bid document may be beneficial. One potential benefit is that the local government may receive an early indication that the services described cannot be purchased with available funds. Bidders at a pre-bid conference will not hesitate to inform local government officials that the requirements demand higher prices than the budget allows. If all bidders take this position, qualified and affordable bid responses might not be received unless the requirements are revised or the budget increased. If the bidders are split in their assessment of the budget figure, the local government will have a better idea of who will eventually respond and can decide either to revise the requirements or proceed with the bid document as written.

Another possible benefit is that when it seems that more providers than expected will compete for a contract and they know the local government's estimate of the cost of the work, competition among them may drive prices down because they know that to be competitive they have to bid lower than the estimate. Do not automatically suppose that a preannounced estimate means that all responses will come in at that estimate.

However, some local governments may be prohibited by law from releasing estimates of probable cost of a contract. Obtain legal advice before releasing a cost estimate for a contract while it is in the bidding process.

contract and the estimated percentage of the contract budget that will be spent on each element of the contract. For example, each size of stump in a tree-stump removal contract is priced differently; replacement of curbs, gutters, sidewalks, and driveways are priced separately in a concrete maintenance contract; and varying thicknesses of asphalt or concrete patches require separate prices in a street maintenance contract. This method is especially useful when bid prices are "all over the place" (Bidder A is high on Item 1 but low on Item 2 and Bidder B is low on Item 1 but high on Item 2, etc.).

The percentage of budget formula establishes the number of units that can be purchased by the local government at the prices submitted by each bidder. When this formula is used, the bid document includes

1. The estimated total budget for the contract
2. The estimated percentage (or dollar value) of the budget allotted for each item or task
3. A description of the calculations made in applying the formula

Exhibit 4-4 illustrates the percentage of budget formula for a contract covering the removal of tree stumps. For this example, the special instructions section of the scope of work must show the sizes of the stumps to be removed, the total budget, and the percentage of the budget expected to be spent for each size.

Removal of tree stumps 12.1 to 20 inches in size represents $20,000 (50 percent of the $40,000 budget). The number of stumps of this size that can be removed is determined by dividing $20,000 by the unit price of the contractor (Bidder A = 200 stumps; Bidder B = 173.9 stumps). The bid price is divided by the dollar value, which yields a product output (number of stumps removed). The number of stumps removed is then summed to arrive at the total product output based on the bid prices for each level of service. When all calculations have been made, Bidder A is identified as able to remove 383.3 stumps at the unit prices proposed. The same calculations are made using the prices submitted by Bidder B. In the examples in Exhibit 4-4, although Bidder B submitted a higher price for the stump size with the greatest budget allocation, the total number of stumps that Bidder B can remove is greater than that of Bidder A (Bidder A = 383.3; Bidder B = 391). Bidder B would get the award.

Price ranking by sample job or past performance   Another method of dealing with the problem of ranking responses with multiple unit prices is to create a fictitious "typical" project based on an average job assignment. For example, when bidding sidewalk repair work, prepare a sample job that shows the number of units required to complete the job (e.g., linear feet of curb and gutter, square yards of driveways, number of handicapped ramps). The job description should be prepared by someone who is knowledgeable about department field operations. It should then be sealed in an envelope by a single department official and should not be released before bid opening. The job description uses only labor categories, equipment, and materials that will be covered by unit prices the bidders will submit. At bid opening, copies may be distributed to bidders so that they can make their calculations and determine where they stand in the ranking. Although distribution to the bidders is not essential, it does help maintain the local government's credibility. The sample job is then priced using the unit prices of each bidder; the totals rank the bidders by price.

Not every unit price item in the bid can be used in the sample job, and the bidders do not know which items have been used. Not knowing encourages the bidders to keep all of their unit prices as low as possible.

Another ranking method is to obtain contractor invoices from the local government files for the previous contract year that represent an average month's billing. The invoices must show the units of work done, the quantity of materials purchased, and the number of labor hours billed for each labor category. Seal the sample invoices and open them at bid opening with the bid responses. Multiply the unit prices of each bidder by the units of work, quantity of materials, and hours of labor shown on the invoices. The award is made to the lowest bidder for the cost of a representative month's work.

Technical exhibits   Technical exhibits, if any, follow the scope-of-work section in the bid document. They can include a map of the area of operation of contract services; reports or studies pertinent to the scope of work; specifications from trade or professional associations used to prepare the scope of work; manufacturer's product descriptions, sketches, or photographs; tables and charts; and applicable laws or regulations. If the technical exhibits cannot be bound with the bid document, insert a page after the scope of work that identifies and summarizes each exhibit.

Scope of work for competitive negotiation and multistep bidding

The scope of work for a competitive sealed bid is considered more difficult to prepare than that for competitive negotiation or multistep bidding. In competitive sealed bidding, much more detail is required in the task description and in the method of ranking price. This section suggests guidelines for preparing the scope of work for competitive negotiation and multistep bidding. It identifies differences between these methods and competitive sealed bidding.

Scope of work for competitive negotiation

The principal difference between competitive negotiation and competitive sealed bidding is that everything the offeror submits under the competitive negotiation method is negotiable, including price. In the following suggested outline for the scope of work for competitive negotiation, only the differences or deletions from the basic outline for competitive sealed bidding are identified. All other sections are the same.

Introduction and general information   The clause in Appendix A entitled "Competitive negotiation solicitation" is suggested as the opening page of the scope-of-work section of the RFP.

Pre-proposal conference   In competitive negotiation, a **pre-proposal conference** is usually mandatory for RFPs covering service contracts to be sure that all potential offerors receive the same information and to obtain as much information as possible from them to help refine the RFP. The pre-proposal conference is also an indicator of the number of responses to be expected. The pre-proposal conference for competitive negotiation performs the same function as a pre-bid conference does for competitive sealed bidding. In competitive negotiation, the local government receives a proposal; hence, it is referred to as a pre-proposal conference. However, it is not uncommon for a local government to call it a pre-bid conference, even when it is soliciting proposals through the competitive negotiation process.

Contractor qualifications Be specific when describing qualifications. The success or failure of any service contract solicitation is as dependent on contractor qualifications and experience as it is on the content of the offeror's proposal.

Task description The task description of the scope of work for competitive negotiation can be very general. Provide as much information about the service as is known at the time of preparation. Be specific when describing the local government's goals. If there are areas of service delivery that must be performed in a certain way or in accordance with federal requirements or regulations, clearly identify these items as nonnegotiable. These areas could include a requirement of electronic billing and data reporting, daily deposits of cash receipts, establishment of work schedules, or special auditing requirements.

Contractor personnel requirements Require detailed resumes for all management and key personnel. Include the minimum qualifications for personnel in the same manner as in the basic outline for competitive sealed bidding.

Contractor responsibilities Include all duties or responsibilities that are known at the time the RFP is prepared. Contractor responsibilities can be a major negotiation item.

Local government responsibilities Local government responsibilities are a negotiable item not required in the RFP unless the local government has identified areas of responsibility that it intends to retain or assume.

Response format Require a specific format to be followed in the proposal to permit easier comparison of proposals during the evaluation process. A typical response format can be structured as shown in the accompanying sidebar. A response format is not in the basic outline for competitive sealed bidding; it applies only to competitive negotiation and multistep bidding.

Evaluation of contractor performance The evaluation of contractor performance is the same as in the basic outline except that the specifics of the process should not be defined completely at this point; they can be addressed during negotiation.

Reporting requirements and procedures Any reporting requirements of the local government that are known at the time the RFP is prepared should be included, although they are subject to negotiation. The local government may want to identify some requirements as nonnegotiable.

Special instructions The special instructions section must state clearly all the factors that the local government uses to evaluate responses; factors that are not identified in the RFP cannot be used. For example, an offeror ranked high on the published evaluation factors who lives in a different city or state cannot be rejected because of location unless the RFP clearly states that the proximity of the offeror to the work site will be used as an evaluation factor. The relative importance of each factor can be indicated by either listing the factor in order of its importance or by identifying it with an appropriate modifier ("critical," "very important," "important").

Whether or not to include a numerical weight for each factor of the RFP is a matter of policy. Some local governments include numerical weights; others do not. First among the advantages of including numerical weights is that offerors are advised of the exact relative importance of each factor. Second, the entire evaluation process

---

Sample response format for an RFP

The information requested in the following sample is basic. Items may be added or deleted as necessary to meet the requirements of each RFP.

Offerors present their responses to the items in the order that the items are listed, identifying each response by the roman numeral.

I   *Management summary*   Provide a cover letter indicating the underlying philosophy of the firm in providing the service.

II   *Proposal*   Describe in detail how the service will be provided. Include a description of major tasks and subtasks.

III   *Corporate experience and capacity*   Describe the experience of the firm in providing the service, give number of years that the service has been delivered, and provide a statement on the extent of any corporate expansion required to handle the service.

IV   *Personnel*   Attach resumes of all those who will be involved in the delivery of service—from principals to field technicians—that include their experience in this area of service delivery. Indicate the level of involvement by principals of the firm in the day-to-day operation of the contract.

V   *References*   Give at least five references for contracts of similar size and scope, including at least two references for current contracts or those awarded during the past three years. Include the name of the organization, the length of the contract, a brief summary of the work, and the name and telephone number of a responsible contact person.

VI   *Acceptance of conditions*   Indicate any exceptions to the general terms and conditions of the bid document and to insurance, bonding, and any other requirements listed.

VII   *Additional data*   Provide any additional information that will aid in evaluation of the response.

VIII   *Cost data*   Estimate the annual cost of the service. Cost data submitted at this stage is not binding and is subject to negotiation if your firm is chosen as a finalist. Include the number of personnel proposed to be assigned to the contract and the total estimated cost of the labor portion of the contract (include a sample staffing chart). Identify all nonlabor costs and their estimated totals.

Note: The cost data section is adjusted to meet the individual requirements of the service under consideration. A separate cost proposal form may be prepared and inserted for offerors to complete. Be aware that some local government regulations may prohibit requesting costs at this stage of a competitive negotiation solicitation.

---

is revealed, indicating the local government's intent to evaluate all responses objectively and openly.

The disadvantages include the following: first, when offerors know the numerical weights, responses will more than likely focus on the areas with the heaviest weights. It may be the skill of the contractor's proposal-writing team and not the contractor's qualifications that make the firm a finalist in the competition. Second, the local government may discover additional information after publication of the RFP that makes the initial estimates of relative importance inappropriate. Third, once published, the weights cannot be changed after the date set for receipt of proposals.

The weights and relative importance of evaluation factors vary in relation to the type of service being purchased. In some services, price has a minor role; in others, it is a major factor in determining award of the contract.

Exhibit 4-5 lists general evaluation factors for competitive negotiation. Besides these general factors, always include those directly related to the service covered by the RFP. Additional factors may include the condition of the offeror's equipment or special certifications and educational requirements for personnel.

Scope of work for multistep bidding

The procedure for creating the scope of work for multistep bidding is similar to that for competitive negotiation. Multistep bidding usually is reserved for use when competitive negotiation is prohibited or when the local government wants the flexibility of negotiation but must make the final award to the lowest responsive and responsible bidder. It also applies to contracts in which the scope of work cannot be fully defined by the local government or for which the local government prefers to have bidders propose their own methods of service delivery for review and approval. These are common conditions when a new service is being established.

In the following suggested outline for the scope of work for multistep bidding, only the differences or deletions from the basic outline for competitive sealed bidding are identified. All other entries are the same.

Introduction and general information　In the introduction to the scope of work, include a detailed description of the bidding method, identifying each step in the process and the procedure for rejecting bidders who fail to meet the requirements at a particular step. Describe in detail the process to be used for discussions with individual contractors in the refinement of their technical proposals. State whether the bidder is to provide a sealed price envelope with the original response or at a later date. Because the first step in the process is a qualifying step as well as the step at which technical proposals are evaluated, qualification criteria included in the introduction must be explicit. Require acceptable references for a minimum of three current contracts of similar size and scope. Require the contract supervisor to be assigned to the contract to have a minimum of two years' experience with a contract of similar size and scope. Use other criteria that are reasonable and relevant to the service being bid.

Task description　Provide as much information as possible, stressing the service goals of the local government. Note that the listed requirements are all subject to negotiation during individual discussions with the contractors.

Local government responsibilities　Include this section in the scope of work only when responsibility for areas that would normally be the responsibility of the contractor will be retained by the local government. Let contractors describe their view of the local government's responsibilities in their technical proposals and during subsequent negotiations.

Response format　To permit easier comparison of the technical proposals, specify a format to be followed in the bidder's response.

Evaluation of contractor performance　Include this section only when the method of service delivery is explicit and the method of evaluation of service delivery is defined. Otherwise, discuss evaluation during negotiation.

Reporting requirements and procedures　Define reporting requirements and procedures during negotiation.

Conclusion

As work on the bid document progresses, more information may be acquired that should be incorporated in the scope of work. The scope of work should not be considered complete until all relevant information has been included. Chapter 5 discusses the preparation of the rest of the bid document and covers the conduct of a pre-bid conference and bid opening. Appendix B contains examples of different types of service contracts and the bidding and pricing methods applicable to each. It also provides suggestions and comments on the resolution of problems that may be encountered when preparing the scope of work for these contracts.

Endnotes

1 Adapted from Society of Local Authority Chief Executives and Local Government Training Board, *Managing Competition: Tendering for Local Government Services* (London: Her Majesty's Stationery Office, 1988).

2 See Harry P. Hatry, *How Effective Are Your Community Services? Procedures for Performance Measurement,* 3rd ed. (Washington, D.C.: ICMA, 2006).

Exhibit 4-1   Model for multilevel performance evaluation.

Level	Standard
Perfect performance	Zero faults
Acceptable performance	No more than three faults per month
Marginal performance	Three to seven faults per month (warning notice)
Unacceptable performance	Over seven faults per month (enforcement of liquidated damages provisions and possible notice of default)

Exhibit 4-2   Performance requirements summary excerpted from a towing contract.

Item	Description
Required performance	Arrive at scene
Performance standard	Never late
Maximum allowable degree of deviation	Late no more than three times per month
Method of surveillance	Police officer's accident report
Amount of deduction	$50 per incident

Exhibit 4-3   Contract activity forecast for a sports field relamping contract.

Item or task	Unit price	Estimated annual use	Extended price
1500W mercury lamps	$ ____ each	120	$ ____
1200W mercury lamps	$ ____ each	75	$ ____
Electrical repairs	$ ____/hour	100	$ ____
Align lights	$ ____/pole	30	$ ____
Install cable	$ ____/linear ft.	900	$ ____
Total			$ ____

Exhibit 4-4 Price ranking for a tree stump removal contract.

Bidder A calculations			
Stump size in inches	Estimated percentage of budget (dollar value)	Bid price	Number of stumps removed
6-12	15 (6,000)	$50	120.0
12.1-20	50 (20,000)	$100	200.0
20.1-30	25 (10,000)	$200	50.0
30.1 and over	10 (4,000)	$300	13.3
Stumps removed			383.3
Bidder B calculations			
Stump size in inches	Estimated percentage of budget (dollar value)	Bid price	Number of stumps removed
6-12	15 (6,000)	$40	150.0
12.1-20	50 (20,000)	$115	173.9
20.1-30	25 (10,000)	$190	52.6
30.1 and over	10 (4,000)	$275	14.5
Stumps removed			391

Note: Budget allocation = $40,000.

Exhibit 4-5 Sample listing of general evaluation factors for competitive negotiation.
The relative importance of each factor varies with the service being procured. For example, the firm's experience may be critical if the principals of the firm are hired to perform the work; however, if they seldom do the actual work but assign lower-level employees (as in architectural or social services contracts), this factor may be rated as only *important* and staff experience may increase to a *critical* value. Similarly, the cost of services may become critical if the local government has limited funds.

Factor	Importance
Staff experience	Very important
Proposed methodology	Critical
Understanding of the project and local government objectives	Important
The degree of completeness of response to specific requirements of the solicitation	Very important
Firm's experience in the service area	Critical
Availability of personnel	Critical
Cost of services	Important
Financial stability	Very important
Other criteria described or included by reference in the solicitation	Important

5

From Boilerplate to Bid Opening

The two previous chapters covered the planning phase of preparing the bid document and the development of the scope of work. This chapter discusses the other components of the bid document: instructions to bidders, general terms and conditions, and the bid form. This chapter also covers procedures for pre-bid conferences, addenda, and the bid opening.

Boilerplate

In this book, "boilerplate" refers to general clauses that apply only to service contracting and (in most instances) to clauses that are tailored to the scope of work of the specific bid document being prepared. It does not refer to the preprinted forms discussed in the accompanying sidebar, which should not be used in service contracting.

The term "boilerplate" is appropriate because these clauses generally remain the same and apply to all bids and services. However, it is important to remember that no clause can be considered standard. When developing the boilerplate for a contract, examine every clause to determine whether it applies to the scope of work in question. Do not publish a bid document until the boilerplate section is tailored specifically to the service being purchased.

The boilerplate is usually developed by the purchasing department while the scope of work is being completed. If there is no purchasing department, the boilerplate can be developed by the legal department.

The boilerplate of a bid document generally includes the **instructions to bidders,** which detail the procedures to be followed in the preparation of the bid response and other requirements of the bidding process, the general terms and conditions, the legal and procedural conditions that will apply to the contract, and other information or documents required by local law or policy.

The instructions to bidders and the general terms and conditions consist of clauses covering a range of topics, from the rules of the public bidding process to the legal terms and conditions of the contractual relationship between the contractor and the

---

Preprinted boilerplate

The term "boilerplate" is often used to refer to the general clauses on a preprinted form inserted in all bid documents whether they are used for the purchase of goods or the purchase of services. The concept of using a single preprinted form developed before the advent of word processing, when extensive retyping of clauses was required every time an invitation for bids or a request for proposals was issued. Even now, when bid documents are usually prepared using word processing, the preprinted form is still used extensively in local governments.

However, many of the clauses on preprinted forms do not apply to the scope of work of a specific bid document or even to the specifications for the purchase of goods. Preprinted forms should not be used to purchase services because they can cause confusion during the bidding process and result in serious misunderstanding during the administration of the contract. For example, a clause in the preprinted boilerplate may require the local government to pay the contractor monthly, but the scope of work or general terms and conditions may state that payments are to be made quarterly.

The purpose of the bid document is to set forth all requirements and conditions of the contract, from the specifics of service provision to the contractor's adherence to employment antidiscrimination laws. Preprinted boilerplate that includes irrelevant or contradictory clauses weakens the bid document and, ultimately, the contract itself.

---

local government. The complete text of each clause discussed in this chapter is listed alphabetically by title in Appendix A. No rules govern the sequence of clauses in the instructions to bidders or in the general terms and conditions.

Besides the basic clauses discussed in this chapter, many local governments have special clauses required by policy or ordinance. For example, local ordinances or federal grants may require the use of minority- and women-owned business enterprises. Before being included in a bid document, any clause, whether it is generated within or outside the local government, should be submitted for legal review.

Instructions to bidders

The instructions to bidders section explains how to submit a response to the solicitation and lists the conditions that must be met in order to submit a bid. Most clauses discussed in this section are typical of those usually included in the instructions to bidders section of the bid document. The economic price adjustment and solicitation for information clauses are used more rarely.

As noted earlier, local policy, ordinances, or procurement procedures may require special clauses. If these clauses specify actions that are required to qualify as a bidder or that otherwise take place before the award of the contract—for example, attending a mandatory pre-bid conference or making a presentation to an evaluation committee—they would be included in the instructions to bidders section of the bid document.

Acknowledgment of amendments   The acknowledgement of amendments clause requires that bidders acknowledge any amendments, either by writing an acknowledgment on the bid form or by returning the amendment with the bid form.

Alternative bids   The alternative bid response clause states that bidders offering service delivery methods other than those permitted in the scope of work in response to a competitive sealed bid may submit an envelope clearly marked "alternative bid." If the local government believes that a service delivery method offered in an alternative bid is valid, this clause permits the local government to cancel the solicitation and re-bid it with a revised scope of work that includes the alternative method. Although the local government is not required to award any contract and can cancel a solicitation at any time before award, an explanation is expected by those who submitted bids. This clause provides an explanation when an alternative bid identifies an exceptional idea or service delivery method.

Discuss this clause at the pre-bid conference and encourage bidders to advise the local government of alternative service delivery methods well before the date set for receipt of bids. Advance notice permits the local government to amend the scope of work before bid opening. Each bidder then has the opportunity to submit a response on the basis of the same specifications (as required under competitive sealed bidding procedures), including acceptable alternatives offered by other bidders, and the local government avoids the inconvenience and expense of canceling and re-bidding a solicitation.

Bid form submission   Submission instructions tell bidders when and where to submit the bid response, how to submit it, and how many copies to submit with the original. The number of copies is usually equal to the number of people who evaluate the responses. Increasingly, local governments are receiving bids electronically. If the bid is to be submitted electronically, the local government must provide detailed instructions, including a designated contact person and a phone number contractors can call if they encounter technical problems in the submission process.

If there is a page length that is not to be exceeded for bids submitted, it should be specified. Also included in the bid submission clause are procedures for the disposition of late bid responses, instructions for how to mark the response envelope, the rules regarding bidders' changes to their responses, and the rules governing withdrawals before and after bid opening.

Bid withdrawal   A bidder is permitted to withdraw or amend a bid response before the date set for receipt of bid responses upon written request to the local government; no reason is required. A bid cannot be amended after bid opening unless the amendment does not affect the price, quality, quantity, or delivery of the service. Bidders occasionally request an opportunity to withdraw a bid after bid opening because of a clerical error. Once withdrawn, the bid cannot be resubmitted. The claim of a clerical error may also be used by bidders who bid the project too low and want to be released from their bid. Unless a bidder can prove beyond a reasonable doubt that there was a clerical error and not an error of judgment, the bid response cannot be withdrawn. This sometimes forces a bidder who does not want an award to accept it. This rule is in keeping with a basic premise of public procurement: once a bid is opened, it cannot be withdrawn without valid reason.

The bid withdrawal clause also specifies the period of time that bid responses remain valid. Bidders are not permitted to withdraw their responses until the specified number of days have passed (usually sixty or ninety days after bid opening). As an additional precaution against collusion, the clause also prohibits a withdrawing bidder from working as a subcontractor for the successful bidder.

Bidder certification   The bidder agrees to accept the award and to enter into a contract if the award is offered to the bidder.

Bidder investigations   Bidders may claim that they have discovered a fact or condition that adds cost only after bid responses have been received or after the contract has been awarded and may request additional payments. To head off this problem, the bidder investigations clause makes the bidder responsible for conducting all the investigations a reasonable firm would make before making a business decision. Of course, the scope-of-work team must include in the scope of work any information that could affect the cost of the service. Failure to disclose known conditions can lead to a claim that the information that was withheld damaged a bidder in some way.

Certification of independent price determination   This clause also protects the local government against collusion. Each bidder is required to certify that the response was prepared independently and that the price submitted will not be disclosed to any other person.

Collusion among bidders   This clause, which is derived from the Sherman Antitrust Act, describes the prohibitions against colluding and submitting more than one response from each bidder. The version of the clause included in Appendix A allows the local government to decide on a case-by-case basis whether to accept bids from contractors convicted of antitrust violations in the past. Strictly prohibiting future awards based on evidence of past collusion may eliminate the only source for the service.

Debarment   By requiring bidders to certify that they are not currently debarred from submitting bids, the debarment status clause helps reduce the possibility of receiving a bid response from a bidder whose past performance led to debarment by another public entity.

Economic price adjustment   The economic price adjustment clause explains how the local government evaluates an economic price adjustment formula submitted by a bidder when the bid document does not include a provision for the adjustment. It also explains how the local government evaluates a bidder's exceptions to an economic price adjustment formula when a formula is included in the bid document.

Exceptions   This clause explains the local government's policy and procedures regarding exceptions to the specifications contained in a competitive sealed bid document. Do not use this clause in competitive negotiation or multistep bidding. The proposals received under these procurement methods are negotiable and seldom match every aspect of service delivery as described in the bid document.

Expenses incurred in preparing bid   This clause states that the bidder is responsible for all costs associated with submitting the bid response.

Informalities and irregularities   Most bid documents include a statement in the advertisement or on the cover page of the bid document that the local government has the right to waive informalities or irregularities. The informalities and irregularities clause defines informality and irregularity as minor defects in a bid response or variations from the exact requirements of the specifications, provided that the defects or variations do not affect the price, quality, quantity, or delivery of the service. The clause can help prevent an otherwise excellent bid response from being rejected because of a minor defect. As in every decision to accept or reject a nonconforming bid response, consult with legal counsel.

Late submissions   Some local governments accept late bids under certain conditions. This clause describes the most common conditions—when the delay is caused by the handling of the mail and when the late bid response is the only one received.

Nonconforming terms and conditions   Bidders sometimes submit responses that include corporate forms, brochures, or sample contracts, any of which may contain terms and conditions that do not conform to the bid document. Examples include a provision that the contract is to be adjudicated under the laws of another state or under corporate requirements for arbitration of contracts, which may not be allowed under state or local law, regulations, or policy. Bidders may be unaware that their boilerplate violates the terms and conditions of the bid document, but some bidders may intend for their boilerplate conditions to supersede the terms and conditions of the local government.

Some local governments reject nonconforming bid responses as nonresponsive. Others ignore nonconforming terms and conditions, consider the bid to be responsive, and proceed with the evaluation process. If the local government awards the contract to a bidder who has submitted nonconforming terms and conditions, the bidder may perform according to the bidder's conditions, not those of the local government. Moreover, the acceptance of a technically **nonresponsive bid** gives other bidders grounds to protest the award. The nonconforming terms and conditions clause allows the local government to ask the bidder to withdraw nonconforming terms and conditions such as corporate arbitration requirements that do not affect the price, quality, or delivery of the service. If price, quality, or delivery is affected, the principles of public procurement require that the bid be rejected as nonresponsive.

Qualifications of bidders   The scope of work defines bidder qualifications specific to the service being requested. The qualification of bidders clause in the instructions to bidders section includes criteria that apply to almost every procurement situation. Include this clause in the boilerplate—even if the scope of work lists general as well as specific criteria—in case some aspect of bidder qualifications is inadvertently left out of the scope of work. For support services that require few specialized qualifications, this clause can serve as the principal qualification clause.

Solicitation for information for planning purposes   This clause is used when the local government wants to obtain information from prospective bidders through a **request for information (RFI).** The clause identifies the solicitation as an RFI only and states that the local government will not pay for any information submitted. The clause protects the local government from claims of a bidder who interprets an RFI as a request for consulting services and bills the local government for services rendered.

Unnecessarily elaborate responses   Some bidders may submit a bound 100-page response with brochures, advertising releases, manuals, and so forth when a two- or three-page attachment is adequate. This clause advises prospective bidders that elaborate responses are not required or advisable. It also helps reduce the amount of material the evaluation team must read.

General terms and conditions

The general terms and conditions section of the boilerplate includes the terms and conditions that will be included in the final contract. In the general terms and conditions section, the bidder or offeror is referred to as the contractor.

The language of the clauses in the general terms and conditions section must be approved by the legal department and adjusted as necessary to comply with local law. Like the instructions to bidders section, the general terms and conditions section of the bid document may include clauses that apply to almost every contract and some that are used only when a contract specifically calls for their use. The "General terms and conditions" sidebar lists clauses that are typically included in most contracts and those that are used only occasionally.

Antitrust   The antitrust clause permits a local government to benefit from an antitrust action if a resulting financial award affects a contractor or items or services provided by the contractor. For example, if a supplier of asphalt paving material to a paving contractor is convicted of an antitrust violation for price fixing, the paving contractor could receive treble damages for the material it purchased from the supplier. If the local government has been paying inflated prices to the paving contractor because of price fixing, the local government has access to the settlement received by the paving contractor as a result of claims against the supplier.

Applicable law   Contractors who are based in another state usually want litigation to be brought in their home state. The applicable law clause specifically requires that any litigation will be brought in the home state of the local government.

Assignment   The assignment clause prohibits the contractor from transferring or assigning the contract to another party without the consent of the local government.

General terms and conditions

Clauses typically included in the general terms and conditions section of the bid document include the following:

Usual and customary clauses
- Antitrust
- Applicable law
- Assignment
- Certificates and licenses
- Changes in scope of work
- Employment discrimination
- Ethics in public contracting
- Failure to enforce
- Force majeure
- Immigration Reform and Control Act
- Indemnification
- Independent contractor
- Nonappropriation
- Oral statement procurement regulations
- Recovery of money
- Right to audit
- Termination for convenience
- Termination for default

Occasional or optional clauses
- Cost reimbursement
- Patents and royalties
- Price adjustments based on the Consumer Price Index
- Renewal of contract requirements contract
- Right of first refusal of employment
- Traffic control
- Vehicle and equipment buyback

Certificates, licenses, and accreditations State requirements for certification, organizational accreditations, business licenses, occupational licenses, professional licenses, exterminating licenses, hazardous waste hauling licenses, asbestos removal licenses, and any other licenses required of the contractor are covered by the certificates and licenses clause. Do not assume that a contractor has the required certificates and licenses. When a professional or government license or certificate is required to perform the contract, require the contractor to submit copies of the documents either with the bid or prior to award.

Change in scope of work The local government must plan for modifications to the contract after the award is made and the contract is signed. This clause sets forth the rules governing changes to the scope of work that the local government makes or requests. It also describes the recourses available if the contractor and the local government disagree about whether changes require additional compensation to the contractor.

Cost reimbursement The cost reimbursement clause prohibits a contractor from marking up the price of material provided under a time and materials contract. The clause specifically prohibits a contractor from using cost plus a percentage of cost pricing methods in the contract.

Employment discrimination An employment discrimination clause is included in every public contract. State or local laws may specify the language to be used in employment discrimination contract clauses and the language of the clause must comply with legal requirements.

Ethics in public contracting This clause is included to advise the contractor of regulations covering gifts, inducements, or kickbacks to government employees. The clause must be adapted to the ethics provisions of state and local laws.

Failure to enforce It is not uncommon for a contract provision to be unenforced for a considerable length of time. The provision may be a minor one or the contract administration staff may have overlooked it. This clause states that past failure to enforce a contract provision does not mean that the local government has waived its right to enforce that or any other provision.

Force majeure The force majeure clause excuses the contractor from failing to perform because of conditions beyond the contractor's control. Use the clause carefully, making sure that it applies specifically to the contract being bid. For example, the clause should not be used unless amended when contracting for services to be provided during emergencies (e.g., natural disasters, hazardous materials incidents, and riots). If a contract contains a standard force majeure clause such as those commonly found in preprinted boilerplate, a contractor whose assistance is expected during an emergency can refuse to provide services. The specific events that excuse nonperformance must be carefully defined for each contract.

Immigration Reform and Control Act This clause restates the requirements of the Immigration Reform and Control Act of 1986.

Indemnification Indemnification clauses are intended to protect the local government in the event of negligent performance or nonperformance by the contractor. Be sure that legal counsel approves any indemnification clause.

Independent contractor   The independent contractor clause establishes the contractor as an entity completely separate from the local government. It is especially important that legal counsel approve the language of this clause.

Nonappropriation   A nonappropriation clause is required whenever a contract extends beyond the end of a fiscal year. This clause permits the local government to cancel the contract if the governing body does not appropriate funds for the service for the succeeding fiscal year. If the local government cancels a contract before the end of the agreed-upon contract term because of lack of funds and the contract does not have a nonappropriation clause, the local government may be liable to the contractor for payment of the contractor's lost profits and the expense of shutting down the contract. Essentially, the local government would be guilty of a breach of contract.

In competitive negotiation, some contractors may propose a nonsubstitution requirement, which means that if the local government terminates the contract because of nonappropriation of funds, it agrees that for a specified period, usually six months to several years after termination, it will not fund a contract for the same or a similar service. They do this in order to obtain assurance that the local government will not cancel the contract and immediately award it to another firm with more advanced technology. The nonappropriation clause included in Appendix A does not include provision for nonsubstitution because this is an issue that should be negotiated. When negotiating, do not accept a nonsubstitution period of longer than six months; ninety days is preferable.

Oral statement   This clause states that written modifications are the only acceptable method for changing the contract and that the contract will not be affected by an oral statement made by any public official.

Patents and royalties   The contractor might use patented or copyrighted material or procedures in performance of the work. A specially adapted hold harmless clause protects the local government from royalty claims resulting from such use, subject to the approval of the legal department.

Price adjustments based on the Consumer Price Index (CPI)   This clause, which defines how contract pricing will be adjusted annually, requires identification of the category of the CPI for goods or services used as the escalator and the base month used to calculate price changes. Do not use the contract anniversary month as the month upon which to base price adjustments; the base month for the calculations should be at least three or four months before the contract anniversary date. This schedule permits time to re-bid if the local government does not want to accept a large price increase resulting from an unusual jump in the CPI. An important provision of the price adjustment clause is that prices change according to the change in the escalator, whether up or down. Do not use the word "increase"; it does not permit price to be adjusted downward.

The CPI is calculated for two population groups, Urban Wage Earners and Clerical Workers (CPI-W) and All Urban Consumers (CPI-U). Figures for the second group are most likely to be used for escalator clauses. Although the CPI figures are adjusted seasonally, the adjusted figures are rarely used in escalator clauses; in the clause, the term "unadjusted" identifies the data to be used. The same clause can be adapted for use with other price indexes.

Procurement regulations   To ensure that procedures for resolution of contract disputes and other pertinent information are a part of the bid and contract documents, incorporate the local government procurement regulations into the terms and conditions by reference.

Recovery of money   The local government may have difficulty obtaining money due from a contractor. The recovery of money due clause allows the local government to obtain money it is owed by deducting it from payments due to the contractor.

Renewal of contract   This clause allows a contract to be renewed for an additional period under the original terms and conditions. The offer of renewal should always be at the discretion of the local government, although the contractor may not be required to accept the offer. If the contractor agrees to renew at the same price, there is no need for a re-bid. Set the date for the decision to renew at least ninety days before the contract expires to allow time for a re-bid if the contractor refuses the offer to renew.

   The renewal of contract clause must be included in the bid document whenever a renewal is contemplated. If the bid document does not include the terms and conditions of a renewal, any continuation of the contract is considered a new contract, which, under procurement regulations, must be re-bid.

Requirements contract   Occasionally a local government can only estimate the amount of a service it will require. Contracts for trade services (those of plumbers, electricians, etc.) or seasonal services (snow removal) are usually structured as requirements contracts. The requirements contract clause states that the local government offers no guarantee of the extent of work (the requirements) during the contract term. The clause protects the local government if the estimate in the bid document is higher than the amount of work actually required.

Right of first refusal of employment   This clause requires the contractor to offer public employees displaced by the contract the opportunity to obtain employment with the contractor before the contractor hires employees on the open market.

Right to audit   The right to audit the contractor's books is a standard element of the contract. In practice, contractors are seldom audited unless there is evidence of fraud or dishonesty, the contract includes the handling of cash or securities, or the contract is based on a percentage of the contractor's revenue. Because contractors are aware that local governments seldom enforce a right to audit clause, they usually pay little attention to it, no matter how stringent the auditing requirements.

Termination   Termination clauses cover either termination for default or termination at the convenience of the government. **Termination for default** allows the local government to terminate the contract when requirements are not met. Although **termination for convenience** of the government may generate opposition from contractors, some contracts should include this clause to protect the interests of the local government. Among these are contracts for projects of an unknown duration; contracts that depend on grants, other outside funding, or enabling legislation; and requirements contracts (for which there is no commitment to purchase a specific amount of services, even when the solicitation forecasts the amount).

   Contractors faced with a termination for convenience clause often request the corresponding right to terminate at will. If this becomes an issue, the local government should forgo the option to terminate for convenience rather than give contractors the same right. Permitting a contractor to terminate on thirty days' notice creates a contract that is, in effect, valid only for each succeeding thirty-day period of the contract term. Such contracts provide no incentive to improve unacceptable performance. A threat to take action against the contractor or to assess penalties for poor performance will often be answered with a notice of cancellation.

The only contractor-initiated termination that should be permitted is termination on the anniversary date of a multiyear contract and then only if the contractor gives notice of the termination at least 120 days before the anniversary date and agrees to pay the local government some form of liquidated damages for early termination. This 120-day period also provides the time necessary to re-bid the contract.

Traffic control If the contractor's operations may affect the flow of vehicle or pedestrian traffic, the general terms and conditions must include specific instructions for traffic management. Without such instructions, a contractor who blocks a main street or sidewalk during rush hour and is directed by the local government to remove equipment or operations from the traffic lanes could file a claim for lost time or added costs.

Vehicle and equipment buyback The vehicle and equipment buyback clause helps establish a fallback position for the local government in the event that a contractor defaults during the contract term. The contractor and the local government agree that in the event of default, the local government can purchase the vehicles or equipment the contractor used to provide the service.

The bid form

The bid form is the response form returned by bidders; it contains bid prices and other information the local government requires. The bid form must be prepared by the local government with the same care and attention to detail as the scope of work because the information requested is essential to pricing the contract accurately. Although many local governments use a preprinted form or a single bid form and attempt to make it apply to all bidding conditions, the bid form should be tailored to the requirements of the bid document.

The format for a bid form proposed in this section does not include every possible entry in a bid response. Certain contracts may require other entries and local governments may have their own requirements for the structure and content of the bid form. The precise format of the bid form, the material to be returned with the bid response, and the number of copies to be returned are all matters of local preference. As noted earlier, there is no best way to construct a bid form, a scope of work, or any other document used for the procurement of services. The best guidelines for a bid form are that it should be clear and to the point and should provide for a rational, fair, and objective comparison of the bid responses.

Bid form heading The bid form heading should include the name and address of the local government, the bid number, the time and date of bid opening, the title, and the number of copies to be submitted if the bids are to be submitted in hard copy rather than electronically. A sample heading is shown in Exhibit 5-1 at the end of this chapter.

General pricing information Each bid form incorporates the pricing structure that applies to the contract.

Lump-sum pricing The bidder enters a lump-sum price in the blank space provided for the first year of the contract term or for each year if multiyear lump-sum prices are requested. If an escalator will be used to determine prices for subsequent years, include space only for the price for the first year (see Exhibit 5-2).

Unit pricing Provide space in the contract for prices for units of service rendered (price per client contact, per physical exam, per household for trash collected, per curb mile for street sweeping, per day cost of inpatient treatment, etc.). If more than one unit price is requested, the bid form must include definite quantities, estimated quantities, or a forecast of contract activity (see Exhibit 5-2); these are necessary to determine the lowest of the bid responses received.

Time and materials pricing In a contract that includes time and materials pricing, one section of the bid form provides space for labor prices and a separate section provides space for prices of materials. The hourly rates for labor are separated by category (principal, supervisor, engineer, laborer, clerical assistant, etc.). Include estimates of the number of hours expected to be used in the bid form and in the scope of work so that the labor costs of the bidders can be fairly compared (see Exhibit 5-2).

In the scope of work, describe when premium pay for overtime, night work, weekends, and holidays will take effect and establish the formula used to calculate premium pay (e.g., time and a half or double time). When the formula is included in the scope of work, bidders need insert only the basic hourly rate of regular time for each labor category in the bid form. For example, the scope of work could define the formula to use as follows:

Regular time	8:00 a.m. to 5:00 p.m. on weekdays
Time and a half	5:01 p.m. to 12:00 midnight on weekdays and 8:00 a.m. to 5:00 p.m. on Saturdays and Sundays
Double time	12:01 a.m. to 7:59 a.m. on weekdays and all day on weekend days and holidays

If material is to be discounted from a manufacturer's published price list, require the bidder to submit a copy of the price list used and provide space for the bidder to fill in the amount of the discount so that bidders' net prices can be compared. An item that is discounted 40 percent from the list price of one manufacturer can be more expensive than an item that is discounted 5 percent from the wholesale, fleet, or dealer prices of another manufacturer (see Exhibit 5-2).

To obtain a valid comparison of the various discounts offered by bidders, either of two methods can be used. The first method requires all bidders to submit discounts to be applied against the list prices and products of only one manufacturer identified in the bid document (e.g., Goodyear tires for a tire contract or General Electric field lamps for a contract to maintain an athletic field). The highest discount offered results in the lowest contract unit prices. However, when specifying the use of a single manufacturer's price list, always demand that the bidders submit their discounts from the list price. Without this caveat, some may bid a discount from the list price and some may bid a discount from the dealer or wholesale price. Both of the latter are types of prices that may appear in addition to the list price in a manufacturer's price list. If there is the possibility of error in identifying the type of price used, use the second method described below.

The second method is used when more than one manufacturer's price list or more than one type of price from a single manufacturer's price list is discounted.

To permit comparative evaluation of items purchased under differing prices and discounts, list in the bid form two or more items that will be purchased frequently during the contract term. For example, in the bid form for a contract for repairing or replacing truck tires, list two or three sizes of the type of tire (since the same generic information applies to all tire manufacturers) and instruct the bidder to use the price list identified by the bidder to price each of the tires, showing type of price (e.g., list, wholesale, dealer), percent of discount, and net (contract) price for each. Even if Bidder A bids Goodyear tires, Bidder B bids Michelin tires, and Bidder C bids Bridgestone tires, each with different types of prices and different discounts offered to the local government, the comparative pricing method shown in Exhibit 5-2 will provide contract prices for each that are fully comparable.

If list prices are not available, require the bidders to price all material at their own net cost (see Exhibit 5-2). Advise the bidders in the scope of work that profit and overhead are not to be included as part of the cost of materials but incorporated into the hourly labor rates or the amount bid for mobilization (the cost a contractor incurs when moving equipment and staff to a job site to perform the assigned work).

If desired, the contractor net-cost method can be used for all time and materials contracts, an approach that minimizes the effect of the cost of materials as an award factor. Require that all invoices for material be accompanied by original invoices (see "Cost reimbursement" in Appendix A). To compare the cost of items, list a few of the most used materials in the bid form and ask the bidders to enter their costs for those materials, supporting the costs with copies of recent invoices from their suppliers. The more high-use items are listed in the bid form, the more accurate the comparisons will be.

Never use a cost-plus or a percentage markup in a time and materials contract. When these markups are used, the more materials used, the higher the contractor's profit and the contractor has no incentive to control costs. Moreover, some legal departments interpret this pricing method as a cost plus a percentage of cost contract, which is specifically prohibited by most local governments.

Unit prices for additional work   There are times when work outside the original scope of the contract is required during the contract term. For example, special events or emergencies can require more equipment or labor than specified in the contract. Asking bidders to enter their unit prices for such work eliminates discussions of price when these services are needed. Include space in the bid form to enter mobilization charges for special assignments and hourly rates for renting equipment, for all contract employees by labor category, and for any other labor or equipment that is available to the contractor but is not required by the contract (see Exhibit 5-2). These entries are for future reference only and are not evaluated when ranking bidders by price. Explain the reason for requesting these prices in the scope of work.

Acknowledgment of addenda   Include a space in the bid form for bidders to acknowledge any addenda issued during the bidding process (see Exhibit 5-3 at the end of this chapter).

References   Require enough references to determine whether the contractor has the experience needed to perform the work. If you ask for a minimum of five, you may find after the bid opening that the most qualified bidder has only four references, requiring the rejection of the bid as nonresponsive. Keep the request for references as flexible as possible. A firm with two excellent references is usually a better risk than a firm with five marginal references. References requested should be for contracts similar in size and scope to the contract being bid (see Exhibit 5-4).

Licenses   Require certification that the bidder has all licenses, certification, or accreditations required to do the work. Bidders should be instructed to include copies of required licenses or accreditations with their bid submission (see Exhibit 5-5).

Required attachments   Include in the bid form a section that describes all the required attachments such as lists of equipment to be used to perform the work, the bidder's proposed staffing plan, organizational charts, estimates of crew size and composition, work plan, quality control plan, resumes of staff, financial statements, and any information that will help in the evaluation of the bid response (see Exhibit 5-6).

Payment terms   It is a good policy to restate the provisions regarding payment terms in the bid form, even though they are included in the boilerplate. If alternative payment terms such as discounts are included in the evaluation of the bid responses, be sure to let bidders know (see Exhibit 5-7). Payment terms are, in effect, price entries because the discounts a contractor offers for prompt payment of invoices affect the contract price. If a contract is for $100,000 and the contractor proposes a 2 percent discount for payment within thirty days or less, savings could be as high as $2,000. Knowing that local governments will process invoices with prompt-payment discounts before those without discounts, contractors may propose payment terms of at least 2 percent; terms of 5 percent or more are not unheard of.

Signature block   In the signature block, request the bidder's business status (corporation, partnership, etc.); federal Employer Identification Number (EIN); minority- or women-owned business status, if these criteria are relevant to bid evaluation; street address; and telephone number (see Exhibit 5-8).

Insurance checklist   It is not unusual to complete the evaluation of bids and then learn that the bidder recommended for award is unable to obtain the insurance required for the contract at the price submitted in the bid response. Including an insurance checklist to be returned as part of the bid response can reduce this possibility. The insurance checklist identifies all coverage required for the contract and requires the bidder's insurance agent to certify that the coverage and its cost were discussed with the bidder. The checklist is attached as the last page of the bid form; Exhibit 5-9 provides an example.

Identification of bid form pages   On each page of the bid form, include a line at the bottom of the page for the firm's name and the bidder's authorized signature or initials. This prevents confusion if the bid form pages are separated and is evidence that the bidder accepts responsibility for each entry on that page.

Preparing and circulating the bid document

Once the scope of work, the instructions to bidders, the general terms and conditions, and the bid form have been prepared, the bid document can be assembled and circulated.

Preparing the bid document

There are no rules governing the order or format in which the components of the bid document are placed. The format shown in this section is simply a suggested outline.

Cover page and legal advertisement The term "legal advertisement" refers to an advertisement placed in the legal notice section of a newspaper. When local government regulations require a legal advertisement to be placed in a local newspaper for each solicitation, the cover page of the bid document and the advertisement should be the same. Nothing in the advertisement can conflict with the contents of the bid document.

The newspaper gives the local government a copy of the advertisement with attached certification of the date of publication. It is kept in the bid file to verify that the advertisement was placed as required by regulations. The cover page includes the following:

- The name of the local government
- The time and place for the bid opening
- The number assigned to the solicitation
- The contract term and a brief description of the service being bid
- Notice that the bid responses will be opened and read in public if bids are to be received in hard copy
- The name of a contact person and instructions for obtaining a copy of the bid document if the cover page is used as the advertisement
- A description of bid, performance, and payment bonds required
- Pre-bid conference information
- A statement on rejection, informalities, and irregularities.

Table of contents A table of contents may be included if the length of the bid document warrants one; it should list only major sections and their page numbers.

Scope of work The scope-of-work section contains the description of services and information the bidder needs to calculate a bid price.

Instructions to bidders The instructions to bidders section applies to the bid process only. It relates to events and actions that occur before the award of a contract. When the final contract is prepared, this section is deleted entirely.

If procedures require that the entire bid document be returned with the bid response, the instructions to bidders section includes the bid form. If only the bid form itself is to be returned with the bid response, the bid form is placed at the very end of the bid document to make it easier to detach and return.

General terms and conditions The general terms and conditions section includes the terms and conditions that will be included in the final contract.

Exhibits and attachments Technical exhibits, maps, drawings, studies, consultants' reports, and similar items are usually too bulky to bind with the bid document. When separate documents are submitted as part of the required information, insert a page just before the bid form that lists and describes them.

Bid form Unless the bid form is incorporated into the instructions to bidders section, it is placed at the end of the bid document. The bid form section includes the bid form and the insurance checklist.

Circulating the bid document

The bidder list is a listing of the names and addresses of firms that may be interested in the work being bid. The principal sources for creating a bidder list are the files of the purchasing department and the department responsible for providing the service or the files of other regional local governments. The names of potential bidders can also be obtained from the Internet or telephone yellow pages, membership listings of chambers of commerce, and lists of holders of local business licenses. If the bidder list is exceptionally long, do not send out the complete bid document to bidders; simply send a notice of the bid, either by regular mail or e-mail. This is generally just a copy of the cover page of the solicitation.

Mailing or e-mailing bid documents to vendors on the bidder list is the beginning, not the end, of a search for bidders. Even if it is not required by local government regulations, advertise a solicitation for a service contract. Use a local newspaper and, if the size of the contract warrants, a regional newspaper. Send notices of the solicitation to local chambers of commerce and regional trade organizations. Include the advertisement on a local or regional cable channel dedicated to local government service. The accompanying sidebar demonstrates how one city circulates the bid document to small and disadvantaged businesses in an effort to level the playing field for these firms.

Pre-bid conference

Pre-bid conferences are held at the discretion of the local government. If the service itself is straightforward and the service description is clear, it may not be necessary to hold a conference. Examples include services provided at the vendor's site for computers, vehicles, or generators and services for temporary help. For contracts that require that the bidder see the site where the service will be delivered—for example, contracts for mowing, collecting refuse, and landscaping—a pre-bid conference is necessary so that prospective bidders can ask questions about the bid document and view the work site firsthand. For contracts involving complex service delivery, such

Diversifying competition

To level the playing field for small and disadvantaged business enterprises (S/DBE) and enhance diversity in its business partners, the city of Shreveport, Louisiana, created the Fair Share Program for Equal Business Opportunity, which committed the city to let 25 percent of all city contracts to S/DBE firms. The city's Disadvantaged Business Enterprise Office certifies local firms with S/DBE status and maintains a comprehensive listing of all S/DBE firms in the city that includes the name, address, and phone number of each firm; the types of work it has been certified to perform; and certification expiration dates. This listing is updated quarterly. Bid documents are circulated to this list, ensuring that notice of contracting opportunities with the city reaches all qualified disadvantaged businesses.

as foster care and adoption or workforce development services, a pre-bid (pre-proposal) conference is recommended.

Mandatory or optional?

Once a local government has decided to hold a pre-bid conference, it must decide whether to make it mandatory or optional. Many local governments make all conferences mandatory. This approach has several advantages. First, a mandatory conference provides the local government with an opportunity to gauge the extent of competition well before the date set for receipt of bid responses. Second, it allows the local government to detect problems with the bid document. For example, a showing of only one or two firms at a mandatory pre-bid conference may indicate that the bid document is unattractive to potential bidders.

On the basis of discussions with the firms that do attend, the local government can revise the bid document, issue an addendum incorporating the changes, and schedule another conference at a later date. If only two or three firms attend the second conference, the local government can either proceed or cancel a competitive sealed bid and re-bid under competitive negotiation procedures, if they are allowed. If only one bidder attends a rescheduled conference, canceling the solicitation and negotiating with that bidder as a sole source may be the wisest course.

Scheduling and planning

The pre-bid conference occurs at the midpoint between publication of the bid advertisement and bid opening. When scheduling the conference, allow at least two weeks after the date the bid document is mailed to give contractors time to work the conference into their schedules. The two-week period also provides an opportunity for contractors that are not on the original bidder list to learn of the solicitation through advertisements, subscription services, or word of mouth.

Conducting a pre-bid conference differs little from conducting any meeting. Planning for registration, late arrivals, and record-keeping is a key component.

If the conference is mandatory, everyone attending must register as proof of attendance and to be eligible to receive any addenda that may be issued. Be certain that all bidders write down their full corporate name, the representative's name, and the firm's address, zip code, telephone number, and e-mail address. Otherwise, you may discover after everyone has left that a firm signed in and attended the conference but left no contact information and cannot be located to receive amendments.

At an optional pre-bid conference, potential bidders who arrive late are usually allowed to participate. At a mandatory conference, potential bidders who arrive after the start of the meeting are generally excluded from participation, although it is common to allow a grace period of five to ten minutes. Each local government must establish and enforce a written policy on late arrivals.

Decide in advance who will represent the local government and respond to questions. Do not let the meeting degenerate into conversations among various public sector representatives and bidders.

The guidelines contained in the accompanying sidebar can help ensure a productive pre-bid conference.

Guidelines for a pre-bid conference

1. Keep the conference as informal as possible.

2. Do not intimidate potential bidders with a bureaucratic approach. A potential bidder who does not submit a bid response because of a poorly run pre-bid conference may have been the best bidder available.

3. The complexity of some contracts requires that every page of the bid document be reviewed. Other contracts require only a general question-and-answer session. Tailor the review to the contract.

4. Keep the discussion focused on the subject matter of the conference.

5. The pre-bid conference is as much an opportunity to sell the contract as to share information. Present the contract as a good opportunity for the contractor and present the local government as a good partner in a contractual relationship.

6. Do not argue with potential bidders.

7. Give accurate and honest responses to questions. If no one on the local government staff knows the answer to a question, advise the potential bidders that all those present will receive a response by letter or in an addendum.

8. If a potential bidder asks whether a specific item will be included in an addendum, explain that after the conference the local government will discuss issuing an addendum and that all present will receive any addendum issued. Do not promise to issue an addendum during the pre-bid conference.

9. Local government staff members must not discuss the merits of a bidder's question during the conference.

10. Begin and end every pre-bid conference by stating that nothing discussed that materially affects the bid document can be relied upon unless it is contained in an addendum issued after the conference.

Issuing addenda

Information obtained at the pre-bid conference, questions raised by potential bidders, ambiguous language, or serious typographical errors discovered after publication of the bid document can be reasons to issue addenda.

An addendum is always required when substantive changes affect the cost, delivery, or quality of the work. Addenda are not required in response to every question raised by a potential bidder. If no pre-bid conference is scheduled or if attendance is optional, any addenda must be mailed to every vendor who received a copy of the original bid document. If an addendum results from a mandatory pre-bid conference, send the addendum only to those who attended the conference. Require in the addendum that the bidder acknowledge its receipt and return the acknowledged addendum with the bid form.

Prepare and issue any addenda as soon as possible after the pre-bid conference, certainly no later than five days before the date scheduled for the receipt of bids. Allow additional time for mail delivery if any potential bidders are not local. Give potential bidders enough time to review the addendum and adjust their bid responses. If the addendum requires a revision to the price bid, consider rescheduling the bid opening.

Bid opening

Bid opening procedures range from an informal opening and tabulation of the bid responses to complex procedures involving lockboxes, official witnesses, or public openings before the governing body. This section covers issues associated with bid openings of any type.

Bid openings are open to the public except in rare cases when local or state laws do not permit public opening for some types of competitive negotiation bid responses. Expect one or more bidders to attend the bid opening. If the service is high profile or controversial, the press and interested citizens might attend as well. The names of all those who attend and the organizations represented should be recorded and made part of the master bid file.

Local government policies vary in regard to how much access to bid responses they give bidders at public openings. Some allow attending bidders to examine the responses immediately. Others deny access until the decision to award the contract is made. Still others permit inspection of the bid responses by appointment after the date of the opening. Whatever procedure is followed, the bid responses must never be marked or altered in any way by the bidders during inspection.

Late bid responses

A late bid response is a response that is not delivered to the designated location by the time set for receipt of bids. The procedures for handling late bid responses are a matter of local government preference, but once they have been put in writing, they must be followed without exception. (See "Late submissions" in Appendix A.) When a bid is delivered late, the most common response is for the local government to reject the bid. Exceptions are rare, even when the bidder is already in the building at the time of the deadline or is delayed by traffic or bad weather or when delivery of the bid envelope is delayed by the postal service. Some local governments are more lenient, however, and accept late bid responses when the envelope is postmarked a specified number of days before the bid opening date or when the bidder is in the building and on the way to the bid opening room.

Defining a signed bid

Some local government officials feel it necessary to reject a bid response that does not have a signature in the signature block or when the signature is written in pencil and not in ink, is typed and not handwritten by the bidder, is an initial and not a full signature, or consists of only a bidder's thumbprint. All these examples of unacceptable bids may be acceptable in court because they may be interpreted to show that the bidder had a clear and present intent to authenticate the bid response as described by state or local law or the Uniform Commercial Code.

Through its legal department, the local government must gain a clear understanding of state and local laws that define the term "signature" and translate that understanding into a written policy that permits as much latitude as possible in accepting bids that the layperson might consider to be unsigned. Without such a policy, a local government official may inadvertently reject a bid that is legally acceptable even though it is not signed in ink. In addition, a written policy provides an appropriate response to a protest of the local government's acceptance of what appeared to a bidder to be an unsigned bid of another bidder. The policy must also include a statement of the acceptability of signatures transmitted by facsimile machine and e-mail; these too may meet the definition even though they are electronic copies of the originals.

Extending the bid opening

Bidders' requests for an extension, which are often made a few hours before the scheduled bid opening, must be addressed individually. There may be instances when an extension of time is appropriate; for example, when a complex addendum was issued a few days before the scheduled bid opening. Evaluate each request for an extension to determine whether it is valid, whether it is being used to cover a bidder's lack of planning, and whether or not granting the extension would result in a "no bid" response from a highly qualified firm. Whatever the merits of the bidder's case, remember that a contractor who cannot plan for a bid opening announced weeks in advance may have similar problems meeting contract deadlines.

An extension given to one bidder is automatically given to all. If an extension is granted, always extend for at least a week beyond the scheduled bid opening date to provide all bidders an opportunity to retrieve their original bid responses for review or revision. A one- or two-day extension unfairly benefits only the bidder requesting the extension.

Receiving bids

Bid responses are usually stamped with the time and date received, and a receipt with a time-and-date stamp is issued to the person delivering the bid. Time-and-date stamping is an effective way to establish exactly when a late bid response was received, which can be helpful if a protest action is filed.

Neither the identity of bidders who have submitted responses nor the number of responses received should be revealed to other bidders before bid opening unless local government regulations require release of this information. Experienced bidders know the general range of their competitors' prices. A contractor that is waiting until the last minute to submit a response may take the opportunity to raise the price after learning that a major competitor has not yet submitted a response. In the same manner, a contractor who learns that no other responses have been received yet may feel that the apparent lack of competition justifies increasing the price.

Maintain the security of bid responses by keeping them in a lockbox or file cabinet. Never open bid responses without at least one witness. If mail room or reception staff accidentally open a response, it should be resealed immediately and marked "Unidentified bid response, opened in error and resealed by [name] on [date]."

Prices are recorded on a spreadsheet or other form that shows the name of the bidder and the price bid. Space can be provided for other information such as proposed payment terms, delivery schedules, and so forth.

Bid responses are usually opened and read aloud to a second staff member, who acts as a witness and who may also be responsible for recording the information on the tabulation form. Advise any bidders attending that the **tabulations** state only what was observed at receipt of bids and that no award recommendation will be made until staff has analyzed each bid response.

If local government regulations permit, copies of the tabulation are made available to bidders immediately after bid opening or within a reasonable time. Whenever a copy is released to bidders or the public, it is a good practice to print or rubber-stamp a disclaimer on the tabulation form. The disclaimer should read as follows:

> This is a draft tabulation. Entries are as recorded during bid opening, may include incorrect price extensions or transcription errors, and are subject to change if conflicting information is discovered during analysis of the bid responses.

After all of the bids are opened, it is time for the local government to turn its attention to the process of evaluating the bids, selecting the winning bidder, and awarding the contract. These topics are covered in detail in the next chapter.

Exhibit 5-1 Sample bid form heading.

> Anytown, USA
> Bid Number 72-99
> Providing Senior Citizen Transportation Services for a Two-Year Period
> Submit a signed original and 4 copies.
> Bids will be opened at 2:00 p.m., January 21, 2007

Exhibit 5-2 Sample entries for the general pricing information section of the bid form.

Lump-sum pricing

Lump-sum price (first year) $_____

Lump-sum price (second year) $_____

Unit pricing

Item	Estimated annual use	Unit price ($)	Extension ($)
Vehicle tows, day	2,500	_____	_____
Vehicle tows, night	3,000	_____	_____
Estimated total annual cost			_____

Time and materials pricing

Hourly labor rates

Labor category	Estimated hours/year	Hourly labor rate ($)	Extension ($)
Journeyman plumber	400	_____	_____
Plumber's helper	400	_____	_____
Estimated total annual cost	_____		

Material at discount from list

Discount offered: _____ percent from list price

Price list used: Manufacturer _____

          Price list no. and date _____

Using the above discounts, price the following items.

Item	List price	% discount	Cost ($)
Windshield, 2004 Chevrolet Caprice	$_____	_____	_____
Rear window, 2004 Chevrolet Caprice	$_____	_____	_____

Material at contractor's net cost

All material shall be charged at contractor invoice cost. Price the following items at contractor cost and attach copies of recent invoices supporting these costs.

Item	Invoice cost ($)
Playground sand (ton)	_____
Bluegrass sod (square yard)	_____

Unit prices for additional work, when required

Labor   Enter labor category and hourly rate for all contract-related personnel and personnel performing related work for the contractor but not included in the pricing for this contract.

Labor category	Hourly rate ($)
Dump truck/snow plow operator	_____
Front end loader operator	_____

Equipment	
Item	Hourly rate, including operator ($)
Dump truck with snow plow	_____
Front end loader	_____

Exhibit 5-3   Sample acknowledgment of addenda.

The undersigned acknowledges receipt of the following addenda:

Addendum number   Date issued

_____   _____

_____   _____

Exhibit 5-4   Sample request for references.

List up to five references for the same type and size of contract described in the bid document. Indicate dates of work. List all governmental references first.

Organization	Dates	Contact Name	Telephone
1. _____	_____	_____	_____
2. _____	_____	_____	_____

Exhibit 5-5   Sample request for certification of possession of licenses.

By submitting this bid response, the bidder certifies that the following required licenses are available for inspection within twenty-four hours of demand by Anytown, U.S.A.

[Describe required licenses and certificates.]

_____

_____

Exhibit 5-6   Sample list of required attachments.

Required attachment	Bidder's initial
[Description]	
_____	_____
_____	
_____	
[Description]	
_____	_____
_____	
_____	

Exhibit 5-7 Sample request for payment terms.

Payment terms: 2% 30 days [or other stated terms]. If alternative terms are proposed, indicate below.

_____

_____

_____

Note: Payment terms [are/are not] considered in price evaluation.

Exhibit 5-8 Sample signature block.

Submitted by:

Contractor name _____

Address _____

City/state/ZIP _____

Authorized signature _____

Name/title (print) _____

Telephone number _____

Tax ID number (EIN/SSN) _____

Initial applicable entry:

Corporation _____   Partnership _____

Joint venture _____   Other _____

Initial applicable entries:

This business is minority-owned _____   woman-owned _____

Handicapped-owned _____   Small business _____

Other disadvantaged status _____

Exhibit 5-9 The insurance checklist supplements the insurance information in the solicitation and shows all the specific coverages required of the bidder for the contract. The checklist is the last page of the bid form and is returned by the bidder with it.

Insurance Checklist

Coverages marked "X" are required if award is made to your firm. "N/A" indicates that the listed coverage is not applicable.

Coverages required	Limits (Figures denote minimums.)
___ 1. Workers' compensation	Statutory limits of [state]
___ 2. Employers' liability	$100,000 accident/disease $500,000 policy limit, disease
___ 3. United States Lands & Harbors (USL & H) endorsement	Statutory
___ 4. General liability	Complete entry no. 25. Items 4-9, 11, and 12 require $500,000 combined single limit for Bodily Injury & Property Damage (BI & PD), each occurrence
___ 5. Premises/operations	
___ 6. Independent contractors	
___ 7. Products	
___ 8. Completed operations	
___ 9. Contractual liability	$500,000 general aggregate (gen. agg.), if applicable
___ 10. Personal injury liability	$500,000 each offense (off.), aggregate (agg.), personal injury (PI)
___ 11. Explosion, Collapse, Underground (XCU) coverage	
___ 12. Broad form Property Damage (PD)	
___ 13. Automobile liability	$500,000 BI & PD, each accident
___ 14. Owned, hired, nonowned	$500,000 BI & PD, each accident
___ 15. Umbrella liability	$1,000,000 BI & PD and PI
___ 16. Garage liability	$ ____ BI & PD, each occurrence
___ 17. Garagekeepers legal liability	$ ____ Comprehensive (Comp.) $ ____ Collision

___ 18. [Local government] named as an additional insured on other than workers' compensation.
___ 19. Other insurance required _____
___ 21. 45 days' cancellation, nonrenewal, material change of coverage reduction notice required.
___ 22. Best's rating ____ or better, or its equivalent.
___ 23. The certificate must state bid number and title.

Insurance agent's statement

I have reviewed the requirements with bidder named below. In addition:
___ 24. The above policies carry the following deductibles

_____

___ 25. Liability policies are *occurrence* __ *claims made* __

_____	_____
Insurance agent	Signature

Bidder's statement

I understand the insurance requirements and will comply in full if awarded the contract.

_____	_____
Bidder	Signature

Note: This version of the insurance checklist shows the abbreviations spelled out. Abbreviations are accepted in the industry and familiar to insurance and risk managers. They permit the local government to keep the insurance checklist on one typewritten page.

6

Evaluation and Award

This chapter addresses the evaluation of responses to a request for proposals (RFP) or an invitation for bids (IFB) and the selection of the contractor. The evaluation procedure depends on whether the purchase is made under competitive negotiation, multistep bidding, or competitive sealed bidding procedures. Although price is always a factor in an award, it is not always the primary consideration. In competitive negotiation, award is made to the most qualified respondent provided the cost is reasonable and acceptable to the local government. Multistep bids are awarded on the basis that a bidder meets minimum qualification criteria and proposes acceptable service delivery methods. When these criteria are satisfied, the award is made to the qualified bidder with the lowest price. In competitive sealed bidding, the lowest bid is evaluated to determine whether it is responsive and responsible. If it meets these criteria, the award is made to the lowest bidder. If these criteria are not satisfied, the bid is rejected and the award is made to the next lowest bidder and so forth until the lowest responsive and responsible bidder is identified.

This chapter is divided into seven major sections. The first deals with the initial review of responses and is applicable to all three bidding methods; the second deals with the composition and duties of the evaluation panels for competitive negotiation and multistep bidding; the next three sections discuss the evaluation procedures for each of the three methods; the sixth deals with protests; and the final section outlines the process of contract negotiations. Evaluation forms that can be adapted for use by most local governments appear as a set of exhibits at the end of the chapter.

Initial review of responses

Before forwarding the responses to the evaluation panel, the purchasing department or panel chairperson examines them to identify those that are clearly nonresponsive, nonresponsible, incomplete, or otherwise unacceptable. These responses are eliminated from further consideration. A written finding of the reasons for rejection is prepared by the chairperson, reviewed by the legal department, and sent to the affected respondents at the conclusion of the selection process or whenever required by local regulations.

Responsiveness and responsibility

Responsiveness refers to the respondent's compliance with all the requirements of the bid process and the solicitation. Responsibility refers to the respondent's ability to do the work called for in the solicitation. The "Qualifications of bidders" clause in Appendix A lists several areas to evaluate in determining responsibility.

If the solicitation includes an "informalities and irregularities" clause or a "nonconforming terms and conditions" clause (see Appendix A), minor variations from the exact requirements of the solicitation may be allowed if they do not affect the price, quality, quantity, or delivery of the services purchased. The nonconforming terms and conditions clause permits the respondent to withdraw terms and conditions that do not conform to the original solicitation. These clauses are particularly helpful in evaluating responses that include nonconforming terms and conditions in brochures or promotional literature attachments. Without these clauses, acceptance of responses with nonresponsive clauses in the attachments could be considered grounds for protest from a respondent whose response contains no exceptions, omissions, or restrictive language.

Rejection of responses

Rejections made by the purchasing department or panel chairperson during the initial review are predominantly due to nonresponsiveness. A number of conditions can warrant rejection of a response, including the following: the firm is suspended or debarred; the response violates conflict of interest laws; the respondent fails to submit the required bid bond or suitable alternative surety; the response lacks requested information (whether this is cause for rejection depends on how much the missing information affects the completeness of the response); the bid is received late (whether a late bid is rejected depends on the regulations and policies of the individual local government); or only one response is received (the policies and regulations of many local governments do not permit the opening of a sole response to a competitive sealed bid or an RFP).

Another legitimate cause for rejection is failure to submit the response in the required format. For example, the respondent may not have used the local government's response forms or may have failed to submit the required number of copies of the response. Errors in the response can indicate poor management and lack of attention to detail and may reflect on the respondent's ability to manage the details of a service contract.

Criteria used to evaluate responsibility

- Does the respondent have the ability, capacity, skill, and financial resources to provide the service?
- Can the respondent undertake the responsibilities outlined in the contract and provide the service within the time specified?
- Does the respondent possess the character, integrity, reputation, judgment, experience, and efficiency the contract requires?
- What was the quality of performance in previous contracts or the quality of services previously delivered?

The decision to reject a response because of errors depends on the magnitude of the error, its effect on the quality of the submission, and the type of bidding method used. Errors occurring in responses to RFPs are often ignored because they can be corrected during negotiation if the offeror becomes a finalist. Errors in bids received under competitive sealed bidding are more problematic. If a bidder makes a clerical error that results in a significantly lower price than intended, the bidder may be permitted to withdraw the bid upon request to the local government. The bid cannot be corrected after bid opening; it can only be withdrawn. Similarly, if a clerical error causes one of several unit prices to be incorrect, the bidder can request permission to withdraw the entire bid; the bidder cannot correct just the incorrect unit price. In competitive sealed bidding, neither partial withdrawals nor changing a unit price after the bid opening are permitted, and total withdrawal is permitted only if the error can be demonstrated to be a clerical error rather than an error of judgment.

A bidder that is denied permission to withdraw a bid may accept the award at the price submitted or refuse to accept the award and forfeit any bid surety submitted. The local government also may initiate legal action against the bidder to recover the difference between the submitted bid and the amount of the next lowest responsive and responsible bid. In competitive sealed bids, errors that are not classified as clerical errors can seldom be corrected unless they are covered by an informalities and irregularities clause.

Evaluation panel: Competitive negotiation and multistep bidding

Evaluating the responses received under the competitive negotiation process and the first steps of the multistep bidding process is usually the responsibility of an evaluation panel. The panel evaluates the responses, selects a finalist or finalists, and makes a recommendation for award of the contract. The panel usually includes the field manager or another person who is experienced in the service area being contracted, a manager who represents the department currently responsible for the service, the contract manager, and a representative of the finance or budget department. Representatives of the legal and purchasing departments participate only as ex-officio members. Their nonvoting status is necessary because their possible future roles as mediators of contract disputes, enforcers of contract provisions, and initiators of litigation against a contractor may require them to render impartial decisions. Their impartiality could be questioned if, for example, they were called upon to resolve a protest involving an offeror or bidder whom they initially voted to reject.

The panel may also include other voting or nonvoting members such as consultants, citizens, or members of governing body advisory committees. For a major service with high visibility or one that significantly affects residents of the community, a mix of local government representatives and citizens on the panel may be desirable and contributes to the credibility of the panel's recommendations. Because of the potential for conflict of interest, citizens selected to serve on an evaluation panel may not have business or personal relationships with any of the respondents and should be required to sign a statement to that effect to be eligible for inclusion in the master files for the solicitation. As an exception to this rule, many local governments select a service recipient or family member of a recipient to serve on the evaluation panel when contracting for social services. If the service is funded partially or fully by federal grant programs, this may be a requirement. Panel members are selected by the purchasing department or the project manager.

Balancing the evaluation panel

The purchasing department or the project manager should approve all panel assignments to ensure that a single department or other group does not have enough votes to overrule the combined votes of the other members of the panel. A department's request for an unusually high number of staff members on the evaluation panel may be granted, but the department representatives should function as a team and should be permitted to cast only a single vote and submit only a single score that is based on consensus. Similarly, if private citizens are included on the panel, the local government manager—who should be involved whenever citizens are selected—should not permit the citizens to be a voting majority of the panel.

The selection of citizen or other nonemployee members of a panel should be approved in advance by the local government manager.

What is being selected?

Selecting the wrong contractor can be just as damaging to the effectiveness and reputation of the local government as providing inefficient and inexperienced in-house staff to deliver the service. Few citizens care whether a service is delivered by a private sector contractor or public employees as long as the service is delivered with reasonable efficiency and effectiveness. However, when problems arise, citizens and governing bodies hold the local government accountable. They demand action by the local government manager, not the contractor. Because the quality of public services is one measure of the effectiveness of a local government, the evaluation panel must decide which of the qualified contractors will improve, not detract from, the citizens' and governing body's perception of local government service delivery.

Responsibilities of the panel

The evaluation panel's overall mission is to develop a well-researched recommendation for award. To ensure that panel members understand their roles and responsibilities in this process, they need at least one training session. Training should include review of a solicitation, coverage of the rules governing the evaluation process, an explanation of the scoring procedures, and instruction in how to complete the evaluation forms. Panel members must know what they can and cannot do legally, procedurally, and ethically during the selection process.

After training, the panel begins its work by reviewing the responses and comparing them to the criteria established in the solicitation. The panel identifies as finalists those respondents whose proposals most nearly meet the criteria and it investigates the contractors' performance in contracts listed as references or in contracts that are not listed as references but that may be known to panel members. The panel's next task is to interview the finalists and evaluate their oral presentations (if presentations are to be part of the award process). After that, the panel conducts cost analyses of the initial response and subsequent information submitted by the finalists and ranks the finalists from most to least qualified.

In addition to making a recommendation for award, the panel has a number of administrative and procedural responsibilities. First, it maintains complete files and records of its own actions. Correspondence, completed evaluation forms, results of reference checks and site tours, and minutes of meetings must be available in the event that the panel's decision is questioned or challenged. Second, the panel provides information and assistance to the purchasing and legal departments if protests are filed by rejected respondents. Third, the panel conducts the evaluation and selection process in strict accordance with the procurement rules of the local government, ensuring that the final recommendation is without bias. Finally, all voting members of the evaluation panel must attend all evaluation meetings and oral presentations. If a member is absent, it may be necessary to void the scores previously submitted by that member and recalculate all panel scores. To ensure that the panel remains intact throughout the evaluation process, each voting member should have an alternate who attends all meetings with the member and serves as a substitute for the member when he or she is absent.

The field manager, contract manager, or another service specialist on the panel must complete a series of tasks in order to assess each respondents' capacity to fulfill the contract requirements. Alternatively, these tasks may be divided up.

1. Evaluate experience and conduct reference checks.
2. Assess the respondent's capacity to do the work. (In competitive negotiation, the field manager also identifies respondents who propose an acceptable service delivery method.)
3. Determine whether the respondent's qualifications meet the published requirements.
4. Investigate prior contractual relationships.
5. Review the respondent's performance with other organizations.
6. Investigate any problems, disputes, or claims in other contracts listed as references.

The panel member representing the finance or budget department serves as the financial advisor to the panel. He or she calculates total contract costs and evaluates the respondents' financial condition. If the contract is the first for a service that was formerly delivered in house, this member also compares the proposed contract prices to the cost of the existing service.

Members of the purchasing and legal departments ensure that the panel follows all the procedures set forth in local regulations or ordinances and provide advice on whether enough evidence exists to support rejection of a respondent as nonresponsive or nonresponsible. In addition, these members review the panel's award recommendation to make sure that it meets applicable legal and procurement guidelines.

Evaluating proposals under competitive negotiation

Most proposals received under competitive negotiation procedures are evaluated by the full evaluation panel. The principal exceptions are proposals for personal services from individual providers such as instructors, architects, engineers, medical professionals, computer specialists, and social services professionals. Personal services contractors are often evaluated only by the professional staff of the requesting department; the purchasing and legal departments serve as resources to assist with any contract issues that arise.

The guidelines that follow apply to competitive negotiation solicitations involving corporate rather than personal services delivery. The forms referred to in the guidelines correspond to the exhibits at the end of this chapter.

Before beginning the evaluation, the panel must review the RFP, concentrating not only on the task description but also on the qualifications required of the offeror and the evaluation criteria. Before the first panel meeting, the panel chairperson prepares scoring forms and distributes them to all members. Members independently review and score the proposals, entering their scores in the column marked "Independent review" on the form. Scoring guidelines and procedures are discussed in the text below and are illustrated in Exhibits 6-1, 6-2, and 6-6 at the end of this chapter.

The panel then meets to discuss the scores assigned during the independent review. During the discussions, members acquire insight into the qualifications of each offeror by listening to other panel members explain the reasoning behind their scores. After the discussions, if a panel member wishes to adjust the scores assigned during independent review, the adjusted scores are entered in the column marked "Review with panel" on the form. If no changes are made, the totals are simply transferred to the column marked "Review with panel."

To identify the offerors who meet the requirements of the RFP and eliminate those who do not qualify, the panel totals the "Review with panel" scores for each offeror. Offerors then are ranked by their total scores, the highest-scoring offeror being first. The panel selects the top-ranked finalists for further evaluation. Although there are no limits on how many finalists may be interviewed, it becomes cumbersome to do all the tasks required to make the final selection when more than five finalists are considered. The remaining offerors are eliminated from further consideration at this stage.

Each finalist is invited to a combination interview and oral presentation. If required by local regulations, the panel chairperson prepares a memorandum that identifies the finalists and explains the rationale for their selection. The memorandum is forwarded to the official responsible for approving this step of the evaluation process.

Some panels schedule oral presentations in order of the scores received. The argument for this practice is that it allows all offerors to be judged against the one who is highest ranked. But when a local government establishes a pattern of always interviewing the highest-ranked firm first, finalists scheduled later in the day may not give the presentation their best effort. A better approach is to assign the interviews alphabetically or by random drawing.

If the evaluation process clearly indicates that only one offeror is fully qualified, that offeror should still be required to make an oral presentation. The panel should have the opportunity to meet the project manager and other team members and examine and discuss the offeror's cost proposal.

In addition to the original proposal, one or more written submissions may be required of the finalists. They should be delivered in time to distribute them to the

---

An interview is worth a thousand words

When the first-ranked finalist's score leaves the competition far behind, oral presentations from other offerors may not appear to be necessary. However, the scores are not absolutely reliable as an indicator of the finalists' capabilities. It is not unusual for offerors who are extremely skilled in preparing written proposals to do poorly in oral presentations, produce marginal references, or submit price proposals that are far higher than available funds. Always keep the process as competitive as possible for as long as possible: no matter what the scoring spread between the finalists, interview and negotiate with at least the two or three top-ranked firms.

panel members at least three days before the date of the oral presentation. The written submission supplements the original proposal, which usually addresses only the qualifications of the offerors. It contains responses to questions about points in the original proposal that may not have been clear to one or more panel members and contains a more detailed response to the specific requirements of the service to be provided, including the finalist's nonbinding estimate of cost of the services, a draft budget, staffing charts, schedules, and an estimate of hours to be spent on the project by principals. The nonbinding estimate of cost provides the local government with a better grasp of how the offerors view the financial aspects of the work; it is negotiable when a finalist is chosen. While some local government regulations prohibit solicitation of cost and hour information in the original submission, requesting the information from finalists is almost always permitted. Exhibit 6-3 shows a sample letter of invitation to an oral presentation (for a sample set of response requirements, see Exhibit 3-1).

One panel member generally checks the references of the finalists selected for interviews. The reference checks should obtain information on how the contractor performed for the organization, the type and extent of claims filed, problems that occurred during the contract term and how they were resolved, and the contractor's reliability and professionalism. Exhibit 6-4 is a sample reference check form.

Immediately before each finalist's oral presentation, the panel member responsible for checking the references reports to the panel. Questions generated by the report are asked during the interview.

The panel's next task is to interview the finalists and evaluate their oral presentations. After each oral presentation, the panel members total the points on their oral presentation evaluation forms for that finalist. Exhibit 6-5 provides a sample evaluation form for oral presentations. The totals determine the ranking of the finalists. If an evaluation form is not used to score the oral presentation, records must be maintained that show the results of panel discussions, any votes taken, reasons for final ranking, and any other information pertinent to the final award recommendation.

If an unsuccessful offeror files a protest, panel members may be required to defend their scoring. Because of this possibility and in order to maintain a complete record of the evaluation and selection process, all scoring forms, panel memoranda, reference check forms, and other documents relating to the panel's deliberations are placed in the contract files.

Using the sample reference check form

Determine the exact nature of the work performed for the reference. Was the contractor's description of the scope of work performed for the reference accurate? Did the contractor meet all the contract requirements on time and within budget? Ask about any claims or contract disputes during the contract term and other problems the reference may have had with the contractor.

Particularly over the telephone, many references hesitate to say that the contractor was unreliable, that the contractor's employees were untrained, or that the work was unacceptable. But references are usually willing to assign a numerical value to professionalism, qualifications, and so forth. Ask for an explanation of a "maybe" or a "no" response to the question of whether the reference would contract with the contractor again and jot down any other comments or observations made by the reference.

When the ranking is made and approvals are obtained from the appropriate authority (management or the governing body), the chairperson contacts the highest-ranked finalist or finalists, depending on local regulations, and schedules the first contract negotiation meeting.

At the negotiation stage, the details of service delivery, the terms of the contract, and the contract price are worked out. The negotiation team usually consists of the contract manager and a purchasing department official; it may include one or more evaluation panel members. Other local government resource personnel participate as required.

Evaluation of multistep bids

There are a number of similarities between evaluation under multistep bidding and competitive negotiation procedures. For multistep bidding, a full panel is assembled that reviews the bid document and evaluates the bidder's qualifications. The same evaluation forms can generally be used under either procedure. Interviews are held with the finalists in both procedures. Under multistep bidding procedures, finalists are defined as respondents whose qualifications meet the evaluation criteria and whose technical proposals can be accepted with minor changes.

At this point, the evaluation process for multistep bidding begins to diverge from that for competitive negotiation. The interviews under multistep bidding are intended less to gather information than to negotiate adjustments to the technical proposals. Several interviews may be held with each finalist until the technical proposal of each is determined to be acceptable. Another difference is that during these negotiations, discussion of price is not permitted. The local government can request amendments to a proposed service delivery method but cannot request the cost of a change or permit the bidder to discuss cost. The only way the local government can obtain an idea of the cost of a proposed change is if the bidder volunteers the information that the change would cost more or less than the original technical proposal.

During the interviews, the panel should not require or negotiate changes to technical proposals that would result in substantial variations among technical proposals. The goal of the negotiation effort is to make the technical proposals as equivalent as possible in their capital outlay and use of resources. The final proposals may all differ slightly, but the differences should not result in wide variations in the contractor's service delivery costs or capital investment.

In the final step of multistep bidding, sealed prices are requested from the finalists or sealed price envelopes submitted with the original bid are opened and the award is made to the lowest bidder.

Evaluation of competitive sealed bids

Because the award under competitive sealed bidding procedures is made to the lowest responsive and responsible bidder and negotiations on price or service delivery method are not permitted, the evaluation procedure is more straightforward than that for competitive negotiation or multistep bidding.

Competitive sealed bids seldom require a full evaluation panel. More often than not, evaluation is undertaken by the department involved and one or more members of the contract administration team. Staff from other departments may be called upon as needed to resolve an issue outside the area of expertise of the panel members. Evaluation forms other than a qualification checklist are generally not used when evaluating a competitive sealed bid.

The bidders are ranked by price. If the contract contains multiple unit prices, the award formula described in the solicitation determines price ranking. If an award formula was not developed for inclusion in the solicitation, it must be prepared before any of the responses are examined.

A common error in evaluating competitive sealed bids is to favor a bidder offering more than what was called for in the bid document. For example, Bidder A offers to sweep four garages monthly for $25,000 per year. Bidder B offers to perform the same service for $25,100 per year and offers to seal the floor of the garages—a $4,000 bonus every second year of the contract term at no additional cost to the local government. Yet Bidder A is the lowest responsive and responsible bidder no matter what Bidder B offers as a bonus. When evaluating a competitive sealed bid, the original specifications and the bid price submitted are the determining factors.

Under competitive sealed bidding, the deliberations of the evaluators center on whether the lowest responsive bidder meets the qualification criteria; a bidder does not receive additional consideration for exceeding them. If one bidder has twice the experience and outstanding references and another just meets the qualification criteria and has merely acceptable references, both are considered equally qualified.

Because qualification criteria are found outside the evaluation section of the scope of work, panel members must examine every paragraph of the solicitation. List all the evaluation criteria identified in the bid document and compare all bidders against this checklist. The "Qualifications of bidders" clause in Appendix A describes the range of evaluation criteria that can be used.

Although many local governments consider a review of financial statements the best indicator of a bidder's financial stability, eliminating a bidder from consideration solely on the basis of a financial statement could be a mistake. Many small and large businesses with weak financial statements (e.g., illustrating poor cash flow or an unusually high debt-to-equity ratio) are skilled at managing cash flow and controlling costs, permitting them to expand into new contract areas with little difficulty. Also, a contractor with limited cash may plan to use the awarded contract as collateral for financing. Before rejecting a bidder because of apparent financial instability, provide an opportunity for the bidder to explain how the contract will be managed financially. The finance and auditing departments should evaluate financial stability.

The intentionally low bid

Although an extremely low price, say 25 percent or more below current market rates, may not be technically improper or illegal, the bidder must be required to demonstrate to the local government through original cost calculations that the price will cover all the costs with at least a nominal profit margin. If the actual cost of service delivery appears to exceed the price submitted or if the bidder does not have a reasonable explanation for an unusually low bid, obtain legal advice before accepting the bid. An unusually low bid may be an attempt to intentionally exclude others from bidding and monopolize a service area, an action that could violate antitrust laws.

As part of the reference check ask how the bidder performed, what problems occurred during the contract term and how they were solved, and what level of professionalism and reliability the bidder demonstrated. Exhibit 6-4 shows a sample reference check form.

An interview may be necessary to fully explore the lowest bidder's qualifications. Require resumes of key staff and staffing plans to help establish the bidder's capability to deliver the service. To evaluate the qualifications of the person directly responsible for supervising service delivery, require that the contractor's project manager or field supervisor be present at the interview.

In competitive sealed bidding, price can be negotiated only with the lowest responsive and responsible bidder and then only if allowed by local government purchasing regulations. Regulations usually allow negotiation with a low bidder only if the price is higher than fair market value or exceeds the funds budgeted for the contract. If the bid price cannot be lowered to an acceptable level through negotiation, that bid and all other bids must be rejected.

Shortly after the bid process has concluded, local governments may wish to hold a debriefing session as a way to help suppliers improve their competitive performance in future bids. Debriefing involves meeting with unsuccessful bidders (or offerers) to provide them with feedback and discuss how the evaluation criteria were applied to make the award. The debriefing process may be beneficial for improving the quality of the contractor pool. The "Benefits of debriefing" sidebar lists additional potential benefits of debriefing for the purchasing government as well as suppliers.

Benefits of debriefing

Debriefing can be an important part of a good procurement process because it offers a useful learning tool for both parties. Effective debriefing requires time and effort and always carries some minor risk of legal challenge, but if it is carefully planned, the benefits far outweigh the costs.

Potential benefits of debriefing for the purchasing agency:

- Identifies ways of improving services for next time
- Suggests ways of improving communication
- Ensures suppliers are updated on best practices not highlighted in their bid, encouraging better bids from those suppliers in the future
- Provides insight into how that segment of the market is thinking
- Helps the purchasing agency establish a reputation as a fair, open, and ethical buyer with whom suppliers will want to do business in the future

Potential benefits for the supplier:

- Helps firms rethink their approach so that future bids are more successful
- Offers targeted guidance to new or smaller companies to improve their chances of doing business in the public sector
- Provides reassurance that the process is fair
- Provides a better understanding of what differentiates public sector from private sector procurement

Source: Adapted from *Supplier Debriefing* (Norwich, UK: Office of Government Commerce, 2003).

Protests

There are few decisions made by public officials relating to contracts that cannot be protested or challenged. Most protests are resolved in house at the first level of protest. Inevitably, a few make it to the courtroom, but a much more common and cost-effective alternative to litigation is to seek alternative dispute resolution (ADR) service when the protest cannot be resolved in house. The sidebar below describes the measures taken by one state agency to use ADR in mediating claims of adverse action.

This section deals primarily with protests—challenges made before the award of a contract. It reviews the common causes of protests and offers suggestions on how to avoid them.

Procedures for addressing disputes and claims filed after award by a current contractor may be different. State laws often govern procedures for resolving contract disputes involving monetary claims against the local government. They usually require hearings before the governing body before the contractor can apply to the courts for relief. Strategies the local government can follow to avoid contract disputes involving performance after the award are addressed in Chapter 8.

Protests are the safety valves of public procurement, enabling bidders to challenge the decisions of public officials that are perceived as unfair or inequitable. Failure to address seriously every protest received can damage the integrity of the local government's bidding process. When bidders perceive a local government as having made arbitrary contract decisions, they have considerably less incentive to participate in future contracts. Prompt, objective, and fair responses to protests are necessary to retain the respect and confidence of bidders and contractors.

Administrative procedures

Administrative procedures for handling protests, contract disputes, claims, and appeals should be part of every local government's contracting program. Formal procedures are necessary to supplement the (often brief) sections on these issues in most purchasing statutes or regulations. Without formal procedures, the simplest protest, dispute, or claim could escalate until it requires resolution by the governing body or the courts. The procedures should address each type of action that may be initiated by a bidder or contractor.

Protests, the most common type of challenge to decisions of the local government, are most often made by bidders before the award of the contract or to

---

Dispute resolution clauses in general building and procurement commission contracts

Given the amount of public funds it spends on building and construction contracts, the Texas Building and Procurement Commission (TBPC) realized that having a means of resolving disputes arising under its contracts could produce substantial savings for taxpayers. In consultation with the Center for Public Policy Dispute Resolution at University of Texas at Austin, the legal staff at TBPC worked to develop an Alternative Dispute Resolution clause for state construction contracts. The clause provides for negotiation, mediation and then arbitration of disputes, pursuant to statutory authority for TBPC to engage in arbitration. The adoption of the ADR clause has been effective for resolving numerous state construction disputes.

Source: Center for Public Policy Dispute Resolution, University of Texas at Austin (www.utexas.edu/law/academics/centers/cppdr).

challenge the contract award itself. The procedures for handling protests should address the responsibility of the local government to notify bidders of actions that may adversely affect their status in the bidding or award process, when a process may be filed, the party who will review the protest, the period for filing and response, the form of the protest, and the causes of protests and their prevention.

Administrative procedures for handling disputes and claims after the award of the contract should address in what circumstances a claim may be filed, who will review the claim, the period for filing and response, and the avenues of appeal available if a contractor does not agree with the decision of the reviewing public official. Because of the legal implications of this area of public bidding, it is essential that the legal department be involved in the development of the procedures and in any response to a protest, dispute, or claim.

Notice of local government action

Providing adequate notice of an adverse action taken by the local government against a bidder is essential to a fair and open public procurement process. Specify that the local government must provide written notice to a bidder when a decision is made that adversely affects the bidder's standing in the solicitation process. This might include a finding of nonresponsibility or nonresponsiveness; rejection of a bid because of an error, late receipt of a bid, or failure to submit a required bid bond; or denial of a bidder's request for bid withdrawal.

When a protest may be filed

Specify whether written protests will be accepted and acted upon before the award of the contract. Some local governments consider the date of award as the date of a protestable decision and refuse to consider protests filed before that date. Most permit protests to be filed at any time during the bidding and evaluation process, which is the preferable approach. Establish a firm period during which a written protest must be filed. Protests received after the specified period has elapsed are rejected. Also, establish a firm period, usually ten to fifteen days after receipt of the protest, within which the reviewing official must respond to the protest.

Reviewing party

Identify the official to whom written protests are to be directed and the next level of appeal if the protesting party does not accept the official's decision. Usually either the local government procurement officer or the contract manager in the department responsible for managing the bidding process responds to an initial protest. The next level of appeal is often the local government manager. A protest denied at this level is then submitted to the governing body or to a protest review board. If the protest is rejected at all levels within the local government, the protesting party is considered to have exhausted all administrative remedies and may then bring action in court.

Form of protest

To be acceptable, a notice or letter of protest must describe the nature of the protest, the specific action that caused the protest, the harm caused to the protester by that action, and the relief the protester seeks.

Effect on contract commencement

Identify the person responsible for deciding whether to proceed with the award and start of the contract or to delay award and start of the contract until the protest is resolved. In many cases, this person is the local government manager. When determining whether the protest will affect the award process, administrative procedures commonly provide that if a protest is received before contract performance begins and delay would not have an adverse effect on local government operations, the award process will be stopped and the start of the work delayed until the protest is resolved. However, if the service affects vital local government operations or the bids received will expire before the protest is resolved, a protest usually is not considered grounds for delay.

If the protest is successful, the relief granted is usually limited to giving the contract to the protesting bidder (any prior award is canceled, even if another contractor has already started work) or reinstating the protesting bidder as a candidate for award in a re-bid of the solicitation. The types of relief available to protesting bidders when their protests are sustained are often governed by laws that vary considerably between local governments.

Causes of protests and their prevention

The most common causes of protests are restrictive requirements for bidder qualification or experience, nonconforming bid responses, submission of deficient bid surety, failure of the bidder to provide required information, late bid responses, and local government errors in procedure.

Restrictive requirements   A protest can be expected if the bid document contains restrictive requirements that prevent all but a few bidders from responding. The best protection against such protests is clear and reasonable requirements and a defensible written justification for requirements that might appear restrictive. The justification should explain how the requirements benefit the local government, how contract performance or price would be affected if they were not included, and what past experience, if any, generated the need for them. The official responsible for the first level of the local government's administrative procedures for protests should approve the justification before a requirement is included in the bid document. If the requirement cannot be adequately justified, it should be deleted or amended.

To ensure that requirements are reasonable and appropriate, avoid arbitrary cut-off points. For example, requiring a minimum of ten years' experience in a service area is unreasonable if it cannot be demonstrated that a bidder would require ten years' experience to obtain an acceptable level of proficiency. A more reasonable requirement would ask the bidder to provide evidence of successful performance in current or recent contracts for the same services. A thorough reference check is more useful than an arbitrary experience requirement.

Nonconforming bid responses   A bid may be rejected if it contains substantive exceptions to the terms and conditions of the bid document that cannot be rectified without affecting the price or the quality of the service delivered. A bid may be accepted, however, if it contains only minor errors or exceptions that do not affect price or quality. Either rejection or acceptance of nonconforming bids may generate protests. If the lowest bidder is rejected because of a response containing substantive exceptions or errors, a protest from the rejected bidder is likely. Similarly, if minor errors or exceptions in the response of the lowest bidder are waived and the bid is accepted, a protest from the next lowest bidder whose response contains no exceptions or errors can be expected. To minimize the risk of receiving protests involving nonconforming bid responses, be sure that procurement regulations specify clearly the rules for rejection of a bidder and that those rules are included in the bid document.

Submission of deficient bid surety Bid surety is a guarantee that the bidder will enter into a contract if it is offered. Bid responses received with less surety than the amount specified in the bid document or without the specified surety should be rejected. Although rejection because of deficient surety usually results in a protest from the affected bidder, the local government's credibility in establishing surety requirements for its solicitations is at stake, and the requirement is too important to waive.

The best protection against protests involving bid surety is, first, to ensure that bid bond requirements are displayed prominently on the cover page of the bid document as well as in any newspaper advertisements for the bid; and second, to unconditionally reject bids accompanied by deficient surety.

Failure to provide required information A bid response that does not include required information may be accepted if the missing information does not affect the price, quantity, quality, or delivery schedule for the service. (See "Informalities and irregularities" in Appendix A.) However, certain categories of requested material— for example, price lists and critical work references—are so closely related to the bid price and to the quality of the bidder's service that failure to submit them may mandate rejection.

To help ensure that all required information is submitted with the bidder's response, include a checklist in the bid form describing all required attachments and require the bidder to initial each entry to certify that the item is attached. Although both inexperienced and experienced bidders may well overlook a response requirement buried deep within the technical portion of the scope of work or in the instructions section of the boilerplate, a bidder who fills in and signs a checklist has little chance of successfully protesting a rejection for failure to submit required documents.

Late bid responses Most local governments reject late bids with no exceptions, but some accept late bids under several conditions: when the bid carries a hand-stamped (not made with a postage machine) postal service postmark dated at least three days before the bid opening date, when the bidder is in the building at the time of bid opening, when the bid is delayed in the local government's mailroom, or when the cause of delay can be clearly traced to the delivery agent (FedEx, UPS, etc.). Accepting a late bid that turns out to be the lowest bid will certainly generate protests from other bidders. The best protection against such protests is a bid clause detailing the conditions under which a late bid may be accepted. (See "Late submissions" in Appendix A.)

Local government errors in procedure If a specific procedural requirement exists in a statute, follow it. If a statute, regulation, or policy needs to be changed, request advice from the legal department; until it is changed, follow it as written. The key to avoiding problems in interpreting statutes, regulations, and policies is consistency in deciding the same or similar issues. When a public official is given discretionary power to accept a bid that is late by only a few minutes or submitted with deficient bid surety, the same rationale should be applied in making a decision whenever that situation arises. Above all, put the decision and the reasons for it in writing and make them part of the bid files.

Written responses to protests

Whatever the nature of a protest, preparing a response can be difficult. A protesting bidder is seldom satisfied with any explanation that supports the rejection of a bid or includes a requirement that prohibits the bidder from responding. Do not lose sight of the fact that the response to a protest could be the first step of a process that may end in court. The response and the original letter of protest eventually may be the key documents public or court officials will use to decide whether to support or reject a protest or an appeal. They too must be convinced that the reason for a restrictive requirement was in the local government's best interest or that a rejection was justified.

In preparing a written response to any protest, separate the elements of the protest. If protest letter raises multiple issues, address each separately in the response. If the response results in an appeal, the bidder may not appeal the decisions on the issues that have been satisfactorily answered and the appeal will then be focused only on the central issue. Compare what the bidder offers and what the local government wants point by point. Failure to respond to a question or issue discussed in the protest letter could generate additional letters, prolonging the process. If there are regulations or portions of the bid document that support the position of the local government, refer to them in the response and attach copies.

Responses should be kept as positive as possible and agree with the protestor's position when warranted. A harsh response may prompt a bidder to pursue an appeal whereas an amiable response may help avert it. Nothing is gained by antagonizing an already unhappy bidder. Finally, be reasonable. If the protestor makes a convincing argument that a restrictive requirement is not necessary, consider amending the bid document.

Negotiating the contract

After the most responsive and responsible bidder/offeror is selected and any protest issues are resolved, the contract administration team begins contract negotiations. Accepting a proposal without negotiating may result in paying too much for the service. Moreover, failing to challenge restrictive terms and conditions may mean that the local government is not an equal partner in the final contract. Because negotiation is so widely used in service contracting, public managers must familiarize themselves with the negotiation strategies needed to support the local government's position.

This section discusses considerations in selecting a negotiator and establishing a negotiating position, offers guidelines for successful negotiating, and addresses the unique challenges of negotiating in sole source and emergency contracting situations.

Choosing a negotiator

One person should serve as the primary agent for the local government in contract negotiations. Other staff familiar with the details of the service area and the in-house costs of the service can participate in negotiations and service as a resource to the primary negotiator. The chief negotiator may be a member of the local government manager's staff, purchasing department, or legal department or may be any staff member familiar enough with the contract area and the basics of negotiation to be effective in the role.

If the local government contracts extensively or plans to do so, training one or more local government staff in negotiation techniques is a good idea. Having trained staff is advantageous not only for negotiating the initial contract but also for mediating contract disputes or negotiating changes once the contract term has begun. Moreover, a trained negotiator can help in other areas of local government such as negotiating development proposals, franchises, and agreements with other local governments or regional authorities.

Understanding the contractor

The contractor's response to the solicitation probably lists one or more local government references. Contact these references and request a copy of the bid document, the contractor's proposal, and the negotiated contract, under the Freedom of Information Act if necessary. It is always easier to establish a negotiating position when the local government staff knows what terms and conditions the contractor has recently agreed to elsewhere. Read and compare the sample contracts obtained and identify points for negotiation. In reviewing the sample contracts, pay particular attention to the cost estimate, hourly rates, unit prices, terms and conditions, and contract type.

Cost estimate   Although the scope of work in the sample contracts may differ from that in the contract to be negotiated, the negotiation team can use the sample contracts to make a reasonable estimate of what the contractor may agree to as an acceptable cost range (factoring in inflation).

Hourly rates   The hourly rates included in the sample contracts can be used to establish the local government's bargaining position, just as the overall cost estimate can. When examining the hourly rates in sample contracts, pay particular attention to the formula or factor the contractor used to determine the hourly rates.

The factor is usually expressed as a percentage to be applied to the net hourly rate (actual salary) paid to each specialized employee (e.g., principal, engineer, draftsman, secretary). A factor of 175 percent means that the net hourly rate is multiplied by 1.75. The factor covers the cost of the contractor's payroll, taxes, employee benefits, overhead, and—unless a fixed fee is separately stated in the contract—profit. If the sample contracts show that in the previous year the contractor accepted a contract with a factor of 175 percent and the contractor is now proposing a factor of 200 percent, there is probably considerable room for negotiation.

Unit prices   Unit prices the contractor charged for additional work may provide a maximum price position for the local government negotiator. For example, a contractor may propose a unit price of $85 per hour for rental of a certain piece of equipment with an operator. But if a sample contract shows that the same equipment with an operator was rented to another local government for $60 per hour, the negotiation team should use $60 plus an allowance for inflation as its maximum price for that item.

Terms and conditions   A sample contract may include terms and conditions that could benefit the local government. For example, if the contractor agreed in the past to pay high liquidated damages for failing to meet contract schedules, the same requirement could be proposed for the current contract.

Contract type   Payment or contracting methods favorable to the local government may not have been included in the contractor's current proposal but may have been negotiated in a sample contract. If a contractor accepted a lump-sum fixed-price contract in the past, consider negotiating for the same arrangement.

Conducting negotiations: Rules of the game

The two negotiation teams have opposing financial goals: the contractor wants the highest corporate profit possible from the contract while the local government wants the best available service at the lowest possible cost. Both parties must be satisfied that the final contract contains all the services required at a fair and reasonable price.

Private sector contractors may be more experienced in negotiation than the local government staff. It is not uncommon for a contractor to inflate a price proposal in anticipation of making price concessions during negotiations. Another strategy is to include in the proposal conditions or general clauses to be used as throwaways—items that can be traded in exchange for items that the contractor values more.

Volumes have been published on conducting negotiations, but there is no one best method that is guaranteed to work in every scenario. Inexperienced negotiators should study the literature available on the subject and develop a technique that best matches their personal style. Whatever the style or techniques used, some basic guidelines apply to all negotiations.

Be prepared   Know the details of the bid document and the contractor's proposal and examine other proposals received for the same solicitation. Study the sample contracts obtained from other local governments and any other material available about the contract or the contractor. Learn as much about the firm as possible and try to anticipate probable topics of discussion (see the "Understanding the contractor" sidebar).

Establish the local government's bargaining position and strategy well before negotiations begin. Decide on the maximum price per contract year that can be paid for the service and the maximum amount for unit prices or hourly rates and identify all aspects of the bid document that are not negotiable. Finally, identify any tasks or obligations in the bid document that could be eliminated from the final contract with little or no effect on the service and use these as bargaining chips during negotiation to retain other provisions that are more important.

Negotiate with someone who has authority   If at all possible, do not negotiate with anyone who does not have the authority to make a binding decision for the contractor. Items agreed on at the negotiating table should not be subject to rejection by a principal of the contractor. Consider canceling the session if no one on the contractor's team has complete authority to negotiate. Do not rely on titles. Many vice-presidents do not have the power to commit their firm to a contract. When in doubt, ask for written evidence of the negotiator's authority to make binding decisions for the contractor.

Negotiate high priorities first   Negotiate the critical elements of the contract first, using less important requirements such as reporting, work schedule, liquidated damages, and payment methods in bargaining. If negotiations start with the discussion of minor issues, take a firm stand on some of them so that they can be traded later when more critical terms are negotiated.

Use the competition   The contractor knows that the local government places a high priority on cost, and the contractor usually expects to be required to lower the cost to obtain the contract. The contractor is also aware that the next-ranked firm is waiting in the wings if negotiations are terminated. Use the contractor's understanding of the local government's position to the best advantage.

Consider the contractor's terms   If the contractor proposes an unacceptable term, condition, or price, do not dismiss it outright. Instead, present an alternative or modification. Although there are times to take a hard line, repeatedly rejecting proposed terms without discussing alternative approaches can antagonize the contractor's team.

Avoid open conflict   Negotiation is a potentially volatile exchange that can unexpectedly escalate into confrontation. Remember that after negotiations are concluded, both sides must work together for the life of the contract. Avoid open conflict with the contractor's team and always work toward an outcome based on respect for the other's position. If a contractor's question or proposal requires research or consultation with other team members, call a caucus and interrupt negotiations, but do this only if absolutely necessary.

Don't be intimidated Do not be intimidated by the presence of powerful executives on the contractor's team. They may have been included for the sole purpose of impressing, awing, or intimidating the local government team. Intimidation works only if the local government team lets itself be intimidated.

Put it in writing To avoid having to renegotiate settled issues, list all the issues resolved at the conclusion of each session and require both principal negotiators to sign the list. When negotiations are complete, the documented results become the basis for the final contract.

Strive for a win/win solution Neither party leaves negotiations with everything it hoped for at the outset. Be prepared to yield on minor points to protect more important requirements. Never try to win it all. Instead, resolve differences through acceptable compromise so that both parties feel satisfied with the outcome.

Sole source negotiation

Sole source contracting does not require unconditional acceptance of a contractor's terms, conditions, or prices; there is always room to negotiate. It is almost certain that the contractor has provided the service to another organization or public agency, and that agency may have paid less than the price currently being proposed or may have eliminated restrictive language from the proposal. It is worth the effort to try to identify and contact other service recipients and obtain a copy of their agreements. Many sole source providers are quick to provide a list of references. Use the public sector advantage to obtain information from public agencies on the list.

The sole source contractor knows that there are no competitors waiting in the wings. What the contractor does not know is exactly how essential the service is to the local government. Acknowledge that the contract is a sole source, then advise the contractor that the final decision to contract depends on cost and level of the service when compared with other methods of service delivery. Remember that sole source contractors are as eager to sell their services as any other contractor, even if the sale requires concessions.

As part of a standard service package, the contractor may provide more services than desired. Calculate the cost of unnecessary frills and enhancements and negotiate to eliminate them from the contract. Deleting unnecessary items from a package can reduce the price without affecting the desired level of service.

Emergency procurement negotiation

The cost of emergency purchase of services can be negotiated even after a contractor has begun delivering the service. Under emergency conditions, services are usually delivered before a purchase order or other contract document has been issued because there is not enough time before performance must begin to make an informed decision about a fair price for the proposed work. When an emergency occurs, the contractor should be asked to begin work immediately with the condition that terms and conditions and unit prices will be negotiated as soon as practicable. The local government that quickly agrees to a price up front without the opportunity to negotiate may find itself paying more than it should for the work. Once emergency work has started, the local government can determine the local market value for the work and negotiate a realistic price with the contractor.

The price charged for emergency services usually depends on the length of time that the service is to be provided. For short-term emergencies of a few days to a week or two, negotiate an hourly cost for labor and equipment rental. If the emergency is expected to last longer, a lump-sum cost per week or month for the service may be preferable in order to take advantage of economies of scale. A longer-term agreement reduces the high cost of mobilization that is often built into a contractor's hourly rates.

Exhibit 6-1   Sample evaluation form: Weight method.

RFP NUMBER _____

TITLE _____

OFFEROR _____

Instructions to evaluator: Complete a separate evaluation form for each proposal reviewed. Each criterion must be assigned a score unless you are instructed otherwise on the form. Make additional notes in the comments section for reference and discussion during meetings of the full evaluation panel.

SECTION 1. GENERAL EVALUATION CRITERIA

A	B	C	D	E
Criterion	Maximum points	Weight factor	Independent review Points × Weight = Score	Review with panel Points × Weight = Score
A. Responsiveness to the RFP	___	___	___ × ___ = ___	___ × ___ = ___
Comments:				
B. Understanding of the project and the objectives	___	___	___ × ___ = ___	___ × ___ = ___
Comments:				
C. Experience and history of firm	___	___	___ × ___ = ___	___ × ___ = ___
Comments:				
D. Methodology and management approach	___	___	___ × ___ = ___	___ × ___ = ___
Comments:				
E. Qualifications and experience of principals and staff	___	___	___ × ___ = ___	___ × ___ = ___
Comments:				
F. Time spent by principals	___	___	___ × ___ = ___	___ × ___ = ___
Comments:				

(continued on page 126)

Exhibit 6-1 Sample evaluation form: Weight method *(Continued)*.

SECTION 1. GENERAL EVALUATION CRITERIA (Continued)				
A	B	C	D	E
Criterion	Maximum points	Weight factor	Independent review Points × Weight = Score	Review with panel Points × Weight = Score
G. Availability and quality of personnel, facilities, and equipment	___	___	___ × ___ = ___	___ × ___ = ___
Comments:				
H. Proximity of base of operations and availability during project	___	___	___ × ___ = ___	___ × ___ = ___
Comments:				
I. Financial stability (Scoring not to be completed by evaluator)	___	___	___ × ___ = ___	___ × ___ = ___
Comments:				
J. Price (Score only when authorized by panel chair.)	___	___	___ × ___ = ___	___ × ___ = ___
Comments:				
Total from Section 1				_____

SECTION 2. EVALUATION CRITERIA SPECIFIC TO THE RFP				
A. _____ _____ _____	___	___	___ × ___ = ___	___ × ___ = ___
Comments:				
Total from Section 2				_____
Total from Sections 1 and 2				_____

Evaluator certification

The point values entered above reflect my best independent judgment of the merits of the identified offeror's proposal.

Signature _____

Date _____

Exhibit 6-1 Sample evaluation form: Weight method *(Continued)*.

Guidelines for using the form

The panel chairperson, assisted by one or more panel members, is usually assigned the task of determining the criteria to be used and establishing their relative weights. The information then is reviewed by the purchasing or legal department to be sure that the form contains all the principal criteria in the original solicitation and that applicable regulations are followed.

None of the evaluation criteria in Exhibit 6-1 is intended to apply to all service contracts. Criteria should be added or eliminated as necessary to adapt the form to a given solicitation. For example, if the solicitation does not request an estimate of the time that principals of the firm will spend on the project, Criterion F in the sample form should not be included.

The principle of fair and open competition in public procurement prohibits the use of any evaluation criteria other than those listed in the solicitation. These criteria must be applied to the responses without change, deletion, or expansion. A protest from an offeror whose proposal was rejected by an evaluation panel that used criteria not identified in the published solicitation has an excellent chance of success.

Assigning points

Points are awarded according to the quality of the response with respect to each criterion. On a 0- to 5-point scale, for example, 0 would represent an unacceptable response; 1, a poor response; 2, satisfactory; 3, good; 4, very good; and 5, excellent. (The 0- to 5-point scale is used as an example because evaluators find it easy to apply, but the panel chairperson can use other numerical values to represent the range of quality in the responses.)

Weighting scores

Criteria that have more importance (weight) than others are assigned a multiplier or weight factor. Weights are fixed values that indicate the relative importance of the criterion, not the quality of the response. The weight factor 5 might represent important; 10, moderately important; and 15, very important. Assign only three weights and do not permit evaluators to adjust them by using other multipliers, such as 7 or 12. Once a weight for an evaluation criterion is established by the chairperson, evaluators cannot change it.

Completing the form

The form has five columns (lettered A through E for purposes of this discussion). When the evaluator receives the form, Columns A, B, and C are completely filled out: Column A identifies the criterion being scored; Column B gives the maximum number of points that can be assigned (on the 0- to 5-point scale shown previously, the maximum was 5); and Column C shows the weight (5, 10, or 15, for example) assigned to each criterion. Columns D and E are partially filled out; so that the evaluator can easily determine the weighted score, these columns show the weight factor assigned to the criterion.

In the first step in the independent review each panel member chooses the best response to each criterion from the responses received. That response is awarded the maximum point value, and the other responses are assigned fewer points according to how they compare with the best response. (In other words, the best response is determined in relation to the other responses rather than in relation to an ideal.) To determine the score for each criterion, the evaluator multiplies the number of points assigned (from 0 to 5, for example) by the weight factor printed in Column C.

(continued on page 128)

Exhibit 6-1   Sample evaluation form: Weight method *(Continued)*.

In order to deal with responses that fail to address certain criteria or that take exception to them, the chairperson may permit evaluators to score below the assigned point range and award zero or negative scores. For example, if an offeror states explicitly that a particular requirement will not be met, a negative score equal to the highest possible number of points (say, -5) is assigned to that criterion and multiplied by the appropriate weight. If an offeror simply fails to address a requirement, a point value of zero is entered on the form. The use of negative or zero scores is covered during panel training.

As part of the independent review, panel members make brief comments under each criterion explaining the reasoning behind their scores. These notes may be used for reference during the full panel discussions if another panel member questions the points assigned. When the review is complete, the scores for each proposal are totaled.

When the full panel meets to review the proposals, some evaluators may wish to change their scores because of information revealed at the panel meeting. For example, if an offeror included information in an attachment instead of in the main section of the proposal, panel members who overlooked the attachment and awarded lower scores because of missing information would need to adjust their scores after evaluating the information. Evaluators enter any adjusted point values in Column E (Review with panel) and calculate the scores as they did for Column D. Scores that are unchanged are simply transferred to Column E. After panel discussions are complete, the scores in Column E are totaled.

The scores entered in Column D must be independently arrived at and not represent a consensus of the panel. The only exception occurs when points are assigned as a result of a professional review (for example, the finance or auditing department reports on the financial stability of each offeror and assigns a score to be entered on all panel members' forms).

Applying the criteria
Section 1: General evaluation criteria

A. Responsiveness to the RFP. Does the proposal address the intent of the RFP or does it deal primarily with generalities? Is it a counteroffer to what the RFP called for and therefore nonresponsive? Does the offeror explain the reason for any variations in content from the information requested in the RFP?

B. Understanding of the project and the local government's objectives. Is the proposal narrative a virtual copy of the RFP or does it indicate that some independent thought was given to its preparation? Does the offer show understanding of the local government's view of the service?

C. Experience and history of firm. This criterion examines corporate rather than individual experience. If the firm limits its work to specialized areas, does the principal area of specialization match the scope of work of the RFP or is the work to be subcontracted? Do the references indicate that the firm can handle the size and scope of the project?

D. Methodology and management approach. How does the offeror propose to perform the tasks? Is the methodology proposed for task management well defined or vague? How well organized is the offeror's effort?

E. Qualifications and experience of principals and staff. Do the qualifications of the principals, project manager, and project staff indicate that the firm can complete the tasks in a professional and satisfactory manner? Are the staff members profiled in the proposal those who will actually undertake the project? If not, their qualifications—no matter how impressive—must be disregarded. Is the experience recent enough to incorporate current changes in service technology?

Exhibit 6-1   Sample evaluation form: Weight method *(Continued)*.

F. Time spent by principals. A company's reputation often rests on the accomplishments of one or more of its principals. The involvement of a firm's principals in smaller contracts is generally limited to approving the proposal, possibly reviewing progress reports, and signing the final report. Does the proposal indicate that the principals of the firm intend to be heavily involved in the performance of the contract or involved only in an administrative or oversight capacity? How much of management's personal time is committed to delivering the service? Pay special attention to the qualifications of staff–particularly the project manager–if the response indicates a low level of involvement by principals. Staff qualifications are much more important to the success of the contract than the qualifications of a principal who has little involvement in day-to-day contract activities.

G. Availability and quality of personnel, facilities, and equipment. Will adequate staff and resources be available for the project? Will most of the work be done by the offeror's employees or is much of the work to be done by subcontractors? Have the subcontractors' qualifications been submitted and are they acceptable?

H. Proximity of base of operations and availability during project. If proximity to the delivery site is important and can be justified, the RFP should require submission of a management plan indicating how the offeror would provide on-site assistance and describing the level of contact with the local government during the course of service delivery. Will the offeror enter into a joint venture with a local firm? Will there be resident local personnel? (This criterion can be included in the evaluation form only if the RFP specifically requests a management plan for nonlocal offerors.)

I. Financial stability. On the basis of financial statements or other documents, the finance or auditing department evaluates the financial stability of each offeror and provides the panel with a score to enter for that criterion. If the financial stability of an offeror is totally unacceptable, the offer should not be given further consideration.

J. Price. Price should not be a major criterion at this stage of the evaluation process. By the time negotiations with the most qualified offeror are complete, the price initially proposed may be much lower–or much higher–than the original estimate. It should be excluded from the evaluation form or assigned a low point value and weight. An offeror cannot predict accurately the cost of a project from an RFP, which typically contains only general descriptions of the work to be performed. In addition, at this stage an offeror may either inflate price estimates to cover all contingencies or purposely understate the cost to ensure placement as a finalist.

Section 2: Evaluation criteria specific to the RFP

Included in Section 2 are criteria such as special experience or qualifications of personnel to be assigned to the contract, experience in dealing with governing bodies or in-house professionals, and the availability of highly advanced technology for service delivery.

Exhibit 6-2   Sample evaluation form: Maximum point method.

RFP NUMBER _____

TITLE _____

OFFEROR _____

SECTION 1. GENERAL EVALUATION CRITERIA

Criterion	Maximum points	Independent review points	Review with panel points
A. Methodology, management approach, technique	____	____	____
Comments:			

_____

Note: Additional criteria are the same as those in Exhibit 6-1.

Guidelines for using the form

The form used for the maximum point method is the same as that used for the weight method except that each criterion is assigned a *different* maximum point value: the more important the criterion, the higher the maximum point value (this compensates for the absence of a weight factor). The evaluator scores each response, using the maximum score as the standard for excellence and a zero for unacceptable responses. Intermediate scores are left to the judgment of the individual evaluators. Negative scores may be used in the same manner as in the weight method or as directed by the panel chairperson. The section entitled "Applying the Criteria" that accompanies Exhibit 6-1 applies to Exhibit 6-2 as well.

Exhibit 6-3   Sample letter of invitation to an oral presentation.

Dear _____:

[Firm name] has been selected as a finalist for [identify RFP]. The final selection will be based on the recommendations of an evaluation panel that will review your written response to this invitation and hear your oral presentation. [Number] copies of the written response are due in [office location] on [date at least three days before oral presentation]. The oral presentation and written response shall address the material covered in the enclosure under "Response Requirements."

All oral presentations will be made on [date]. You firm's presentation is scheduled to begin at [time] and to end at [time] on that date. [Number] minutes of this period shall be set aside for your oral presentation and up to [number] minutes for questions from the panel. A principal of the firm and the project manager proposed for assignment to the project must be part of the presentation team. The oral presentation will be held at [location]. The purpose of the oral presentation is to obtain a better understanding of your qualifications and to assess the project team proposed to be assigned to the contract.

If you have any questions concerning the process or the submission requirements, please contact [name and telephone number].

Cordially,

Exhibit 6-4   Sample reference check form.

RFP NUMBER _____

TITLE _____

OFFEROR _____

Reference _____   Person spoken to _____

1. Describe the scope of work of the contract awarded by your firm to this contractor.

2. Was the project completed on time and within budget?

3. What problems were encountered (claims filed, etc.)?

4. How would you rate the contractor on a scale of *low* (1) to *high* (10) for the following?
   Professionalism _____   Final product _____
   Qualifications _____   Cooperation _____
   Budget control _____   Reliability _____

5. Would you contract with this contractor again?
   Yes _____   No _____   Maybe _____

6. Comments

Reference checked by _____   Date _____

Using the sample reference check form
Determine the exact nature of the work performed for the reference. Was the contractor's description of the scope of work performed for the reference accurate? Did the contractor meet all the contract requirements on time and within budget? Ask about any claims or contract disputes during the contract term and other problems the reference may have had with the contractor.

Particularly over the telephone, many references hesitate to say that the contractor was unreliable, that the contractor's employees were untrained, or that the work was unacceptable. But references are usually willing to assign a numerical value to professionalism, qualifications, and so forth. Ask for an explanation of a "maybe" or a "no" response to the question of whether the reference would contract with the contractor again, and jot down any other comments or observations made by the reference.

Exhibit 6-5 Sample evaluation form for oral presentation.[a]

RFP NUMBER _____

TITLE _____

OFFEROR _____

Use the values indicated as the maximum points allowed for each section.

Criterion	Score
Personnel	
1. Were key management and the project team identified?	____
2. Did the presentation clearly describe the roles and responsibilities of management and the project team?	____
3. Will the project manager communicate well with elected officials, staff, and public?	____
4. Do you have confidence in the project manager?	____
5. Do you have confidence in the individual team members?	____
6. Do you have confidence in the group as a whole?	____
7. Are they a team? Will they act as a team?	____
Maximum point value	____
Score	____
Past work	
1. What is your overall impression?	____
Maximum point value	____
Score	____
Management	
1. Has the firm assigned roles and responsibilities to specific individuals?	____
2. Do the lines of responsibility seem reasonable and logical?	____
3. Is team leadership apparent?	____
4. Does team appear to be able to manage suggestions from the public or other groups?	____
Maximum point value	____
Score	____

Exhibit 6-5   Sample evaluation form for oral presentation *(Continued)*.

Criterion	Score
Understanding	
1. Does team understand the nature of the service?	____
2. Has the team specifically identified the issues to be dealt with in this project?	____
3. Has the team gained your confidence?	____
Maximum point value	____
Score	____
Total score	____

Evaluator certification

The scores indicated above reflect my best independent judgment of the offeror's presentation.

Signature _____ Date _____

Using the sample evaluation form for oral presentations

The criteria for evaluation are personnel, the offeror's project team; past work, the offeror's experience with other clients; management, how the tasks will be performed; and understanding, the ability to work with the local government team. The score awarded for each criterion is an overall evaluation based on all information received to date: the original proposal, the written submission, and the oral presentation.

Before the presentation the panel members assign a maximum point value to each criterion (25, 50, 75, or 100 points) according to its importance. After an offeror's presentation, each panel member assigns a score to the criterion between zero and its maximum point value. All of the entries under each criterion are taken into consideration for the total score.

At the conclusion of the oral presentations, the scores are totaled. The total of all scores of the panel ranks the finalists in order of panel preference. (The forms shown in Exhibits 6-1 and 6-2 can also be adapted for use in evaluating oral presentations.)

[a] This sample evaluation form for oral presentations is based on a form developed by King County, Washington, for its consultant selection procedures as cited in *Contracting Municipal Services,* ed. John Tepper Marlin (New York: John Wiley & Sons, 1984), 136-137.

Exhibit 6-6   Short form evaluation method.

Short form evaluation, probably the evaluation system used most often under competitive negotiation or multistep bidding procedures, establishes four to six general evaluation criteria, assigns maximum point values to each, and allows evaluators to assign scores at or under the established maximums. Short form evaluation is used when the time and effort required for the more complex scoring methods are not warranted. However, the simplicity of the method occasionally generates protests from offerors claiming that not enough criteria were used to score the responses fairly.

In the following example of short form evaluation, the values in the "Maximum score" column indicate the maximum number of points that can be assigned to each criterion. (The values shown are only examples that should be increased or decreased to reflect the contract being bid and the weight assigned to each criterion. The maximum scores for Criteria 3, 4, and 5 can vary considerably according to the contract.) Although the scores in the example total 100, there is no reason to limit the total to any particular number. Five criteria are shown in the sample, but others can be added—for example, the completeness of a respondent's quality control plan or the quality of the equipment to be used. If more than six or seven criteria are identified, however, the more detailed scoring systems should be used.

Short form evaluation method

Criterion	Maximum score	Score
Qualifications of firm	20	_____
Qualifications of staff	15	_____
Experience in this area	25	_____
Service delivery method	10	_____
Cost	30	_____
Total score		_____

7

Preparing the Contract

The final step in the award process is the preparation of the contract, the only document that governs performance and price during the contract term. No oral or written communication between the contractor and the local government can affect performance or price unless it is incorporated into the contract. Because the contractor is required to perform only those duties set forth in the contract document, the document should never be released to a contractor for signature or comment until it has been reviewed for completeness by all members of the contract administration team and approved by the legal department. Occasionally in a contract let under negotiation, the contractor may take exception to a clause or task described in the final contract document, requiring renegotiation of the contested areas. If changes are made, the internal review and approval process must be repeated.

Attention to detail is more important during the preparation of the contract document than during any other part of the contracting process. A misplaced word or punctuation mark may drastically change the meaning of an entire paragraph. Errors discovered after a contract is signed are sometimes impossible to correct without renegotiation and added expense to the local government. The underlying lesson of this chapter is that the contract manager or the department issuing the contract must not rely solely on their understanding of the contract and its terms. They must work closely with their legal department to be certain that the language is correct, the terms and conditions of performance are clearly described, and the document is in legal form.

This chapter describes the principal types of contracts: the purchase order contract, the short form contract, the standard contract provided by the contractor or by a third party, and the formal contract.

The formal contract is the type preferred by most local government legal departments, and it is also the most complex to prepare. This chapter covers the development of a formal contract in detail, including the preparation of two exhibits: the scope of work, which is the foundation of the contract, and the unit price exhibit, the pricing reference that sets forth the hourly labor rates and allowable charges for reimbursable expenses during the contract term. Finally, the chapter offers guidelines on insurance and contract bonds. The contract should not be signed until it has been determined that these documents conform to contract requirements.

Purchase order contract

The simplest contract format is the purchase order, which is used primarily for uncomplicated, moderate cost, competitive sealed bidding contracts. A purchase order contract includes an encumbrance-of-funds statement, the local government's acceptance of the contractor's bid, information such as the contract term and the name of the local government contact person, and the contract amount, including unit prices if applicable. Documents incorporated into the purchase order include the scope of work, the general terms and conditions of the bid document, the bid form, and any sections of the bid document or the contractor's bid response that have a direct bearing on performance or price. Exhibit 7-1 is a sample format for a purchase order contract.

Short form contract

The short form contract is normally reserved for awards made under an invitation for bids (IFB) or request for proposals (RFP) for personal services. Although the short form contract is similar to the purchase order contract, it is somewhat more detailed and, unlike the purchase order contract, requires the signatures of both parties. The short form contract specifies the number assigned to the original solicitation, the date of execution, the parties to the contract, the contract term, the contract amount, and the payment terms. The contract documents include the original bid document (identify any amendments) and the contractor's bid response. Exhibit 7-2 is a representative short form contract.

Contractor's standard contract form

Architects, engineers, and other professionals often request that standard contracts or clauses developed by their professional associations or corporate contracts prepared by their legal departments be used.[1] Whenever possible, avoid preprinted or standard contracts, which may contain clauses favoring the architect, engineer, or corporation. Preprinted contracts may contain clauses governing mandatory arbitration, indemnification of the contractor by the local government, the contractor's ownership of materials produced and delivered to the local government, and the granting of broad powers of decision to the contractor.[2]

Sometimes the local government cannot avoid using a standard contract form submitted by the contractor. For example, the contractor may insist on using the form as a condition of acceptance of the award or local government staff may not have enough time to prepare its own contract document. If a preprinted contract is used, review it carefully with the legal department, identify unacceptable language, and alter it by amendment. The accompanying sidebar lists provisions in contracts provided by the contractor that may not be in the interest of the local government.

The formal contract

Local government legal departments usually prefer a formal contract. All terms and conditions are physically incorporated into the contract document, which then constitutes the complete agreement between the parties. The conditions of performance are included in a scope-of-work exhibit and other exhibits, such as unit prices and special conditions, are added as necessary. The content of a formal contract document is specific to the service. Material not directly related to performance, such as the instructions to bidders and award evaluation sections of the bid

Provisions to watch for in standard contracts provided by contractors

Applicable law　Enforcement and interpretation are to be according to the laws and the courts of another state.

Limitation of liability　The contractor's liability for damages is lower than required by the local government. Some provisions may prohibit consequential damages of any kind, however caused; others may limit the contractor's liability to an amount equivalent to the value of the contract.

Termination　Renewal or termination clauses may conflict with the bid document. Clauses allowing the contractor to terminate at its convenience on short (30- or 45-day) notice are not uncommon.

Arbitration　An arbitration clause may require contract disputes to be submitted for resolution by a professional arbitrator, a procedure that could deny the governing body its right to settle contract disputes without the intervention of a third party.

Indemnification　The local government may be required to indemnify the contractor for acts or omissions of the local government, pay attorney's fees or costs of collection, reimburse expenses, or pay damages to the contractor for termination of the contract by the local government, even if the termination was the result of an action of the contractor.

Unusual rights of the contractor

The contract may permit the contractor unusual discretion in making unilateral changes to the work rather than making recommendations for decision by the local government contract manager.

Limiting services　The contract may limit contract services to a level below that agreed to during negotiations.

Nonsubstitution　A nonappropriation clause may contain a nonsubstitution requirement that prohibits the local government from obtaining an equivalent or better product or service for several years after cancellation by the local government for nonappropriation. The local government should not agree to more than a six-month nonsubstitution clause, if any.

Insurance　The contract may require the local government to purchase builder's risk or contractor's liability coverage or other insurance at its own expense instead of having the contractor provide it and may limit the contractor's liability for damage directly caused by the contractor.

Payments　The contract may require advance or down payments. Public funds should not be used to pay for a service that has not yet been received.

document, or resumes, brochures, organizational background statements, preliminary cost proposals, and promotional material included in the contractor's original proposal should not be part of the contract document.

Exhibit 7-3 is an example of a formal contract illustrating the various contract elements that are typically included, although each local government legal department has its own preferred language and order. First, the contract must be identified with the name of the local government and the contract title, number, and date to distinguish it from any other contract that may be in effect. A contract document can be dated in several ways. A blank date block can be inserted on the first page or in the signature block section and filled in when the document is signed by the local government representative after the contractor has signed and the required documents have been received and approved (e.g., performance and payment bonds, insurance certificates, etc.). The date of execution (i.e., the date when the local government representative signs the contract) is identified as the contract date. The contract date should not be the date the contract document was prepared by the local government. Because contract events are often based on the contract date, it is more prudent to use the date of execution as the official contract date, after all bonds, insurance, licenses, and other required submissions have been received and approved.

Next, the various exhibits and attachments that constitute the contract documents are listed. A priority statement specifying which documents prevail over which is necessary to prevent future contract disputes in the event of any inadvertent discrepancies among them.

Insert the time for completion of the contract (contract term), identifying specific beginning and ending dates. Specify the total amount of the contract (contract amount) as a firm fixed price or, in the case of cost reimbursement, the maximum amount to be paid under the contract for services delivered during the contract term. Often included in the contract amount are general references to payment provisions or conditions governing the frequency of payment (e.g., monthly, upon completion of certain tasks, or based on an estimated percentage of completion of the work). The scope of work or special provisions exhibit can also include payment clauses that refine or expand these general statements (e.g., reports that must accompany an invoice, the format of the invoice to be used, specific invoice dates).

Contracts for consulting or professional services awarded on a cost reimbursement basis often include a provision that the local government will reimburse the contractor for expenses incurred in the performance of the contract. Such expenses might include printing, travel, postage, telephone, photocopying, and so forth. The types of allowed reimbursable expenses and the maximum expenditure approved for each are often listed in a separate exhibit in the contract. The contract should specify that the contractor may not incur reimbursable expenses without the prior approval of the contract manager. As an alternative, the contract can specify a dollar limit for reimbursable expenses incurred by the contractor.

Last, the general terms and conditions of the bid document are physically incorporated into the contract document. The special terms and conditions section of the original bid document are often incorporated into the scope of work or they may be kept together as a separate exhibit within the contract. Include spaces for the signatures of the local government representative, the contractor, and witnesses and for the date signed.

Preparing the scope-of-work exhibit

The scope-of-work exhibit details how the service will be performed and the duties and responsibilities of the contractor. The scope of work from a competitive sealed bid is the simplest element to convert from its form in the bid document to the form required for the contract. It is transferred intact from the original bid document because negotiation is not permitted. Only clarification of the original scope of work of a competitive sealed bid is allowed; substantive changes that affect the contract price or quality of the service delivered are not. Few changes are required other than deleting references to bidder qualifications or to activities that preceded the award of the contract and changing the word "bidder" to "contractor."

The scope of work for a solicitation let under competitive negotiation or multistep bidding requires a bit more effort. In these processes, the original scope of work and the terms and conditions of the solicitation are refined and expanded during negotiations between the local government and the contractor. Drawing from all notes, memoranda, and e-mail communications, the contract administration team prepares the negotiated scope of work that will be inserted into the contract. The contract administration team might consider requesting that the contractor provide the original proposal on disk or electronically to use as a starting document from which to prepare the negotiated scope of work. This will save time and prevent the contract administration team from having to start from scratch.

The local government is responsible for preparing the contract, including all exhibits and attachments. If the contractor is responsible for preparing any part of the contract documents, the documents must be compared with the prior versions word for word from beginning to end to ensure that the contractor has not made any unauthorized changes.

Another important benefit of having the document within the local government's word-processing system is its availability for reuse in future contracts. For example, the scope of work negotiated with the contractor probably is more complete than the one contained in the original solicitation, especially if it is for a new service. Once it is in the local government system, it can be retrieved, modified as needed, and used again as the scope of work for the next solicitation for that service, saving considerable time for the next scope-of-work team and clerical staff.

A contractor might be requested to prepare the first draft of a negotiated scope of work when the changes to the original scope of work in the solicitation are not extensive. However, if the scope of work has already been put into written form by the local government during negotiations or the changes to the original scope of work are extensive, the local government should prepare the first draft.

If the local government prepares the negotiated scope of work for the final contract document, it must be as detailed as possible. The procedure for preparing the scope-of-work exhibit for a contract is the same as that used to prepare the scope of work for a competitive sealed bid: identify and describe each phase, stage, or task separately; specify the date for the completion of each; identify how and when contract deliverables will be presented to the contract manager; and summarize the review and evaluation procedures the local government will use.

Exhibit 7-4 shows an excerpt from a scope-of-work exhibit for an architectural/ engineering (A/E) contract. Exhibit 7-5 is the scope-of-work exhibit for a security services contract.

Preparing the unit price exhibit

Many contracts have several types of prices. The base contract price can be the cost for the total contract term or the first year of the contract term if subsequent years' prices are developed by use of a formula such as that for the application of the Consumer Price Index. The base contract price can be further described as the monthly contract cost or the cost per unit of service delivered during the contract term (e.g., when the contract is based on one or two hourly labor rates, cost for custodial services for each building in a multiple building contract, or cost for refuse collection at the curb or from backyards of residences). When the exact requirements of the local government cannot be determined (e.g., in requirements contracts for tree removals, transportation, social services, etc.), the base contract price may be an estimate or a not-to-exceed price.

The base contract price usually is identified in the main section of the contract document under the heading "Contract Amount" (see Exhibit 7-3). In addition to the base contract price, a unit price exhibit may be included in the contract when the contractor uses many individual prices in invoices for services (e.g., hourly labor rates for various classes of workers, equipment rental charges, percentage discounts that apply to materials used); when the local government obtains emergency noncontract services from the contractor (e.g., hourly labor rates for personnel or hourly rental rates for equipment); or, in a lump-sum contract, when the contractor lists hourly labor rates for all personnel to be used to calculate the cost of any future amendments to the scope of work. A separate unit price exhibit may also be prepared to list all approved reimbursable expenses for a contract that includes a cost reimbursement provision. Exhibits 7-6 and 7-7 are suggested formats for a unit price exhibit for a professional services or consulting contract and for a street repair contract.

Approving insurance and contract bonds

An important detail of the contracting process is the review and approval of any insurance certificates, performance bonds, or payment bonds that the contractor is required to provide. The contract should not be signed until these documents have been reviewed by the risk manager or the legal department to ensure that they conform to contract requirements.

Insurance certificates

It is common practice for contractors to submit their standard business insurance coverage for approval, even though that coverage may not meet the contract requirements. Because adequate protection against loss caused by a contractor is a critical concern in service contracting, insurance certificates must be carefully reviewed to determine whether required coverage is provided.

Chapter 5 includes an insurance checklist to be completed by the bidder and the bidder's insurance agent and submitted as part of the bid response or offer (see Exhibit 5-9). When the bidder and the bidder's agent sign the form, they certify that the bidder can obtain the required coverage. The checklist also gives the insurance agent an opportunity to advise the bidder if any additional coverage has to be purchased to meet the contract requirements. The cost of the premium for the added coverage is then factored into the contractor's bid price.

In an ideal situation, every contractor awarded a contract would submit an acceptable insurance certificate. In reality, even with the insurance checklist, the first certificate of insurance submitted is seldom acceptable and must be returned for correction. The next nine sections discuss areas where problems may arise.

Name of the insured If the certificate was issued for the parent organization of the contracting firm, it may not include the contractor's (the subsidiary) name. Do not accept the certificate unless the name of the bidding contractor is on the certificate.

Insurance company rating If the local government requires the insurance carrier providing coverage to have a minimum Best's rating,[3] the risk manager should determine whether the company's rating meets the stated minimum.

Policy effective dates All certificates must show the expiration date of each policy carried by the contractor. If any of the policies are scheduled to expire during the contract term, contact the contractor at least thirty days before the expiration date and obtain a current certificate that shows that coverage is extended at least to the end of the contract term or require that the effective dates of the initial policy cover the full contract term—if possible, without an increase in premiums.

General liability endorsements   The insurance package that contractors usually purchase for their businesses may not include all the endorsements (special provisions that expand or modify the coverage of an insurance policy) or specific types of liability coverage required. Be sure that the insurance certificate identifies the endorsements required in the checklist (e.g., hold harmless endorsement, Motor Carrier Act endorsement) and each type of liability coverage required as part of the comprehensive general liability insurance (e.g., independent contractors, products, completed operations, contractual, personal injury). If there are any doubts about the coverage provided, request a copy of the contractor's policy to find out whether there are any exclusions that could affect the coverage required for the contract. Do not wait until an accident or loss occurs to find out that the contractor does not have the specified insurance.

Liability limits   Under competitive sealed bidding, the price of required insurance should be factored into each contractor's original bid price and the amount of coverage must meet or exceed contract requirements. If, after bid opening, the lowest responsive and responsible bidder refuses to provide the required coverage or claims to be unable to do so, the local government has two choices: reject the bid and award the contract to the next lowest responsive and responsible bidder who can provide the required coverage or reconsider the amount of coverage required and re-bid the contract with reduced insurance requirements. Because insurance is always a cost factor in a bid, never waive an insurance requirement after the opening of a competitive sealed bid. The local government always should address the insurance requirements of a contract at the pre-bid conference. If prospective bidders appear unanimous in their inability to obtain a required coverage, the coverage could be reduced by bid amendment before bid opening.

When evaluating requests for exceptions from insurance requirements under competitive sealed bidding and competitive negotiation, carefully examine why the request was made. It is possible that the bidder or offeror is considered a high risk by insurance carriers because of a poor claim history.

The local government risk manager can help obtain this information. If the bidder or offeror has a poor claim history, it is prudent to retain the original coverage requirements, effectively excluding the bidder or offeror from participating in the solicitation.

Additional insured   The insurance certificate must clearly identify the local government as at least an additional insured. The statement "The [local government] is an additional insured" typed on the insurance certificate by the issuing insurance broker indicates that the contractor's insurance carrier will defend the local government along with the contractor in the event a claim is filed. The cost to a contractor for an additional insured endorsement is, at most, slight and may be provided at no cost by the carrier.

Some local government risk managers require the local government to be a named insured, which means that the contractor's insurance policy designates the local government as an insured party along with the contractor. The local government is then a client of the carrier. Making the local government a named insured often costs the contractor more than obtaining an additional insured endorsement. Because bidders include insurance premiums in the contract price, making the local government a named insured may increase the contract cost. The decision to make the local government an additional or named insured should be made by the local government risk manager or legal department.

Identification of contract   The contract number and title must appear on the insurance certificate. The title of the contract on the certificate alerts the insurance agent to the nature of the work the insurance will cover. The agent can then check the contractor's coverage to be sure that the specific service being insured is not excluded from the contractor's policies. A local government should not permit a contractor's insurance agent to issue a certificate without knowing the nature of the contract and the risks that may affect the contractor.

Certificate holder   The complete legal name of the local government and the name and address of the person or office responsible for approving the contractor's coverage must be included on the certificate of insurance as the certificate holder. The responsible person or office could be the purchasing department, the risk manager for the local government, the contract manager, or the contract administrator. Cancellation notices are mailed to the person named at the address given.

Cancellation notice   Most insurance agents use a standard insurance certificate form (ACORD form) to certify to a third party—the local government—that the contractor has the insurance coverage required by the contract.[4] This preprinted form also contains a clause that releases the insurance agent from responsibility for notifying the certificate holder of a cancellation of the listed policies, though insurance companies always notify their insured party—the contractor—and the contractor's insurance agent of cancellations. Insurance agents favor the clause because it frees them from having to notify the local government of cancellation of the contractor's coverage, but neither insurance agents nor insurance companies are likely to object to a modification requiring the agent to notify the local government. Request a written explanation from the agent if any objection is raised to modifying the clause. The examples that follow show the standard ACORD clause and the recommended version.

Standard ACORD clause:

> Should any of the above described policies be canceled before the expiration date thereof, the issuing company will endeavor to mail [X] days' written notice to the certificate holder named to the left, but failure to mail such notice shall impose no obligation or liability of any kind upon the company, its agents, or representatives.

Recommended version of the ACORD clause:

> Should any of the above described policies be canceled before the expiration date thereof, the issuing company will mail [X] days' written notice to the certificate holder named to the left.

Performance and payment bonds

Like insurance certificates, performance and payment bonds must be reviewed carefully to ensure that they are executed properly, that they are in a legal form that includes the required power of attorney, and that the bonding company is authorized to conduct business in the state where the work is performed.

Performance, payment, or bid bonds may be signed by local representatives of the bonding company or by insurance brokers or agents who have been assigned this authority by power of attorney, a legal instrument authorizing one party to act on behalf of another. Power of attorney for the person signing the bond must accompany every bond submitted to the local government. Exhibit 7-8 is a sample performance bond.

Combination bonds Some contractors submit a combination performance and payment bond, which may have abbreviated language and limited information about the procedures to follow in the event of default and about the extent of the bonding company's liability. Always require separate performance and payment bonds and have the legal department review the language of each. Some local governments create their own bond forms, which are included as exhibits in the contract for the contractor to complete.

Incomplete forms All blank spaces on the bond forms must be filled in. Contractors often submit bonds with blank spaces where the bonding company requires contract identification, contract starting date, or other information. Return all incomplete bonds to the contractor for completion. A bonding company agent that has been called about an incomplete form will often ask the local government to fill in the blanks. Do not complete the entries in house to speed up the process. When such changes are made without written authorization of the bonding company, they may become an issue if the bond is used in a default proceeding.

Endnotes

1 Examples of standard contracts of professional associations include design or construction contract forms prepared by the American Institute of Architects or the Engineers Joint Contract Documents Committee.

2 The section on contractors' contract forms is drawn extensively from the General Services Administration, *Agency Procurement and Surplus Property Manual* (Richmond, Va.: Department of General Services, Division of Purchases and Supply, 1998).

3 A. M. Best Company is a publisher of guides that rate the financial and management strength of insurance carriers. The contact information for its world headquarters is Ambest Road, Oldwick, N.J. 08858; (908) 439-2200; www.ambest.com.

4 ACORD Corporation, Certificate of Insurance, ACORD Form 25-S, 1988, available at www. acord.org. This form is the one most used by independent insurance agents for reporting coverages carried by a contractor. Other insurance certificate forms, which generally are issued by insurance companies through their own agents, have similar language.

Exhibit 7-1 Sample purchase order contract.

This purchase order encumbers funds in the amount of $40,200 for a contract awarded to Green and Green Landscaping, Inc., on June 15, 2010, in accordance with your response to Any City Bid No. 74-94, Landscape Maintenance Services for the South Point Mini Park. The following are incorporated into and made part of this purchase order by reference: the bid submitted by your firm including the unit price attachment; the scope of work, special conditions, and general terms and conditions of IFB No. 74-94; map of the park; maintenance schedule; staffing plan.

Contract term: From 7/1/10 through 6/30/11

Contract price: $40,200 payable in equal monthly installments Unit prices: As set forth in the bid unit price attachment Payment terms: 2% 30 days after receipt of correct invoice

City contact person: Jim Harris, Contract Manager (777) 555-3434

Exhibit 7-2 Sample short form contract.

Any City, U.S.A.
CONTRACT NUMBER 77-94

This Contract is entered into this 15th day of June, 2010, by Pete's Pet Posse, Inc., hereinafter called "the Contractor" and Any City, hereinafter called "the City."

The Contractor and the City, in consideration of the mutual covenants, promises, and agreements herein contained, agree as follows:

Scope of work: The Contractor shall provide to the City the services set forth in the Contract Documents consisting of providing animal control services for the City for a two-year period from July 1, 2010, through June 30, 2012 (Contract Term).

Contract documents: The Contract Documents consist of this signed Contract, Exhibit A (Invitation to Bid No. 77-94, Animal control service) and Exhibit B (the bid of the Contractor), all of which are incorporated herein by reference.

Compensation and method of payment: For satisfactorily providing all services described and required in the Contract Documents, the Contractor shall receive 24 equal payments of $8,600 for every month of the Contract Term from the City, payable monthly in arrears for a total contract amount of $206,400.

In witness whereof the parties have caused this Contract to be duly executed, intending to be bound thereby.

Any City	*Pete's Pet Posse, Inc.*
Authorized signature: _____	Authorized signature: _____
Title: _____	Title: _____
Date: _____	Date: _____
Witness: _____	Witness: _____

Exhibit 7-3   Sample formal contract.

Any County, Virginia
Contract No. 308-91: Transportation Services for Senior Citizens

This Contract is made on the date of execution by Any County, Virginia, 333 N. Main Street, Any City, Virginia (County) between Green Side Cab Company, Inc., 100 Main Street, Any City, Virginia (Contractor) and the County.

The County and the Contractor, for the consideration specified, agree as follows: The Contractor shall perform the services described in the Contract Documents consisting of providing transportation services for senior citizens to three senior centers and one adult day care center.

Contract Documents

The Contract Documents consist of this Contract and Exhibit A (Scope of Work). Where the terms of this Contract and Exhibit A are at variance, the provisions of this Contract shall prevail.

Contract Term

Work under this Contract will commence on November 1, 2010, and will be completed no later than October 31, 2013 (Contract Term), subject to any modifications provided for in the Contract Documents. No work shall be deemed complete until it is accepted by the County's Contract Manager (Project Officer).

Contract Amount

The County will pay the Contractor an amount not to exceed $224,000 for each year of the Contract Term for transportation services actually provided to senior citizens subject to the terms and conditions in the Contract Documents. The rates charged shall be the rates allowable under County ordinances less a 10 percent discount. This is a requirements contract.

Payment

Payment will be made by the County to the Contractor within thirty days after receipt by the County Project Officer of a biweekly invoice for transportation services provided that are allocable to the Contract and that have been performed to the satisfaction of the Project Officer.

Reimbursable Expenses

No reimbursable expenses will be incurred without the prior written approval of the County and the issuance of a purchase order detailing the specific expenses expected to be incurred by the Contractor and their estimated amount.

General Terms and Conditions

Antitrust	Immigration Reform and Control Act of 1986
Applicable law	Indemnification
Assignment	Independent Contractor
Change in scope of work	Insurance Requirements
Contractor personnel	Nonappropriation
Employment discrimination	Right to Audit
Ethics in public contracting	Termination for Convenience
Failure to deliver	

Witness these signatures:

ANY COUNTY, VIRGINIA	GREEN SIDE CAB COMPANY
AUTHORIZED SIGNATURE _____	AUTHORIZED SIGNATURE _____
NAME _____	NAME _____
TITLE _____	TITLE _____
DATE _____	DATE _____

Exhibit 7-4   Sample scope-of-work exhibit for an A/E contract.

This figure is a scope-of-work exhibit for one task (Task 3) in an architectural project. A complete scope of work for an A/E design project has five or more principal tasks: predesign (establishing initial design parameters), design development (implementing the design decisions), construction document preparation (preparing the plans and specifications for the work), assistance during the bidding and award process (responding to contractor's technical questions, evaluating responses and bidders, etc.), and providing construction administration services (monitoring the construction contractor's adherence to the design drawings). In the full scope of work exhibit, the requirements for each task are formatted in the same manner: a single format for all tasks highlights the contractor's responsibilities, the time of completion of the task, the deliverables required, and the local government's role in reviewing performance. The format used in the excerpt can be adapted for use in many consulting or professional services contracts. In this example, the local government representative is called the contract manager. In many contracts, however, the term "project officer" is used to identify this individual.

Task 3. Construction document preparation

Completion date   Task 3 will be completed 90 calendar days after completion of Task 2.

Process   The Contractor shall prepare final technical specifications and construction drawings for the work and coordinate with the City's Contract Manager in their development.

Deliverables   Construction drawings and specifications shall be prepared and submitted for approval to the City Contract Manager at the following completion levels:

Benchmark	Completion date
50% completed	4/1/10
90% completed	6/1/10
100% completed	8/1/10

Five copies of the product at each completion stage shall be delivered to the Contract Manager.

The construction documents submitted at the 50%, 90%, and 100% stages will be accompanied by estimates of probable cost of the project divided into the following components of the project: structural, mechanical, electrical, interior finishing, landscaping. The estimate of probable cost submitted at the 50% stage will not be exceeded by the Contractor during the balance of the task. If the estimated cost at the 90% or 100% stage exceeds the estimated cost at the 50% stage, the Contractor agrees to redesign the project at its own expense to meet the 50% cost estimates.

At the 90% stage, the Contractor will submit a construction plan showing the phases of the construction work.

After the acceptance of the 100% completion stage of the construction plans, the Contractor will provide a complete set of reproducible copies of the drawings and a complete set of original technical specifications to the Contract Manager. The Contract Manager will provide the general conditions, insurance requirements, instructions to bidders, and the bid form sections for inclusion in the bid document for construction of the project.

Review   The Contract Manager will, in conference with the Contractor at least every two weeks during the progress of the task, review and approve project progress. The Contract Manager may conduct other reviews of the Contractor's work.

Exhibit 7-5   Sample scope-of-work exhibit for a security services contract.

Scope of work   The Contractor shall provide security services as defined herein for a two-year period. Services shall be provided at the XYZ Health Center, referred to as "the Facility."

Hours to be worked   The Contractor shall provide one guard to perform the services during the hours specified below. The Contract Manager may change the hours slightly from time to time during the contract term, but the hours worked will remain within the same general time frames.

Monday through Thursday:
Evening from 5:30 p.m. to 11:00 p.m.   Staff the security post located in the Facility lobby, greet and assist clients who come to the building, and maintain overall security by making at least three random walk-through inspections of the Facility during the working hours and immediately before closing the building. Lock and secure the building at 11:00 p.m. Control any disturbances that arise with minimal use of force, calling the police department for assistance if necessary.

Night from 11:00 p.m. to 7:00 a.m.   Conduct motorized surveillance patrols throughout the parking lots and perimeter of the Facility at least every hour. Investigate any suspicious activities and enlist the assistance of the police department if necessary.

Friday:
Evening from 5:30 p.m. to 9:00 p.m.   Same as evening duties above.
Night from 9:00 p.m. to 7:00 a.m.   Same as night duties above.

Saturday:
Day from 8:30 a.m. to 4:00 p.m.   Unlock the building and continue with duties performed in evening, as above.

Weekend from 4:00 p.m. Saturday to 7:00 a.m. Monday   Same as night duties above.

Uniform   The security person shall wear a low-profile security uniform consisting of slacks and a blazer with the Contractor's corporate logo visible on the blazer pocket. The security person shall not carry a firearm, a nightstick, mace, or any other offensive or defensive device.

Security system   The Facility has an ultrasonic alarm system. Listening devices are located in hallways and in some offices within the building. On weekdays, building personnel are responsible for opening the building and notifying the alarm service that the opening was made by an authorized person. On Saturdays, the security person shall be responsible for opening the building and notifying the alarm service. The security person shall also be responsible for closing and securing the building every evening after notifying the alarm service that the building is about to be closed. Entry by building personnel to the premises is prohibited during the time that the security guard is present unless a written exception is granted in advance by the Contract Manager and the Contractor notified of the exception.

Duties of the security person   The security person shall be responsible for making sure that all perimeter doors are locked and that the building is secured before leaving each night. This includes visual inspection of the building to ensure that all spaces are cleared of visitors and employees, all windows are closed, all lights are turned off, and all outside doors are locked.

The security person shall staff the post at the building lobby, give accurate information to callers on the telephone and to visitors, and greet and assist clients. The security person shall conduct random checks of the building at least three times during each shift. The security person shall accompany staff and clients to their vehicles in the parking lot upon their request.

Motorized patrols shall be conducted at least once every hour during the hours that the Facility is closed, including holidays. Police assistance shall be requested if any activities are observed that appear to jeopardize the security of the building.

Exhibit 7-6 Unit price exhibit for professional services or consulting contracts.

Hourly rates

The Contractor shall be paid for work done on the basis of the number of hours that the persons in the job categories shown below do work allocable to the Contract and accepted by the City.

Position	Hourly rate
Principal	$134.00
Project Manager	$104.00
Architect	$96.00
Clerical	$44.00

Reimbursable expenses

Reimbursable expenses are limited to the following:

Expense category	Unit price
Photocopying	$.15 per sheet
Air travel	At Contractor's cost, coach class
Lodging/Meals	At cost, not to exceed $130.00 per day
Traffic consultant	$22,320 maximum allowable cost

Expenses itemized above are reimbursable only if pre-approved by the City as reasonable and allocable to the Contract. No expenses for subcontractors or consultants shall be allowed without the City's prior approval of the work, the subcontractor or consultant to be engaged, and the terms of the engagement.

Exhibit 7-7 Selected unit prices for a street repair contract. Format can be adapted to other general services contracts.

Contract unit prices

Hourly rates

The following contract unit prices will apply to services ordered, delivered, and accepted during the contract term:

Item	Rate
Crew foreman	$52.00 per hour
Concrete worker	$37.00 per hour
Asphalt worker	$35.00 per hour
Laborer	$26.00 per hour
Asphalt in place, 9"	$90.00 per square yard
Asphalt in place, 5"	$74.00 per square yard
Curb/gutter in place	$24.00 per linear foot
Sidewalk in place, 4"	$30.00 per square yard
Asphalt roller rental	$90.00 per hour with operator

Overtime will be paid at one and a half times the straight time rate. Labor for night and weekend emergency service will be paid for at twice the straight time rate.

Exhibit 7-8   Sample performance bond.

The Big Bonding Company
Dallas, Texas
PERFORMANCE BOND

Know all men by these presents that Jones Custodial Services Corporation, Principal, and The Big Bonding Company, Surety, are held and firmly bound onto Any City, U.S.A., Obligee, in the amount of three hundred fifty-eight thousand dollars ($358,000) for the payment of which we bind ourselves, our legal representatives, successors and assigns, jointly and severally, firmly by these presents.

Whereas, Principal has entered into a Contract with Obligee, dated July 1, 2010, for providing custodial services at various sites in Any City, U.S.A., in accordance with the provisions of Any City Contract No. 148-94 for a period of one year effective 10/1/10 through 9/30/11, a copy of which Contract is by reference made a part hereof.

Now, therefore, if Principal shall faithfully perform such Contract and any and all duly authorized modifications of said Contract that may hereafter be made, notice of which modifications to Surety being waived, or shall indemnify and save harmless the Obligee from all cost and damage by reason of Principal's failure to so do, then this obligation shall be null and void; otherwise it shall remain in full force and effect.

Signed, sealed, and dated July 1, 2010.

Jones Custodial Services Corporation

By _____ (Seal)

Jacob Jones
Principal

The Big Bonding Company

By _____ (Seal)

Peter Bond
Attorney-in-fact[1]

[1] Power of Attorney attached.

8

Monitoring Contract Performance

To monitor a contract effectively, each member of the contract administration team must understand the duties associated with his or her position on the team and must understand a number of basic issues that are common to public and private service delivery: customer satisfaction, timeliness, productivity, and performance problems. The team must understand the importance of pre-performance conferences in laying the groundwork for efficient and effective performance and monitoring. Despite the care that has gone into the preparation of the contract documents, most contracts require amendments, and the team must understand when and how to issue them.

To monitor a contract effectively, the team must select appropriate measures of output or outcome, choose suitable monitoring methods, carefully document performance, and work cooperatively with the contractor.

Preparing for contract monitoring

This section delineates what the contract administration team needs to know and do before performance begins. It begins with the structure of the contract administration team and the responsibilities of the members; looks at several issues of basic importance in monitoring a contract; discusses the first step in contract administration, the pre-performance conference; and concludes with an overview of the contract amendment process.

The contract administration team

Chapter 2 described several organizational models for a service contracting program. Under the centralized model, a single contract manager is responsible for contracts in several or all departments and is assisted by a contract administrator and field manager for each contract established. In the decentralized model, each department has its own contract manager and supporting teams that draw on the resources of the legal, purchasing, and finance departments for technical direction. In the more common combination model, some contracts are handled centrally and others by individual departments. In the network model, a local government department contracts with one or more core providers who may in turn rely on subcontractors to meet the complex service needs outlined in the scope of work. Whether they function in a centralized, decentralized, combination, or network model, all contract administration teams have the same goal: to work with the contractor(s) to develop and maintain an environment in which the contractor can succeed in delivering high-quality public services at the agreed-upon cost.

Because of the variety and flexibility of organizational structures used in service contracting, the term "contract administration team" used throughout this chapter does not refer to a large static team that handles all service contracts but to individual teams composed of a contract manager and/or a contract administrator and/or a field manager and persons who do not bear these titles but perform similar duties. For the sake of consistency, the emphasis in this chapter is on the duties of the contract manager, contract administrator, and field manager.

Contract manager responsibilities   The contract manager reports to the local government manager, project manager, or—in a decentralized model—a department head. As the team leader, the contract manager is responsible for the success of the contract administration activities for each contract. The contract manager functions as coordinator, organizer, evaluator, mediator, and enforcer of the contract administration program.

As coordinator, the contract manager

- Coordinates the activities of contract administration teams
- Conducts scheduled meetings at least monthly with each team to review the status of individual contracts and the progress of the contracting program
- Reviews and acts upon the requests of all parties involved in a contract, working closely with the contractor and with the auditing, finance, legal, and purchasing departments.

As organizer, the contract manager

- Establishes what is to be evaluated for each contract and devises rating systems and monitoring methods to be used
- Establishes evaluation criteria, rating systems, surveys, and other monitoring methods to be used for each contract
- Assembles and trains the contract administration team
- Establishes procedures for review of contract problems or disputes
- Responds to management requests for new services or changes in existing services
- With the team, prepares default contingency plans for each contract
- Prepares and updates a contract administration procedures manual.

As evaluator, the contract manager

- Determines the acceptability of reports or other deliverables provided by the contractor
- Reviews contractor payment requests and approves or rejects them as required
- Monitors the performance of the contractor in person when possible, working closely with the field manager
- Reports to the local government manager on contractor performance
- Evaluates the effectiveness of the contract administration teams in reaching their goals

- Establishes inspection schedules for performance monitoring
- Plans and manages surveys of citizens and department clients
- Analyzes information collected during the contract term to identify ways to improve the effectiveness and efficiency of the service, implements the improvements with the current contractor either by mutual agreement or by contract amendment, and incorporates the improvements into future specifications for the service.

As mediator, the contract manager

- Resolves conflicts between the contractor and citizens or local government clients when such conflicts cannot be resolved by the field manager or contract administrator
- Monitors team members, departments, and user agencies to prevent the development of an adversarial relationship that could affect the contractor's performance
- Negotiates and approves amendments to the scope of work and attempts to resolve disputes with the contractor
- Negotiates and resolves agency demands on contractors that may be beyond the contractor's responsibilities.

As enforcer, the contract manager

- Interprets contract provisions for the contractor, contract administration team members, and departments
- Decides what liquidated damages provisions or other default actions will be taken if serious service problems arise.

Contract administrator responsibilities   The contract administrator functions at the department level and reports to the department director or the contract manager or both. The contract administrator also functions as the contract manager in the manager's absence. There is usually one contract administrator in a department; this person is responsible for providing administrative support to the department field managers and administrative oversight for all the service contracts in the department. A department with many contracts may require more than one contract administrator, each providing administrative support to several field managers and oversight for their assigned contracts.

The contract administrator

- Directs, monitors, and reviews the field manager's performance
- In cooperation with the field manager, assesses the contractor's performance
- Ensures timely submission of required reports from the contractor and field manager
- For cost reimbursement and unit price contracts, monitors the contractor's expenditures to ensure that they stay within expenditure forecasts and budget
- Reviews the contractor's payment requests and the field manager's payment recommendations, processes approved payment requests, and forwards requests that have been disapproved by the field manager or the contract administrator to the contract manager for review and disposition
- Tracks payment requests as they travel through the accounts payable system to ensure that the local government meets the promised payment schedule
- Assists the field manager in reviewing the contractor's requests for amendments and forwards to the contract manager recommendations for action on the changes

- Makes recommendations to the contract manager regarding enforcement of liquidated damages provisions or default procedures
- Maintains the master contract files and ensures that insurance certificates, bonds, licenses, and other contract-related documents are current
- Monitors the contractor's compliance with small and minority-owned business plans and Equal Employment Opportunity goals if applicable
- Helps prepare default contingency plans.

Field manager responsibilities The field manager reports to the contract administrator and is the team's principal link with the contractor. Field managers may be responsible for one or more service contracts. The field manager is in more frequent contact with the contractor's crews than any other team member and must be alert to identify service problems in the early stages. Of the three team members, the field manager is generally the most familiar with the operations of the contract and the exact duties and responsibilities of the contractor.

The field manager

- Checks the qualifications of the contractor's personnel against contract requirements
- Conducts scheduled and unscheduled inspections of the contractor's work to ensure that it is done as required
- Reports on contractor performance
- Monitors the contractor's quality control program
- Reviews payment requests to be sure that items or hours charged match the contract prices and accurately reflect the services that were received
- Alerts the contract administrator to developing problems
- Helps develop default contingency plans
- Advises the contract manager of improvements that could be made in the scope of work in current and future contracts.

Service delivery issues

The key to effective contract administration is to identify and address all problems before they become unmanageable. The following discussion addresses issues common to both public and private service delivery and offers guidelines to assist the contract administration team in dealing with them.

Customer satisfaction All customers deserve satisfactory service. To help ensure that they receive it, the contract administration team should assess customer satisfaction. If evaluation systems and procedures were used to monitor in-house service delivery, they should remain in place to evaluate customer satisfaction with private service delivery, particularly when a service is delivered to private citizens. If no systems are in place to measure and evaluate customer satisfaction, incorporate customer surveys, interviews, customer service lines, or some other similar mechanism into contract administration activities.

Timeliness Monitoring delivery schedules to prevent or minimize lapses in service is a critical function of the contract administration team. The team reviews, approves, and monitors contractor work schedules to ensure that acceptable services are delivered when and where promised. When a service is delivered in house, schedule slippage can often be corrected by shifting employees from other

---

Record-keeping

Record-keeping increases significantly under service contracting. Preparing performance reports, keeping bond and insurance files current, tracking contract payments, and responding to contractor claims and disputes consume a considerable amount of the contract administration team's time.

To simplify record-keeping, the contract manager should maintain an individual master file for each contract that contains the complete history of the contract, including all correspondence, reports, evaluations, insurance certificates, and so forth. Do not mingle correspondence relating to several contracts in a general correspondence file. Place correspondence regarding each contract in its own file. To keep paperwork to a minimum, do not require a standard report or procedure if it is not essential for the monitoring of a specific contract.

The contract administrator (or the person who fills the equivalent position) is responsible for preparing and maintaining the master contract file. Although the field and contract managers may maintain their own files, everything in those files must be copied to the master file. The master contract file is the central reference for the contract and should contain (at a minimum) all contract documents, including the contractor's bid response, the scope of work, amendments, bonding documents, current insurance certificates, and required licenses and permits, and all performance documents, such as correspondence, evaluations, reports submitted by the contractor and the contract administration team, payment requests, and copies of invoices.

---

assignments to the problem area until the service is back on schedule. In the case of contracted services, slippage must be addressed by the contractor, and a contractor is seldom amenable to spending the money necessary to bring a slipped schedule up to date. It is not uncommon for a contractor to demand extra payment for correcting slippage, claiming that the local government contributed to the problem. The contract administration team must be alert to correct slippage problems immediately.

Productivity   Specific productivity standards—for example, the amount of work to be performed by a work crew during one shift—should be part of every contract. These standards must be at least as high as those established for local government employees who formerly provided the service.

Careful monitoring is necessary to make sure that the contractor meets productivity requirements. When productivity falls below the established standard, the contract administration team must act quickly to prevent further decline and to ensure that productivity is brought back to contract minimums.

Performance problems   Most problems that arise with public or private delivery of a service are based on poor performance on the part of individuals. It is important to be aware that when problems arise with a contractor, the attempt to resolve even simple issues can potentially result in a formal contract dispute. A contract manager's request to a contractor to correct a problem or perform a task may have little or no effect unless it is made clear to the contractor that there has been a breach of a specific term or condition of the contract or that the task is part of the contractor's obligations under the contract. If the contractor does not agree with the contract manager, the problem may eventually require resolution by the governing body or the courts.

The contract administration team, particularly the field manager, should intervene to prevent problems or conflicts from developing into formal disputes. Examples of intervention include meeting with a contractor whose repairs to equipment are being rejected at an unacceptable rate or informing a contractor that an employee has behaved belligerently toward a client.

Pre-performance meeting

Pre-performance meetings clarify the procedures to be used throughout the contract term and enable all parties to better understand one another's perspective and expectations. These meetings are especially important because members of the contract administration team may have different views of the contract due to their different responsibilities. The contract manager, for example, focuses on the relationship between the contractor's performance and service delivery goals. Both the department and the contract administrator are principally concerned with whether the contractor's performance meets department goals, contract requirements, and the project budget. A major part of the contract manager's job is to ensure that these sometimes-conflicting views do not interfere with the administration of the contract, that team members understand that the contract document alone should govern their actions, and that contract administration must be a team effort to succeed.

The contract administration team holds two separate pre-performance meetings: the first with the department or departments involved and the second with the contractor.

Department meeting   The department meeting is facilitated by the contract administration team and attended by staff from all the departments involved. In this meeting, the contract manager defines the roles of the team members, reviews the forms and procedures to be used, and responds to any concerns or procedural questions department staff may have. Particularly when contract administration is centralized, this meeting helps assure department managers that although the details of monitoring and administration may be handled by team members outside the department, the department will continue to influence how the contract is administered and the quality of service delivery.

The meeting allows a department to question, comment upon, or recommend changes to the procedures that have been developed before the team commits itself to them at the pre-performance meeting with the contractor. This is especially important when the contracted service is closely related to the central mission of a department. For example, a contract for temporary clerical help is usually assigned to a central contract administration office and may be monitored by each department using the service. Although the contract is seldom monitored exclusively by the personnel department, it represents a service that is like the service provided through that department. Although not charged with overall contract administration and monitoring responsibilities, the personnel department is concerned about such issues as the minimum qualifications of personnel hired under the temporary help contract, the rate of pay for temporary personnel, and benefits of temporary personnel. The personnel department wants assurance that all employees, including temporary contract help, are qualified to perform their assigned tasks, are aware of their rights and responsibilities, and are treated fairly. Involvement of the department in the pre-performance meeting enables it to provide input during the contract administration process and establishes it as a resource for the team.

Contractor meeting After the department meeting but before the start of contract performance, a pre-performance meeting is held with the contractor. The purpose of this meeting is to establish a common understanding of contract requirements and the responsibilities of both the local government and the contractor under the contract. The meeting also helps make service start-up as smooth as possible.

The participants and the structure of the meeting can vary considerably. Typical participants include the contract administration team, staff from the departments involved, the contractor, and the contractor's staff person responsible for monitoring service delivery. In contracting for trade services (plumbers, carpenters, etc.), equipment repair services, or mowing services, a meeting between the contractor, the department involved, and a member of the contract administration team is sufficient. Services that affect essential operations, such as public transportation, refuse collection, or recycling, may require the attendance of the entire contract administration team, representatives from the departments involved, a representative of the local government manager, and possibly a member of a citizens' advisory committee.

An agenda should be prepared that includes topics such as the following: the identification of participants and a description of their authority, review of the contract documents, the local government's responsibilities, the contractor's responsibilities, performance expectations and monitoring, quality control, resolution of service complaints and contract disputes, contract enforcement, and payment procedures. When appropriate, combine the contractor's conference with a site tour to review field conditions that could affect performance. The accompanying sidebar describes these agenda items in more detail.

Amendments to the contract

The local government and the contractor are required to perform only those duties described in the contract documents. Because even the most comprehensive contract documents may fail to address clearly some aspects of service delivery, the responsibilities of the parties, or other important issues, amendments are almost inevitable.

Either the local government or the contractor may request an amendment, but both parties must agree to it unless the contract specifically allows unilateral changes by the local government (e.g., the incorporation of new legislation that does not affect the contract price, the time of performance, the quality of service, or the establishment of a new price structure for subsequent years on the basis of a formula set forth in the contract). Amendments must be approved by the legal department to be sure that the rights of both parties are protected. They are binding only if signed by the principals of the contractor's firm and local government officials authorized to execute contracts for the parties to the contract. Local government department heads, contract managers, contract administrators, and field managers are seldom, if ever, authorized to approve or sign contracts or contract amendments.

Although minor changes or clarifications that do not affect price, time of performance, or quality of service are sometimes made informally through a letter of understanding, the safest course is to issue a formal amendment to the contract. The letter of understanding—which is usually signed by only one party to the contract—has considerably less legal status than a formal amendment, which must be executed

Pre-performance conference agenda items

Authority of participants   Identify representatives of both the local government and the contractor and state the limits of their authority.

Review of the contract documents   Review the contract documents in detail. Clarify any ambiguities and make the clarifications part of the written record of the meeting. If necessary, amend the contract to avoid future problems of interpretation. Review the contract amendment process. Stress the need for written amendments and remind attendees that verbal changes are not binding on either of the parties. Define what the local government considers adequate justification for an amendment.

Local government responsibilities   Review the local government's obligations under the contract. Assure the contractor that the local government will abide by the contract and will provide an environment in which the contractor can provide the service with the least interference.

Contractor responsibilities   Review the contractor's responsibilities described in the contract. They generally include following contract requirements: following the established staffing plan; providing a responsible on-site manager; assigning qualified personnel to the contract; providing the equipment required to do the assigned tasks; maintaining records of expenditures, deliverables, and progress; submitting required reports on schedule; and maintaining a clear line of communication for prompt resolution of problems.

Performance expectations and monitoring   Describe the level of performance expected and provide the contractor with copies of the forms to be used for evaluation and monitoring. Review the forms in detail so that the contractor understands the performance standards and the evaluation methods. Encourage the contractor to recommend improvements in service delivery methods or productivity during the contract term. Establish a schedule for follow-up meetings to review both contractor and local government performance.

Quality control   If the contract requires the contractor to have a quality control program, review and discuss the program. A contractor's quality control program may be similar to a local government's contract administration and monitoring or quality improvement program. It should have the same elements: inspection and observation on a scheduled and unscheduled basis; procedures for early identification of service delivery problems; and provisions for written records and reports.

Resolution of service complaints   Review the procedures for prompt resolution of complaints generated by citizens or local government clients. Review any complaint forms devised for the contract and the information required from the contractor to complete them. If the contractor is responsible for managing the complaint process independently, describe the nature and frequency of any reports required.

Contract disputes   Review the procedures for handling disagreements between the local government and the contractor. Provide the contractor with copies of ordinances, regulations, or procedures governing disputes. Review the time limits for dispute resolution, identify the local government staff responsible for settlement of disputes, and describe the administrative appeals procedure.

Contract enforcement   Explain the liquidated damages provisions of the contract and describe the conditions that trigger their enforcement or enforcement of other similar provisions of the contract.

Payment procedures   Because many contractors are not familiar with local government payment procedures, review the payment process from the time payment is requested by the contractor to the issuing of a check. Explain how processing of the check can be delayed by errors such as inserting incorrect payment terms on an invoice, failing to properly identify the department for which the work was performed, or failing to give a purchase order number. Discuss the level of detail or format of the invoice required under the contract.

by both parties. A seemingly inconsequential issue that is dealt with through a letter of understanding may open the door to later contract disputes.

It is not unusual for a contractor to attempt to use the amendment process to correct a pricing error in the bid response. Requests from the contractor for additional compensation or a change in the level of service must be examined carefully to determine whether the request is valid and reasonable. If the request for an amendment stems from the fact that the contractor underestimated the effort or expense required to do the work or overestimated its capacity to provide the service, the amendment is not justified and should not be agreed to.

Valid amendments have a common element—the work covered is beyond the scope of work defined in the original contract documents. If the local government requests work that is not clearly within the scope—for example, adding a new building to a custodial services contract—an amendment is justified. If an amendment affecting the contract price is determined to be valid, the contractor must provide a detailed breakdown of the proposed cost increase to demonstrate that there are no unwarranted extras built into the amended price.

Performance monitoring

This section covers the basics of performance monitoring, focusing on two approaches: measuring outputs and measuring outcomes. Measuring outputs involves a relatively straightforward method of counting service components produced. This might include number of intakes conducted in a given month, number of acres mowed, number of meals served, number of curb miles paved, number of health screenings performed, and so on. Outcome monitoring, also known as performance measurement, is a much more difficult task. Assessing outcomes involves asking whether clients were helped and what impact the service is having.

Information on output is generally gathered by the contract administration team. Information on outcome, or results, may be derived from multiple sources, including data collected from users of the service.[1] Both output and outcome monitoring are based on information that must be gathered and recorded, and this chapter covers a number of approaches to obtaining data and documenting performance, including observation records, discrepancy reports, field diaries, surveys, and customer hotlines.

Any monitoring method or combination of methods may be appropriate for a given contract. Part of successful contract administration is selecting the method that will provide the most timely and accurate information to the local government at the least cost.

Whatever the method used, it is important to remember that a single monitoring report provides only a snapshot view of performance; inspections and observations over time are required to create a comprehensive picture of average contract performance.

Getting started

The first thirty days of the contract term influence the character of the long-term relationship between the contract administration team and the contractor. For any contractor new to the local government, erratic performance during the first month is to be expected. Being patient and working with the contractor to resolve contract start-up problems will help create a long-term relationship characterized by cooperation and mutual respect.

Contract documents usually establish a range of acceptable performance, but contractors seldom perform at the upper end of the range, particularly when beginning a new contract. For example, even an experienced contractor may have underestimated the effort required to perform some aspects of the service and overestimated others. These miscalculations may cause performance to be uneven until the contractor makes the necessary adjustments in personnel and equipment to balance service in all contract areas.

During the start-up period, the contract administration team needs to monitor intensively but leniently. The point is to help the contractor get on the right path but not to interfere with the contractor's work. Performance problems are sure to arise, but the team should assist rather than criticize the contractor. Whatever idealized notions the team may have had about service contracting will quickly be tempered by the realization that the contractor faces the same service delivery problems that the local government faced with public service delivery—and may make the same mistakes in trying to resolve them.

Monitoring output

There are several choices for gathering information on outputs. One option is direct monitoring, which occurs while the work is being performed. Another option is follow-up monitoring, which occurs after the work is completed. Monitoring by exception is another approach, which may incorporate either direct or follow-up monitoring but is triggered only by specific complaints about service. Both direct and follow-up monitoring can be conducted according to a schedule or at random. The next five sections explore these options in detail.

Direct monitoring   Direct monitoring is used mainly during contract start-up and occasionally during the contract term to ensure that the work is being performed according to established procedures or standards. Although it can be helpful in determining exactly how the contractor delivers the service, excessive use of direct monitoring can antagonize the contractor's employees and create tension between them and the observer.

Follow-up monitoring   Follow-up monitoring is the inspection method used most often. Its purpose is to answer general and specific questions such as the following:

- Does the work meet contract requirements?
- Is the contractor on schedule?
- Have the required number of units of service been delivered?

The monitor's monitor

Responsible contractors place as much or more value on effective monitoring as the local government and their internal quality control measures may be more stringent. For some contractors, elaborate internal monitoring mechanisms may be a requirement of accreditation, certification, or membership in industry-specific associations. In addition, to protect their investment in the contract and to prevent undue interference, contractors often familiarize themselves with contract law, local ordinances, and state and federal regulatory requirements. Essentially, they monitor the local government monitors to be certain that they do not overstep their authority.

- Are clients satisfied with the service?
- Has the work area been left in acceptable condition?
- Is the grass mowed to the correct height?
- Are all the rest rooms clean?
- Has all trash been removed from the curbside?

Monitoring by exception   Monitoring by exception is a common and often necessary part of a contract administration program. Monitoring all contracts with the same attention to detail is costly, and the local government that can afford to do so is rare. For every contract requiring intensive monitoring there are probably several candidates for monitoring by exception.

If a service is essential to the community or if there is a risk that a client can actually be harmed by services of poor quality (refuse collection and social services are examples), then monitoring by exception cannot be relied on as the sole monitoring method. However, monitoring by exception is usually acceptable for contracts that meet two criteria: (1) the work performed is easy to measure and is conducted primarily at a contractor's site rather than on local government property (fleet repair and blueprinting services are examples); and (2) the delivered product (e.g., the work of a painting or plumbing contractor) is the criterion by which the contractor's proficiency is evaluated. Monitoring by exception is also appropriate for services that users evaluate continuously as a matter of course. For example, in the case of personal services (those delivered by a specified individual), a user will simply not rehire an unsatisfactory contractor; in the case of temporary help, a dissatisfied user will dismiss the assigned employee.

The principal disadvantage of monitoring by exception is that the contractor and the contract administration team may be caught off guard by a problem that might have been picked up by more intensive monitoring. For example, if a contract for repair of a small bus fleet used for supplemental public transportation is monitored by exception and a vehicle breakdown occurs as a result of the contractor's use of rebuilt transmission or engine components rather than new components, as called for in the contract, the entire fleet could require extensive repairs to correct prior unauthorized work—a situation that might have been prevented by periodic examination of the contractor's repair work orders. Periodic examination can be helpful in identifying a problem early enough to prevent a crisis later.

Scheduled monitoring   Scheduled monitoring for some types of services is necessary to ensure systematic review of performance. Generally, scheduled monitoring occurs on a monthly or quarterly basis. The contract may have a plan for scheduled monitoring

---

When an increase in productivity creates a problem

Although one goal of service contracting is to improve productivity, increased productivity can signal trouble. In lump-sum, fixed price contracts, it is in the best interest of the contractor to increase productivity because all productivity increases contribute to profit. But when productivity increases are achieved by lowering the quality of service, what benefits the contractor may harm service recipients. Thus, the contract administration team must examine unusual improvements in productivity as carefully as it would a drop in productivity.

built in from the beginning or may initiate scheduled monitoring if service problems begin to develop or if the local government receives significant complaints from service recipients.

Scheduled monitoring is arranged in advance with the contractor's project officer or field supervisor and can occur during or after performance. At the specified time, the local government's field or contract manager inspects or reviews the service with the contractor's representative. Because scheduled inspections allow the contractor to alert employees beforehand, the service is often an example of the best the contractor can deliver. This can be a benefit: problems identified during a scheduled inspection—when the contractor has presumably made a strong effort—indicate that the contractor may be misinterpreting contract requirements and should review them with the field or contract manager. Similarly, if the level of quality achieved for the scheduled inspection is higher than that noted in previous reports, it may indicate that the contractor is capable of improving performance, particularly when monitored closely. The contractor should be advised that the performance observed during the inspection is a welcome improvement and will be the new standard against which future work will be measured.

Random monitoring   Random monitoring is direct or follow-up inspection of the contractor's performance undertaken without the contractor's advance knowledge. Although random monitoring should not be relied on as the sole indicator of performance quality, it does provide a view of performance that is not usually obtainable through scheduled inspections. Another advantage of random monitoring is that it encourages the contractor to maintain acceptable service levels even when local government observers are not present. The sidebar on this page provides an illustration of random monitoring using "mystery shoppers."

Monitoring outcome

As noted earlier, outcome monitoring is the analysis of the results of a service. In a street maintenance contract, for example, the number of potholes repaired is a measure of output, whereas an outcome analysis might focus on the smoothness

Mystery shoppers

To ensure that contractors' interactions with clients fulfill contractual performance requirements, Genesee County Community Mental Health (GCCMH) in the state of Michigan uses a "mystery shopper" program to randomly monitor its contractors. The Customer Services unit of GCCMH enlists the help of client volunteers who are provided with training and a set of protocols for randomly assessing how the contractor responds to client requests for help. The client is assigned a set of expectations to evaluate during a single encounter with the contractor. For example, the client may contact the agency by phone or visit the site in person and make a request for service. The client may be asked to report on whether they were treated with respect; how long they were put on hold if they phoned; whether they were given an appropriate response to an emergent care request; and, if they presented a request in a foreign language, whether the contractor followed the appropriate protocol for accessing a translator. This program has been highly effective in helping GCCMH monitor contractors and involve clients in the process, and it keeps contractors "on their toes." Contractors find the feedback helpful and use it as a performance improvement tool.

What does an outcome measure look like?

Outcome measures assess the extent to which a program has achieved its intended results. The principal question in outcome measurement is: Has the program or service made a difference? Outcome measures should assess some aspect of the effect, result, or quality of a service. They are outcomes the public would likely be interested in, not merely the amount of work done or resources consumed. Typically, outcomes are broad program goals that are measured through a series of measurable indicators. Some examples include:

Outcome: Timely access to services

   Indicator 1:   Intake appointments scheduled within 48 hours of initial request for services

   Indicator 2:   Clients assigned a caseworker within 7 days of initial intake

   Indicator 3:   After-hours emergent care calls answered within 15 minutes

Outcome: Economic revitalization

   Indicator 1:   Number of new businesses start-ups

   Indicator 2:   Reduction in unemployment rate

   Indicator 3:   Clearance of 25 percent of blighted land area

Outcome: Client satisfaction

   Indicator 1:   Number of complaint calls received per month

   Indicator 2:   Number of repeat complaint calls

   Indicator 3:   Average client satisfaction rating of service on annual survey

Source: Adapted from Compassion Capital Fund National Resource Center, *Measuring Outcomes* (Washington, D.C.: National Resource Center, 2005), available at www.acf.hhs.gov/programs/ccf/resources/gbk_pdf/om_gbk.pdf.

of the repaired roadway or on the reduction of hazards to pedestrians. As another example, social services contracts commonly examine recidivism rates, employment attainment, client satisfaction, and quality of life indicators as outcome measurements. The sidebar above provides more examples of outcome measures. Criteria for measuring outcome should be included in the contractor evaluation section of the original scope of work. The sections on surveys and hotlines later in the chapter are particularly pertinent to outcome monitoring.

Few contracts today are established without detailed performance expectations. However, local governments must exercise caution in the way these expectations are structured. Outcomes and performance expectations must be carefully structured so as not to stifle innovation with excessive rigidity or create incentives for the contractor that are at odds with the interests of clients. The sidebar on page 164 highlights some strategies for avoiding these risks.

Documenting performance

Because no single method of data collection can present a complete picture of a contractor's day-to-day performance, objective evaluation of performance must be based on information received from several sources. A random inspection, for example, may provide a snapshot view that does not necessarily represent average performance. A complaint may be groundless or unrelated to actual service delivery. Contractor reports and deliverables required under the contract may or may not be reliable.

Overcoming the problems of performance contracting

Specifying the type and level of performance expected from contractors can go a long way toward structuring the monitoring process, but it is not a foolproof method. Performance contracting has several downsides, including the fact it may inhibit contractors' creativity, stifle overachievement, and encourage innovation in cost-cutting but not in service delivery. Robert Behn and Peter Kant offer eight strategies for avoiding these and similar pitfalls associated with performance contracting:

1. Link performance measures that are used to monitor contractors to the local government's mission. This reminds the contract administration team of the underlying purpose of contracting.

2. Create contracts based on outputs that are linked to mission; are easy to measure, understand, and reproduce; and facilitate benchmarking.

3. Start with measures that are simple and adjust the complexity with time and experience.

4. Monitor many indicators of performance and monitor them frequently

5. Be prepared to learn, change, and adapt. Use knowledge gained through the process to improve future versions of the contract as well as new contracts.

6. Work collaboratively rather than adversarially with contractors.

7. Pay contractors not just for final outputs but also for significant and well-defined progress.

8. Choose contractors with a track record of desirable performance.

Source: Adapted from Robert D. Behn and Peter A. Kant, "Strategies for Avoiding the Pitfalls of Performance Contracting," *Public Productivity and Management Review* 22, no. 4 (June 1999): 470-489.

This section discusses a number of approaches to gathering and recording information on performance—from forms to diaries, surveys, and hotlines. Whatever the source of information, the goal of the contract administration team is to tie together all available information to create a comprehensive picture of a contractor's performance. The forms and techniques described can be adapted for use in any service contracting program.

One important note to remember: good record-keeping procedures are as essential to service contracting as they are to any other local government function. For example, any written material relating to a contract—a memorandum issued by the field manager or contract manager, for example—must be forwarded to the contract administrator and stored in the master file for that contract. Similarly, if the contract administrator receives a document that affects the contractor's performance or amends the contract documents, the administrator should forward a copy to the field manager for information and reference.

Contract administrator's checklist   The contract administrator's checklist (Exhibit 8-1 at the end of the chapter) lists the licenses, certificates, bonds, and insurance and the reports, forms, and other deliverables required of the contractor during the contract term. The checklist is prepared by the contract administrator at the beginning of the contract term and is reviewed at specific intervals—anywhere from monthly to annually—to ensure that all items are current. Although the contractor's failure to provide the required items on time is a factor in the evaluation of performance, the checklist is more an aid for the contract administrator than an evaluation form in the strict sense.

Observation record An observation record (Exhibit 8-2) is used to document observations of contractor performance, primarily by the field manager but also by the contract administrator and contract manager whenever they observe service delivery.

Complaint record The complaint record (Exhibit 8-3) is used to record and follow up on complaints received from citizens or local government clients. To permit easier tracking of a complaint from receipt through final disposition, a separate form is used for each complaint.

Discrepancy report A discrepancy report (Exhibit 8-4) is used to document a condition that is or could lead to a breach of contract. It is prepared by the field manager or contract administrator, approved by the contract manager, and forwarded to the contractor for corrective action with a cover letter if necessary. If the contract manager thinks that a written response is necessary, he or she recommends in the discrepancy report that the contractor respond to the complaint in writing. A copy of the original complaint report may also be sent to the contractor with the discrepancy report. If the local government does not have an official discrepancy report form, a simple memorandum citing the discrepancy should be issued to the contractor and a copy placed in the contract file. The key is to put the problem in writing so that it becomes part of the performance history.

On the discrepancy form, the contract manager requires the contractor to respond within a specified time. After reviewing the contractor's response, the contract manager decides whether further action should be taken to prevent recurrence of the problem. A copy of the completed form is then returned to the contractor with a cover letter expanding on the entries, if necessary.

Depending on the nature of the discrepancy, it may be appropriate to ask the contractor to submit a brief corrective action plan. The corrective action plan does not need to be lengthy but should address why the discrepancy occurred and describe action taken to prevent future discrepancies.

Summary evaluation report The summary evaluation report (Exhibit 8-5) is a brief evaluation of performance during a given period. It should be prepared 30 or 60 days after contract start-up and every 90 to 120 days after that. Summary reports are prepared more frequently when performance threatens to fall below contract standards.

The report is prepared by the contract manager using information received from all available sources during the evaluation period (personal observations, team member observation reports and memoranda, complaints received, etc.).

Contract status report Depending on the type of service, the local government may require status reports from contractors on a routine basis as part of the performance monitoring process. If the local government is paying the contractor for the service fully or in part through federal funds, status reports from contractors are probably required. A monthly narrative status report prepared by the contractor may fulfill a grant requirement or provide management or the governing body with information on contracts of special interest to them. All reports are reviewed thoroughly by the contract administration team and the affected department for completeness and accuracy.

Do not require a report without a valid reason. Reporting is not necessary or practical, for example, for contracts for trades services or any short-term personal service or consulting contract. When in doubt about whether to include a reporting requirement, require a quarterly report "at the discretion of the contract manager." It is much easier to waive an existing reporting requirement than it is to ask for a report that was not required in the contract.

Establish an outline of the topics or areas that must be addressed in any contract status report required and let the contractor choose the response format. The outline may include items such as the following:

- Specific tasks, units of service provided, number of clients served, or deliverables provided since the last reporting period and a summary of activities to date
- Problems encountered in service delivery or in adhering to budget or project schedules and how they were resolved
- In cost reimbursement contracts and contracts under which work is to be completed in phases, a comparison of the progress to date with targeted and actual contract dollars spent
- A forecast of tasks, deliverables, or services to be provided during the next reporting period
- An assessment of the quality of cooperation received from the local government staff
- Recommendations for improvements in service delivery, level of local government involvement, and so forth.

Field diary Field notes include information on weather conditions, favorable and unfavorable observations of contractor performance, and records of telephone and face-to-face conversations with the contractor. Because the observations recorded in field notes are included in more formal documentation of performance such as discrepancy reports and evaluation forms and may be required to justify the assessment of liquidated damages or to support legal action against the contractor, it is essential that they be accurate.

One way to help ensure accuracy and protect the integrity of field notes is to record them in a field diary. Traditionally, a blank hard-covered book has served this purpose. Increasingly, construction inspectors rely on electronic systems to record observations in the field. Specialized software such as Field Manager allows inspectors to record inspection details on an electronic reporting pad while in the field and later transfer the information to the local government's main computer system.[2]

The field diary provides a dated record of each inspection, observation, and problem encountered during the contract term. Every entry must be accurate and defensible: the diary is not to be used to express opinions or repeat hearsay but to record events or activities directly observed. Like most contract administration documents, the diary may be a part of the public record under freedom of information laws.

The sidebar on page 167 lists recommended procedures and typical entries for a field diary. The field manager should use a separate diary for each contract. Contract administrators and contract managers, who have less frequent contact with individual contractors, do not have to use a separate diary for each contract. They can insert their observations and comments into a single diary, identifying the contract to which each comment applies. However, when monitoring highly visible or sensitive contracts, it is advisable for each member of the contract administration team to have a separate diary for each such contract.

Maintaining a field diary

Procedures

1. Number all pages consecutively in ink.

2. Make entries in ink, if possible. Do not erase entries. Cross out errors and enter the correct information.

3. Do not tear pages from the diary. If an entire page needs to be corrected, cross it out with a large "X" and mark it "VOID."

4. Make entries directly into the diary at the time that events are observed. Do not make separate notes to be entered into the diary later.

5. Make an entry for every calendar day. If nothing of significance occurred that day, enter "No significant activity," "Sunday," "Holiday," etc.

6. Sign or initial each day's entries immediately after making the last entry for the day. Do not leave a space between the last entry and the initials or signature.

7. The diary may be supplemented with photographs that should be numbered, marked with the time and date the photograph was taken and the photographer's name, and stored permanently (along with the negatives) in the master contract files. Digital cameras are useful because they can store photos electronically and provide a backup for this component of the field diary. Photos should be identified in the diary by date and number, and electronic files containing photos should be labeled the same.

8. If a single diary is being used for several contracts, enter the contract number and date immediately before each entry.

Typical entries

1. A description of the weather, if weather affects contract performance.

2. A record of the type of monitoring (direct, follow-up, exception, scheduled, random).

3. All favorable and unfavorable observations.

4. A summary of any substantive contract-related telephone conversations.

5. A description of any event or activity not in keeping with contract requirements, including the name of the contractor's supervisor who was notified, the date and manner in which the contractor was notified, and any other action taken or observations made.

6. A summary of the content of any substantive discussions held with the contractor, on or off the job site.

7. A description of any problems with reports or incorrect invoices submitted by the contractor, including notes on whether they were returned for correction

Surveys   Surveys are effective ways to monitor services provided to citizens or to clients within the local government. Because citizen surveys are usually outcome oriented, constructing them may be comparatively difficult and may require professional assistance. Surveys of local government clients are generally simpler to construct, conduct, and evaluate than citizen surveys. They usually address basic issues (e.g., whether the citizen is satisfied or dissatisfied with the service) or the number and quality of contract outputs.

Citizen or client surveys capture feedback from service recipients and are therefore a valuable means of monitoring contract performance. However, a reliable survey requires some understanding of survey techniques, statistics, and data analysis—skills

---

The contractor's employees

The contractor—not members of the local government contract administration team—is responsible for the supervision of its employees while performing contract tasks. During the monitoring process, team members must be careful not to do anything that would interfere with the relationship between the contractor and its employees. Avoid direct communication or contact with the contractor's employees and discuss contract matters only with the contractor's supervisor or field representative. Do not direct a contractor's employee to perform or to stop performing any task. Directions given to a contractor's employees by a local government employee could be interpreted as the local government's direct supervision of the work crew and could excuse the contractor from liability for damage that may result from the order.

However, when dealing with emergency situations, a local government employee may be forced to order the contractor's supervisor or employees to perform or not perform a task. Before an emergency arises, the contract manager should obtain the advice of the legal department on the liability of the local government if an emergency condition requires a team member to order a contractor's supervisor or employees to perform or stop performing a task.

---

that the local government contract administration staff may not have. An improperly conducted citizen survey may have side effects that offset its potential benefit. For example, the selection of one sample group may provoke resentment among groups not selected to participate or a poorly worded survey question may be perceived as biased or misleading. When the results of a survey are criticized by citizens or the governing body, its value can be diminished, no matter how valid the results.

To create the best climate for acceptance of a survey and protect the integrity of the results, the survey must be properly planned, conducted, and evaluated. The best course of action is to obtain the endorsement of the governing body to hire an independent professional survey firm. For local governments that find this cost-prohibitive, those on the contract administration team responsible for survey design should familiarize themselves with survey methods.[3]

Internal surveys are usually one- or two-page questionnaires that ask users to record their level of satisfaction with the service, describe any service problems they encountered, and comment generally on service quality and contractor performance. They are circulated to department users at least once during the contract term (at contract midpoint) or, if needed, twice during each contract year, usually in the fourth and eighth months. Some department surveys ask for the user's level of satisfaction with the contractor each time a service is delivered. This works well, for example, when evaluating contracts such as temporary help contracts, trades contracts, and others under which the service is provided intermittently.

A useful by-product of a user survey is that it creates a record of contractor performance that can be used to help qualify or disqualify the contractor the next time the service is let for bids. As is true for the results of every contract monitoring method, the contract administration team must share both positive and negative survey results with the contractor. Use positive results to encourage continued good performance and negative results to establish a plan for improvement.

Hotlines   Hotlines, toll-free numbers, and customer service lines are dedicated telephone numbers for registering service complaints. This method of monitoring allows service delivery problems to be detected quickly and anonymously if the service recipient does not wish to be identified. Hotlines are particularly helpful when the service covers a large geographical area that cannot be constantly monitored by contract administrators (e.g., park maintenance, mowing, tree trimming, refuse collection, transportation) and for vulnerable client populations who may otherwise be reluctant to report complaints. To obtain the best results from a hotline, be sure the number is broadly publicized where users are likely to see it—in news releases, Web sites, department publications, and newsletters and at the worksite.

Conclusion

A contract administration program is held together not by forms, surveys, diaries, or other monitoring tools but by the contract administration team. Effective contract monitoring depends more on the skills of the contract monitors than on the particular monitoring methods or forms used.

The contract administration team must work to accurately observe and record performance but it must also work with contractors to maintain acceptable performance and correct poor performance. Although most contractors cooperate readily with the team to resolve problems, some are more difficult to work with. Team members must be able to recognize the different styles and needs of contractors and apply the tools of contract administration flexibly in order to encourage the best possible performance from each contractor.

Contract monitoring can be one of the most labor-intensive aspects of contract administration, and funds and personnel must be carefully rationed and put to best use. A service that required only casual and infrequent inspection under a previous contractor may require constant attention when delivered by a new one. Contract managers must balance the time and money required to monitor a contract against the potential for disruption of essential service delivery. If the risk of disruption is low, less intensive monitoring may be adequate. Each contract and each contractor is different. There is no single right way to monitor a contract.

Endnotes

1 For a helpful source of information on how to collect and analyze outcome data, see Harry P. Hatry et al., *How Effective Are Your Community Services? Procedures for Performance Measurement*, 3rd ed. (Washington, D.C.: ICMA, 2006); and Harry P. Hatry, *Performance Measurement: Getting Results*, 2nd ed. (Washington, D.C.: Urban Institute Press, 2007).

2 Information on the format, content, and use of field diaries is based in part on the discussions of field diaries in Edward Fisk and Wayne Reynolds, *Construction Project Administration*, 8th ed. (New York: Prentice Hall, 2005), 55-57.

3 Local governments that have qualified staff and want to conduct their citizen surveys in house can find methods and guidelines for conducting citizen surveys in Thomas I Miller and Michelle Kobayashi, *Citizen Surveys: How to Do Them, How to Use Them, What They Mean*, 2nd ed. (Washington, D.C.: ICMA, 2000).

Exhibit 8-1 Sample contract administrator's checklist

Contractor Smith Contracting	Contract number 7893	
Contract requirement	Due date	Comments
1. Update insurance certificate and payment/performance bonds 30 days before expiration	Insurance: *June 30* Bonds: *June 30*	*OK 6/15* *OK 6/15*
2. Obtain bond renewals	On contract anniversary date	
3. Provide monthly reports on vehicle accidents	No later than 10th of following month	
4. Provide monthly personnel accident reports	No later than 10th of following month	
5. Provide evidence of license renewals (business, professional, technical) within five days of renewal date	Professional: *10/30* Business: *6/30* Technical: *6/30*	*OK 6/15*

Contractor reports

Monthly vehicle accident report	10th of each month
Monthly employee accident report	10th of each month
Quarterly summary of activity	1/1, 4/1, 7/1, 10/1

Prepared by *P. Johnson, Contract Administrator*   Date   *7/1*

Signature _____

Exhibit 8-2 Sample observation record

---

1. Contractor *XYZ Mowing Service*   Contract number *3493*
    Type of monitoring Direct _____
                            Follow-up _X_
    Cause
    Complaint from cycling club that bike trail is littered excessively between mile markers 1 and 3.

2. Date of observation   Location   Comments
    _____

    July 21   *Mile marker 1*   *Heavy concentrations of clippings.*
    July 21   *Mile marker 2.5*   *Same as above.*

    Additional comments
    Clippings and light trash on path throughout trail length, worst at above locations. Safety hazard exists.

3. Action recommended/taken
    Contractor called 7/21 and told to clean up trail. Discrepancy report attached.

Report prepared by *John Smith, Field Manager*   Date *July 21*

Signature _John Smith_____

Completing the form   The numbered notes below correspond to the numbered sections of the figure. The sections of an actual form would not be numbered.

1. Identify the contract, contractor, and type of monitoring.
2. Describe what was observed and when. Record both favorable and unfavorable observations.
3. Note action recommended or taken at the site. Attach other reports as required.

Exhibit 8-3 Sample complaint record

---

1. Contractor *Smith Contracting*   Contract number *7893*
   Date and time of complaint   *7/21–10:15 a.m.*
   Source   *Tel. call–Mrs. Jones–1400 Main*
   Nature   *Refuse truck backed into and broke fence.*

2. Valid/invalid   *Valid–2 fence sections cracked*
   How verified   *Physical inspection on 7/21*
   Date contractor informed   *7/21–2:15 p.m.*

3. Who informed   *Mr. Brown, vice-president of firm*

   Action taken by contractor *Brown promised to repair within ten days and will deal directly with Mrs. Jones.*

4. Disposition *Undersigned will follow up by phone in ten days (7/31) to verify repair. Suggest that a warning letter be sent to the contractor. This is the third incidence of damage to property by vehicles in the past month.*

Form completed by *B. White, Field Manager*   Date *7/22*

Signature *B White*

Completing the form   The numbered notes below correspond to the numbered sections of the figure. The sections of an actual form would not be numbered.

1. Whoever receives the complaint completes the first section of the form, entering the date, time received, source, and nature of the complaint.
2. The form is sent to the field manager, who investigates and rules on the validity of the complaint. If the complaint is ruled valid, the date that the contractor was advised of the complaint is entered by the field manager.
3. After discussing the complaint with the contractor, the field manager enters the contractor's action or promised action to correct the problem or prevent its recurrence.
4. The field manager enters actions recommended to prevent recurrence of the problem, such as further observation or surveillance, meetings with the contractor, or warnings to the contractor.

Exhibit 8-4 Sample discrepancy report

To *Smith Contracting*   Date *7/23*

Attention of *Mr. A. Brown, V.P.*

Contract title and number *Refuse Collection–7893*

From *D. Fredericks, Contract Manager*

1. Discrepancy or problem
   Please review the following and respond by *8/1.*
   On 7/21, refuse vehicle damaged fence at 1400 Main Street. On 7/14, same vehicle damaged steps
   at 3500 Washington Street. On 7/11, a refuse vehicle was involved in an accident at a transfer
   station. All incidents involved the same driver. Corrective action must include removal of this
   driver from contract duties. Please advise what action will be taken.

   Signature ~~D. Fredericks~~   Date *7/23*

2. Contractor response
   Operator suspended from driving for 60 days and assigned as crew member. All damages have
   been repaired or are now being repaired. See attached letter for further details.

   Contractor signature ~~a brown~~   Date *8/1*

3. Disposition/action taken
   Response not acceptable. Please remove driver from contract duties immediately in accor-
   dance with Section II-3.4 of contract.

   Contract manager signature ~~D. Fredericks~~   Date *8/6*

Completing the form   The numbered notes below correspond to the numbered sections of
the figure. The sections of an actual form would not be numbered.

1. The field manager or contract administrator enters the specifics of the problem, then forwards
   the form to the contract manager for approval. The contract manager signs and sends the
   form to the contractor.
2. The contractor is required to describe the corrective action to be taken.
3. After reviewing the contractor's response, the contract manager enters the action taken or
   required and returns a copy of the completed form to the contractor.

Exhibit 8-5 Sample summary evaluation report

Contractor *XYZ Mowing*   Contract Number *3493*

Report for period *7/1* to *8/1*

1. Customer complaints   *Four complaints received, three regarding debris on bike trail and one regarding a crew supervisor using abusive language to bike trail user.*

2. Contract checklist deficiencies   *All documents OK and current.*

3. Performance goals not met   *1. "No more than 3 complaints per month." Four received. One complaint satisfactorily resolved when contractor discharged supervisor who had used abusive language. See "Contract Manager Recommendations" below.   2. "Schedule maintained within two days." Schedule continually off by one or two days. Contractor is required to maintain approved schedule.*

4. Contractor discrepancy reports
   Three discrepancy reports issued. All resolved satisfactorily.

5. Performance rating
   Responsive/cooperation   *5+*   Cost control   *N/A*
   Quality of work/deliverables   *3*   Other_____
   Timeliness of work/deliverables *4*   _____

6. Performance summary
   Work is generally satisfactory except for maintenance of mowing schedules and occasional failure to clear bike trail of all debris. Contractor's responsiveness and cooperation are outstanding.

7. Contractor manager recommendations
   Contractor must ensure that bike trail is free of trash and clippings. Repeated violations may lead to cash penalties.

Contract manager *D. Fredericks*   Date *8/10*

Signature *D. Fredericks*

Completing the form   The numbered notes below correspond to the numbered sections of the figure. The sections of an actual form would not be numbered.

The contract manager will complete the form and

1. Record the number and nature of any valid complaints.
2. List any instances of failure to meet the requirements of the contract requirements checklist.
3. Identify performance goals that have not been met during the reporting period.
4. Review any discrepancy reports and their final disposition.
5. Determine whether the contractor's performance is unacceptable, acceptable, or exceptional. A point value ranging from *acceptable* (5) to *unacceptable* (1) may be used instead of a descriptive term.
6. Summarize the contractor's performance for the period covered by the report and for the contract term to date either in a narrative or by assigning a point value.
7. Recommend actions to be taken by the contractor to improve performance or correct deficiencies and specify any liquidated damages that may be assessed for the performance period covered by the report. If the report shows acceptable performance, congratulate the contractor.

9

Dealing with Poor Performance

Service contracting is a partnership. Maintaining the performance standards established in the contract is a responsibility shared by the contractor and the contract administration team. When discrepancies arise between performance and stated contract requirements, the local government must communicate verbally and in writing with the contractor to ensure that expectations are clearly understood. In dealing with problems that will inevitably arise, the team should try not to assign blame but rather seek prompt and fair resolution. Failing to treat the contractor as an essential part of the local government's service delivery program can undermine the performance of even the best contractor. However, if the team and the contractor work together to address problems, enforcement of liquidated damages provisions, cancellation, and default can usually be avoided.

Most of the time of the contract administration team is spent resolving what may appear to be insignificant problems, such as crew members' inexperience, the improper placement of barricades, or faulty equipment. However, this is the proper use of the team's time because small problems unattended can easily escalate into major ones: an inexperienced crew member may cause a chemical spill, poorly placed barricades may cause a serious traffic accident, and faulty equipment may delay delivery of essential services. The contract administration team must be prepared to tackle all problems, whatever their size or source, to make the contract succeed.

This chapter first describes a five-stage approach to dealing with performance problems. It then covers steps that can be taken in case of default and offers guidelines on establishing a default contingency plan. It addresses debarment and suspension, which are actions to be taken in extreme cases (such as conviction of a contractor for a criminal offense related to obtaining a contract) to prohibit the contractor from participating in local government contracting. Because it is possible that the local government may be the source of poor performance, the next section describes five performance problems common among local governments and suggests ways to avoid them. The next chapter provides advice on how to proceed through contract termination and other transitions in service contracting.

> **Partnership**
>
> A contract for goods generally results in an impersonal relationship between a buyer and seller that is concerned solely with price and specifications. The buyer is interested more in the safe and timely delivery of the specified product than in how the product is manufactured, packaged, or shipped. In service contracting, the buyer-seller relationship is much more personal. The buyer and the seller are concerned with every facet of the service from raw material (labor and equipment) to the finished product (the delivered service). The successful service contracting relationship is a public-private partnership that is cooperative and interactive throughout.

Dealing with poor performance: A five-step plan

If a performance problem occurs, the contract administration team should address the problem immediately. Deal with it in a calm, rational manner and strive to resolve it at the lowest management level possible.

Dealing with a performance problem generally involves five steps. In the first step, the field manager attempts to resolve the problem by working directly with the contractor's on-site supervisor. If this is unsuccessful, the second step follows, in which the field or contract manager calls the contractor. The third step is more formal, involving meetings of the contract manager, field manager, and contractor. If the problem is still not resolved, the process moves to the fourth step, in which liquidated damages or similar provisions of the contract are put into effect.

The enforcement decision is usually the responsibility of the contract manager. No more than three weeks should pass between the time the problem is first identified and the decision to enforce is made. After consulting with the legal department, the contract manager mails a notice to the contractor requiring the problem to be corrected by a specified date, usually within ten days, and describing any liquidated damages or financial penalties authorized by the contract that the local government intends to assess after the notice period. The contractor is also advised that failure to comply will trigger cancellation of the contract.

If enforcement does not produce the desired result, the process moves to the fifth and final step: cancellation. All attempts to resolve the problem have failed, and action is taken to cancel the contract.

Of course, not every performance problem can be addressed strictly according to this model. In custodial, medical, food service, or other types of contracts that affect clients' health or welfare, the second and third steps may be eliminated. On the other hand, if a contractor promises to resolve a problem within a certain period and then fails to do so, the contract manager may choose to schedule additional meetings with the contractor rather than assess liquidated damages immediately. When the nature of the problem permits, it is best to use whatever time is necessary to resolve it. The nature of the problem and its impact on service delivery determine how and with what speed a performance problem is addressed.

In the example shown in the sidebar "The five-step process in action" on page 178, a company had been awarded a contract to repair, replace, and maintain sidewalks, curbs, and gutters. The contract required all work to be done according to the requirements published in a booklet put out by the local public works department. The circumstances are simple: the contractor failed to follow a requirement that new curbs and gutters match the existing curbs and gutters. The narrative

---

Due process and damages

Due process is the phrase to remember when considering enforcement of liquidated damages provisions or any other action against a contractor. If performance falls below an acceptable level and the contract administration team believes that assessing liquidated damages is warranted, the team should first consult the legal department before taking any action. Legal guidance is necessary to ensure that the local government's actions adhere to any state or local laws governing due process. For example, before assessing liquidated damages, the local government may be required to allow the contractor a specified period in which to correct performance. The contractor may be entitled to advance written notice of the local government's intent to make a cash deduction from the next payment due. All due process procedures set forth in the contract or in applicable laws or regulations must be followed to the letter.

---

details of the steps taken to resolve the problem, beginning with its initial discovery in the field and ending with the local government's declaration of default and cancellation of the contract. The next section of this chapter addresses default and explores options for dealing with it.

Handling default

If a contractor is performing poorly and is on the brink of default, the local government can either bide its time or cancel the contract.

Biding time

When the team has reached the conclusion that the contractor cannot fulfill the terms of the contract, monitoring must be intensified to the point that the contract administration team is, in effect, "carrying" the contractor to the end of the term or at least until the contract is re-bid and a new contractor is selected. Although this option creates more work for the contract administration team than cancellation does, this may be the only option available if one or more of the following conditions exist:

- The contractor does not have a performance bond or the contractor's bonding company refuses to acknowledge the validity of the local government's claim of default.
- There is no provider available to take the service for the rest of the contract term.
- The local government does not have the personnel, equipment, or funds available to provide the service in house.
- Only a few months remain in the contract term.

A local government forced to bide its time should put the experience to good use. Try to determine what went wrong and why, without assuming that the performance problems were solely the fault of an unqualified or inexperienced contractor. Use the remainder of the contract term to plan for a successful re-bid. Critically examine the quality of contract administration and its effect on the contractor's performance. Study the original scope of work: Did it include conditions or tasks that contributed to the contractor's poor performance? If the contract is too large or too complex for available contractors, simplify the scope of work or divide the service area into smaller sections before re-bidding the contract.

The five-step process in action

Step 1. Field contact

As is often the case in contract management, the local government field manager is the first to notice that the curbs and gutters installed by the contractor do not match the curbs and gutters described in the specifications. Instead, the contractor is casting the concrete in forms designed for the curb and gutter used in a nearby city. The field manager advises the contractor's onsite supervisor of the problem and proposes a quick solution: the local government will rent some of its surplus curb and gutter forms to the contractor until the contractor can obtain its own. The contractor's supervisor declines the offer and says that the home office will purchase the correct forms within ten days. The field manager orders the contractor to stop work on curbs and gutters meanwhile and directs the contractor to work only on sidewalk maintenance until the correct forms are received.

Two weeks later, the curb and gutter forms have not arrived. The contractor's on-site supervisor tells the field manager that he put in the request for the forms but that the home office did not order them. At this point, the field manager decides that the on-site supervisor cannot resolve the problem within a reasonable time and notifies the contract administrator of the problem and the action taken to date.

Step 2. Telephone call

After talking with the contract administrator, the field manager notifies the contractor's onsite supervisor by telephone of the problems encountered and asks for corrective action within a week. A week later, the curb forms still have not been delivered to the job site. The field manager makes a second telephone call to the contractor.

In a memorandum to the contract manager, the contract administrator and the field manager summarize all the actions taken to date. The contract manager prepares a written discrepancy report and mails it to the contractor, citing the contract provisions violated, establishing a one-week deadline for correction of the problem, and scheduling a meeting with the contractor at the end of the same week if performance does not improve by the stated deadline.

Step 3. Contractor meeting

By the end of the week, the curb forms have still not arrived. The contract manager, the field manager, the contractor's on-site supervisor, and a principal of the contractor attend the meeting called by the contract manager. Because action against the contractor could result from the meeting, minutes are taken.

The meeting begins with a statement of the specifics of the problem. The contractor is given the opportunity to explain why the problem still exists, what action has already been taken, and what further measures will be implemented. The contractor is reminded of the possible courses of action authorized by the contract documents if corrective action is delayed any further, including enforcement of liquidated damages provisions. The contractor is reminded of the failure to deliver clause in the contract, which permits the local government to have another contractor complete the work, charging any extra costs to the present contractor. The minutes of the meeting, including corrective actions proposed by the contractor, are sent to the contractor and to the contractor's bonding company.

Step 4. Enforcement

Still the contractor fails to obtain the required curb and gutter forms, and the contract manager issues a notice of default to the contractor with a copy to the bonding company requiring the contractor to correct the default within ten days.

Step 5. Cancellation

The contractor does not satisfy the conditions of the notice sent by the contract manager, thereby remaining in default.

The contract manager considers the do-nothing option but decides it is unacceptable. The replacement curbs and gutters cast in the contractor's forms do not match the profile of the existing curbs and gutters, and the difference is especially obvious where the new work abuts existing curbs and gutters. Moreover, because the local government forms do not match the contractor's forms, when the replacement curbs and gutters eventually require repair, demolition and removal of all of the contractor's work will be necessary. If the contractor had used the correct forms, simple repairs of short sections could have been made.

The contract manager therefore cancels the contract and initiates action through the legal department to attempt to collect enough of a settlement from the contractor's bonding company to finance the rebuilding of the curbs and gutters already installed and to complete the contract.

Canceling the contract

Canceling a contract is always a risky option. If the contractor contests the cancellation, the local government must have supporting documentation strong enough to convince a bonding company (if the contract required a performance bond) that the cancellation was valid and strong enough to support any litigation the local government may bring against the bonding company if it does not agree with the local government's position.

Never assume that a bonding company will come to the rescue of the local government. As an agent of the contractor and not of the local government, a bonding company may claim that the local government's cancellation is premature or unfounded. It is not unusual for a bonding company to defend the actions of the contractor and refuse to satisfy a local government's claim of contractor default. When this occurs, abandoning the default action, negotiating with the bonding company, or litigation are the only avenues open. Settling the issue through negotiation or litigation may take several months. This may be far too late to address the immediate problem of providing the contracted service.

Cancellation is an action of last resort and should be used only when contract performance has deteriorated or shows signs of deteriorating to the point that no other action—even biding time—is possible.

Default contingency plan

Every important contract should have a contingency plan to provide for continued service if a contractor defaults. Prudent contract managers plan for default even before award of the contract. A number of options are available for a default contingency plan: contracting with the next lowest bidder from the original solicitation, using

---

The default notice

If meetings, correspondence, and application of liquidated damages provisions do not improve performance and the local government feels that termination of the contract is the only viable course of action, a notice of default is issued, usually by the contract manager.

The first step in issuing the notice is to advise the legal department of the circumstances leading to the default; the legal department then prepares or reviews the notice to ensure that it conforms to contract and legal requirements.

A notice of default includes at least the following:

1. A description of the problem

2. A chronological recapitulation of events leading to the notice, including telephone calls and meetings with the contractor

3. A description of actions the contractor took to resolve the problem and their outcome

4. A statement that the contractor has defaulted and that the contract will be canceled if the default is not corrected completely by a specified date

5. Specific reference to the contract provisions that have been violated and that support the issuing of the notice.

If a bond was required of the contractor, the contractor's bonding company also receives a copy of the default notice. Although the bonding company should already have received copies of any previous correspondence related to the default notice, additional copies should be sent to the bonding company along with the notice of default.

another current contractor, delivering the service in house, and intergovernmental contracting. At least two possible courses of action should be included in any default contingency plan. When faced with default, implement the option that best suits the circumstances at the time of default.

Next lowest responsive and responsible bidder

The most common approach for replacing a defaulting contractor is to turn to the next lowest responsive and responsible bidder from the original solicitation. Put this option into place at the time of award. Ask the next lowest bidder if the firm will accept a backup award in the event of default. If the firm is large enough, it should have the capacity to mobilize resources needed to take over on relatively short notice. By openly making a formal backup award, the local government may help deter poor performance on the part of the firm awarded the contract. If the original contractor is terminated, the backup contractor will be available to deliver the service either for the balance of the original contract term or until a new contract can be awarded. Another advantage of issuing a formal backup award is that the backup bidder's original prices are held firm for the entire contract term.

When the local government does not make a formal backup award, negotiation may be required with the next lowest bidder to replace a defaulted contractor at a later date. If these negotiations take place in the first six months of the defaulting contractor's contract, the local government should contact the next lowest bidder to determine if they are able to assume the work at the price submitted with their original bid. However, if they take place toward the end of a service contract and only a short time remains in the contract term, the next lowest bidder may refuse to accept an award at the price originally submitted. Prices may have increased since the contract started, rendering the original price unprofitable. (Contractors often inflate prices to produce a higher profit margin during the first months of a contract. If costs escalate unexpectedly during the contract term, the higher prices help offset potential losses from the escalation.) If the next lowest bidder refuses to honor the original contract unit prices, it may be possible to negotiate a price under emergency award procedures or to apply an escalator to the original prices. Obtaining the service for at least the period needed to prepare and award a new contract may be well worth a reasonable price increase.

Using a current contractor

A default contingency plan is built into a contract awarded to several different contractors on a geographic or phased-in basis. If one of the contractors defaults, the others should be able to absorb the added work on short notice. If more than one contractor is available, either award the new work to the contractor that offers the best unit prices or split the work among the remaining contractors. If the other contractors cannot provide service for the rest of the contract term, a short-term commitment from one or more of them may be all that is needed to provide time to re-bid and award a new contract.

Delivering the service in house

Bringing the service in house is typically less feasible, even if the local government provided the service initially. However, if the local government has retained a portion of the contracted work or has enough equipment and trained staff to expand its service delivery capabilities rapidly, this option should be considered. The local government can later decide whether to keep the service in house or re-bid the contract.

If a service requires specialized equipment, it is wise to include in the default contingency plan a contract provision allowing the local government to buy back equipment from a contractor in case of default. The "Vehicle and equipment buyback" clause in Appendix A outlines a method for selling and transferring specialized equipment or vehicles used in the performance of the contract to the local government. To soften the impact on the budget, finance the buyback over the remaining life of the equipment or require the next contractor to assume payments for the equipment.

If the default contingency plan did not provide for a buyback clause, it may be possible to expand in-house capability by obtaining equipment locally; rental rates may be comparable to charges for vehicles in the in-house fleet.

Personnel from professionals to laborers may be available from temporary help contractors. To supervise and train temporary workers effectively and reduce the time it takes for them to master their assignments, pair them with experienced members of the in-house work force.

Intergovernmental contracting

Establish a mutual assistance plan with a regional or neighboring local government in which the governments agree to pool their resources if one is faced with service disruption resulting from emergencies, disaster, or a defaulting contractor. Staff or equipment from a neighboring local government may also be available under a rental or direct cost reimbursement agreement. If the other local government has a similar contract with the private sector, an emergency award to their contractor can solve the problem until the defaulted contract is re-bid.

Debarment and suspension

Debarment and **suspension** are similar procedures that local governments use to prohibit a contractor from participating in local government solicitations. The

---

Reasons for debarment or suspension

To determine whether debarment or suspension is appropriate, most local governments use guidelines similar to those set forth in the American Bar Association's *Model Procurement Code for State and Local Governments*. The ABA guidelines list the following as possible reasons for debarment or suspension:

- Conviction of the contractor for commission of a criminal offense as an incident to obtaining or attempting to obtain a public or private contract or subcontract

- Conviction of the contractor for embezzlement, theft, forgery, bribery, falsification or destruction of records, receiving stolen property, or any other offense indicating a lack of business integrity or business

honesty which currently, seriously, and directly affects responsibility as a local government contractor

- Conviction under state or federal antitrust statutes arising out of the submission of bids or proposals

- Violation of contract provisions of a character that is regarded by the local government to be so serious as to justify debarment, including a deliberate failure without good cause to perform in accordance with specifications or within the time limit provided or a recent record of unsatisfactory contract performance

- Any other cause the local government determines to be so serious and compelling as to affect responsibility as a contractor for the local government, including debarment by another governmental entity.

Source: Adapted from American Bar Association, *The Model Procurement Code for State and Local Government* (Chicago, Ill.: American Bar Association, 2000), Article 9, Parts A and D; Article 12, Part D.

grounds for debarment or suspension are very broad, ranging from unsatisfactory performance to the contractor's conviction for a criminal offense.

Debarment

Debarment, the more formal and severe of the two processes, prohibits business dealings with the local government, usually for at least two years and occasionally for an indefinite period. Debarment is the usual course of action for major violations of the guidelines provided by the American Bar Association (see the "Reasons for debarment or suspension" sidebar). If debarment is considered, legal assistance is required to guide the local government through the administrative procedures that state and local laws require and to establish a solid defense against any future legal action by the contractor against the local government.

The procedure for debarment includes sending written notice to the contractor of the decision to debar that gives the reasons for the proposed debarment and advises the contractor of any rights to a judicial review or administrative hearing guaranteed by state or local law. Local laws or regulations generally require that a formal hearing with the contractor precede the final debarment decision.

Debarment is, in effect, a finding of nonresponsibility that can damage a contractor's reputation and chances for future contract awards unless it is overturned. Thus, a contractor is likely to challenge a debarment decision. The larger the firm, the more likely it is to take legal action against the local government. Expect challenges from larger corporations even if the debarment action is based on a gross violation of the contract or otherwise clearly meets the ABA guidelines for debarment.

Suspension

Suspension of a contractor follows a written finding by a local government that the contractor should be denied participation in local government solicitations for a specific period, generally six to twelve months. The decision to suspend is made by the local government manager or purchasing official after review of the written finding by the legal department. A formal hearing with the contractor is usually not required. However, local laws and regulations may permit the suspended contractor to request a hearing. Because the period during which the contractor cannot participate in local government business is shorter for suspension than for debarment, requests for hearings or legal challenges to suspension decisions are rare. However, larger and more sophisticated firms may view any suspension decision as sufficient reason to protest or initiate legal action to overturn the decision.

Poor local government performance

When the local government fails to meet its contract obligations and that failure affects the quality of the contractor's performance, the local government is encouraging contract disputes and may be paving the way for the contractor to abandon the contract. For example, a local government is obligated to provide correct information and specified support services to the contractor and to pay the contractor within the time promised. If it fails to do so, the contractor may have the right to stop work or terminate the contract. Moreover, a local government that contributes to or causes a default by failing to follow its contract obligations may develop a reputation for poor payment, sloppy performance, or unfair dealings and may then have a difficult time attracting qualified bidders.

The issues most likely to lead to additional contract costs or action against the local government are slow payment, denial of access to the work site, delays in reviews or approvals, changes in the work schedule, and excessive conflict between the contract administration team and the contractor.

Slow payment

The contractor has a right to be paid for work performed and accepted within the time promised in the contract documents. Failure to meet payment schedules may force the contractor to borrow money to meet payroll or pay suppliers, which can cut into the contractor's profit. More important, delayed payments can affect the contractor's ability to keep full work crews and equipment available for delivery of the contracted service.

Occasional delays at the department level in approving and forwarding the contractor's invoices for payment are inevitable, but this problem is often compounded by the local government's accounts payable procedures. To ensure that payment requests are processed quickly enough to clear the accounts payable, purchasing, or budget review procedures by the time payment is due to the contractor, the contract manager must ensure that no delays in payment occur at the department level by enforcing strict limits on the time for department review of the invoices.

Denial of access to work site

Denial of access to a work site can occur when a recreation event conflicts with the date scheduled for landscape maintenance, when a building superintendent fails to unlock a facility scheduled for service, or on a holiday. The field manager must notify the contractor of any conditions that could hamper access to a work site and cooperate with the contractor to resolve any problems quickly and effectively.

Delays in reviews and approvals

Required local government reviews of contract deliverables such as draft reports, budgets, and completed work must be made within the time established in the contract. Delays in approvals can be costly to a contractor, particularly when the next phase of performance cannot be started until the review is complete. Because contractors schedule their employees' workloads far in advance, failure to provide timely reviews or approval may mean that employees are idle while the contractor waits for the local government to make a decision, conduct an inspection, or approve a critical document. Local government delays are a major cause of contractors' demands for additional compensation.

Work schedule changes

Advise the contractor well in advance of any planned changes in the work schedule to allow time for the contractor to plan for effective use of its work force. The contract is often only one of many accounts served by the contractor, so the contractor may be unable to accommodate sudden schedule changes.

Conflict with the contract administration team

The contract manager must monitor the contract administration team members to make sure that they do not overstep their authority or harass or antagonize a contractor. Personality conflicts between the contractor's crews or supervisors and members of the team are not uncommon, but if such conflicts are not resolved they can lead to deterioration in contract performance. The contract manager must ensure that the contract administration team members perform their duties objectively and without personal bias.

10

Transitions in Service Contracting

This chapter offers guidelines for handling four types of transition likely to be encountered by a local government: contracting for a new service, changing an established service from one contractor to another, renewing a contract, and changing from private to public service delivery. Two alternatives to private sector contracting are also discussed: public-private competition and optimization, or public provision of services with an eye on lessons from the private sector.

Contracting for a new service

Contracting for a new service is seldom trouble free, and the problems associated with it may come from unexpected quarters. For example, contrary to expectation, labor organizations seldom protest contracting out unless the new service encroaches on or is very similar to an in-house service. Elected officials often prefer contracting out to increasing the number of employees on the local government payroll, and citizens are more interested in the quality and cost of a service than in the identity of the deliverer. The problems that arise in planning and implementing a contract for a new service stem primarily from three other sources: contractors' inexperience, internal opposition from managers and middle managers in the department that would provide the service if it were delivered in house, and inexperience on the part of local government staff.

Contractors' inexperience

Local governments in or near large metropolitan areas seldom have difficulty finding experienced contractors. Smaller, rural, and more isolated local governments that cannot find enough experienced contractors can use a number of strategies. They can conduct a market search, develop intergovernmental agreements, limit the scope of work, and allow contractors to learn on the job.

Conduct a market search Do not restrict the market search for a contractor to the local area. Use bidder lists from other local governments to conduct a statewide search for firms that may be interested in expanding into new geographical areas.

Develop intergovernmental agreements   Pooling the requirements of several adjacent local governments may yield a multijurisdictional service contracting package large enough to attract regional or national firms. Similarly, if another local government has extra capacity and can provide the service at a reasonable price, contracting directly with that local government may be an option.

Limit the scope of work   Conduct a written survey of area contractors who deliver the type of service desired and invite each contractor to an interview to determine the level of experience and expertise available. If the survey and interviews indicate that the scope of the new service is too broad or too complex or covers too great a geographical area and that no state, regional, or national contractors are interested, consider reducing the size or complexity to match the capabilities of area contractors. A limited scope of work may be the best approach when a local government first contracts out. After the contractor has gained some experience, it may be possible to increase the contract to its original scope.

For example, although traffic island maintenance contracts are usually envisioned to include total maintenance of every traffic island in the community including decorative islands, a contract of this scope is often scaled back once the local market is surveyed. The market may contain many contractors who can perform small-scale general maintenance such as mowing, watering, and trimming, but qualified contractors who can provide both basic maintenance and landscaping of the decorative traffic islands that appear in almost every community may be rare.

Allow contractors to learn on the job   If available contractors can perform the basic service but do not have the special skills desired, plan to allow the contractor to learn on the job by phasing in the more difficult tasks or areas of responsibility one at a time.

For example, in a traffic island maintenance program, if available contractors do not have the skills to handle the maintenance of decorative islands, the contract can be structured so that the islands are added to the contract gradually over two or three years as the contractor's crews are trained and their skills improve. The local government can provide thirty to sixty days' instruction in any special techniques required. Close supervision during and after the training period is needed to ensure that the crews meet the local government's standards for maintenance of traffic islands. To accommodate this process, the contract must provide for increases in the contract price as the workload is increased and the skills of the contractor's crews improve. Incentive payments can be included to compensate the contractor for meeting standards within a pre-established period.

In a market where few or no firms have the requisite experience, contract terms should be for at least three years to enable the local government to obtain the benefits of the investment made in educating the contractor. The disadvantage of a long-term contract is that when the contract comes up for re-bid, the current contractor may be the only one qualified to provide the service and the contract may have to be negotiated on a sole source basis. It is also possible that after two or three years, the competitive environment will have changed enough to allow competitive purchase of the service.

Internal opposition

The problems that can result from internal opposition to a service contract from department and middle managers are noted in Chapter 1. The impact is usually minor but can sometimes be a serious impediment to the success of a contract. If opposition creates significant problems, management should consider assigning contract management responsibility to a centralized contract manager, thus preventing a department manager who opposes the contract from having control over it.

Inexperienced local government staff

The best strategy for dealing with inexperience on the part of local government staff is to obtain training for them. Many consulting firms provide training for contract administration teams and can also provide technical advice to the scope-of-work team. All that should be required for a local government to develop an effective contract administration team is training followed by periodic reviews of the team's progress by the consultant.

Changing from one contractor to another

When a contract changes hands, the contract administration team is likely to face two problems. The first problem is deterioration of the current contractor's performance as the current contract term comes to an end, extending in some cases even to sabotage. The second problem is uneven performance by the new contractor at the beginning of the new contract term.

Deterioration of performance

Intentional damage to property or disruption of service delivery is rare, but it is likely to be the act of an angry current contractor when it does occur. If deliberate sabotage is suspected, immediately report the incidents to the appropriate agencies for investigation. For example, fire or police departments should be notified of mysterious fires, property damage, or missing personal or public property. A sudden drop in revenue from a concession stand should generate an immediate audit by the local government. Swift official action and intensified monitoring can deter more serious sabotage of local government operations.

Some degree of deterioration of performance is to be expected when a contractor loses a re-bid. Few contractors are happy to turn over a profitable contract to a competitor. The strategies described in the next four sections can be of help in improving performance that is poor enough to affect the quality of service.

Use the threat of a bad reference   Threatening to give the contractor a poor reference for future work is seldom an effective means of improving performance. A bidder that is asked for references by a potential employer will simply exclude previous employers who might give a poor report. The threat will likely be effective, however, if the local government informs the contractor that unless performance improves, a report will be sent to local trade organizations and chambers of commerce and the purchasing offices of nearby local governments.

Regional public purchasing organizations, such as the procurement committees of councils of governments, should be encouraged to maintain a file of contractors their members use, including members' evaluations of the contractors' performance. A clearinghouse at the regional level enables any member local government to find out about other members' experiences with a contractor, including those members that a contractor would be reluctant to include in a list of references.

Intensify monitoring   At the first sign of deteriorating performance, step up monitoring. Review performance expectations with the contractor and establish a schedule for follow-up reviews of the contractors' performance. The field manager may need to temporarily increase the frequency of site visits to monitor the contractor's progress in performance. The field manager must provide regular progress reports to the contract administrator, who in turn should communicate with the contractor's on-site supervisor to report whether the contractor is meeting expectations about performance improvement.

Enforce liquidated damages provisions Strictly enforce any liquidated damages provisions of the contract. If there are no specific liquidated damages provisions in the contract and the contractor's work does not meet performance standards, withhold from payments due the contractor an amount equal to the value of the difference between the work actually performed and the work required by the contract. Do not pay full price for partial performance.

Terminate the contract The threat of early termination, which can cost the current contractor a considerable sum of money, may be effective in restoring service quality. If performance is poor enough to seriously disrupt the service and the threat of termination fails to produce results, do not hesitate to follow through and cancel the contract: simply issue an amendment to extend the new contractor's term by the amount of time left on the incumbent's contract and start the new contractor earlier than the scheduled starting date.

If the performance of the current contractor is deteriorating badly, send a written notice to the new contractor with a copy to the incumbent contractor. This action may be advantageous to the local government for several reasons. First, a written notice prepares the new contractor for the possibility that the new contract will begin earlier than originally planned. Second, the notice indicates to the new contractor the strength of the local government's commitment to performance standards.

Uneven performance

Expect problems when a new contractor first begins the contract term. The contractor needs time to become accustomed to local government policies and procedures and the details of the service.

There are a number of ways to smooth the transition from one contractor to another. One is to monitor intensively and supportively, particularly during the first thirty days of the contract term. A second strategy is to ensure that good documentation of contract activities is made available to the new contractor.

Good documentation of past contract activity must be planned for in advance. The contract administration team must ensure that all required reports of contract activity are clear and accurate and in a format that can be used by subsequent contractors. Documentation of contract activities should be created and stored electronically, and such files should be made available to the new contractor.

Changing contractors can be an especially difficult process if the contractor owns specific equipment that is essential to the delivery of the service. If the local government plans to contract for a critical service on an ongoing basis, it may be in the local government's best interest to retain ownership of essential infrastructure, such as computer hardware and software, and lease it to the service contractor. Then if it becomes necessary to change contractors, the local government can do so with minimal disruptions to service continuity. The accompanying sidebar describes how one city has successfully used this approach.

Infrastructure ownership eases transitions in contractors: Weston, Florida

The city of Weston, Florida, has a population of 63,000 and contracts for public and private providers for all of its services. Realizing the importance of service continuity in the event that it became necessary to change contractors, the city has moved toward retaining ownership of essential infrastructure needed to perform the work. For example, the city contracts with a firm to do its accounting, accounts receivable/payable, and budgets. In the past the work was done on the contractor's hardware and software, but when the city contemplated changing contractors, it realized that changing software and data from one contractor to another was a complex, cumbersome, and time-consuming task. At that point, Weston determined that it was essential for the city to own the hardware and software so it would have the ability to change contractors in a relatively short period of time and still maintain continuity in data management abilities. The city ultimately chose to purchase the hardware and software necessary to perform the work and lease it to the contractor.

Source: John Flint, city manager of Weston, Florida.

The city also contracts with the county sheriff for emergency medical, fire protection, and fire prevention services. In the past, the sheriff's department has provided the emergency medical services and fire apparatus and charged the city for the apparatus as part of the contract. However, the city became concerned when the sheriff's budget failed to allow for replacement of the aging apparatus for a period of several years. In an effort to ensure that the city's residents are served with the best emergency medical services and fire apparatus, the city chose to lease brand-new apparatus from the manufacturer and have the sheriff's employees operate the equipment. The sheriff will no longer charge the city for apparatus within the contract. This gives the city control over how the equipment will be used, including for mutual aid purposes.

Lessons learned: Consider the infrastructure needed when contracting for services. It is a lot easier to change people than it is to change infrastructure. Control the infrastructure when it comes to services that will be needed on an ongoing basis.

Renewing a contract

Either of two types of renewal clauses may be included in a contract. The first is renewal at the discretion of the local government and the second is renewal with contractor right to decline. Renewal occurs at the local government's discretion in either case, but in the second type, the contractor is not obligated to accept the local government's offer of another contract term. This section offers suggestions for proper timing of the decision to renew, which is necessary to make the best use of the renewal option.

If renewal is anticipated, the local government should include in the original contract a clause that allows it to exercise a renewal option (see Chapter 5). The contract may specify renewal prices, terms, and conditions identical to those pertaining to the original contract term or it may specify an escalator or other formula to calculate firm prices for subsequent years.

In a service area where costs may change quickly (e.g., a contract requiring extensive vehicle use when gasoline prices are fluctuating rapidly), a renewal clause requiring the contractor to maintain the same price for a second contract year usually permits the contractor the option of declining to renew. Concern about rapid fluctuations in price might make a contractor reluctant to agree to a firm price for a second year, and the option of declining gives the contractor an alternative. In the event that prices do not fluctuate during the contract term and the contractor therefore accepts the renewal option, the local government has spared itself the costs of re-bidding and possibly starting from scratch with a new contractor.

When a published escalator is used to determine successive years' pricing in a multiyear contract or in one with an option to renew, the contract document must include three key dates:

- The escalator date—the date used to calculate the prices for the subsequent year's contract
- The anniversary date of the contract—the date on which the contract expires unless the local government has taken action to renew
- The decision date—the date by which the contractor must decide whether to accept a renewal offer.

The decision process begins long before the decision date. At least thirty days before the decision date (and well before that for essential services), the local government must decide whether it wants to renew the contract. If it does and if the contractor cannot decline the offer, the contract costs for the renewal year are calculated according to the original contract formula and the contractor is notified of the renewal. If the local government decides to renew a contract and the contractor has the option to decline, the local government sends the contractor a notice of its intent to renew that includes the contract costs of the renewal year. The contractor is asked to respond no later than the decision date established by the local government. When negotiation is permitted, notice should be sent at least ninety days before the anniversary date to allow time to negotiate the cost of the services for the renewal year.

The contract must include enough time between the decision date and the anniversary date to allow the local government to re-bid the contract if it chooses not to renew or if the contractor declines the renewal offer. If a local government does not want to exercise an option to renew—for example, because the escalator applied to the original price yields an unacceptable price increase—but the contract does not allow sufficient time for a re-bid, the local government may nevertheless be forced to accept another contract year at excessive prices.

Ideally, the escalator date should be three or four months before the anniversary date. If the Consumer Price Index (CPI) is used as the escalator, a four-month lead time is required. In the following example, the escalator date is based on the March CPI, which is not published until the end of April: so the decision date is May 1. A May 1 decision to cancel the contract allows ninety days to re-bid before the contract expires on July 31.

Escalator date	April 25 (receipt of March CPI data)
Decision date	May 1
Anniversary (expiration) date	July 31

If a contract does not include an escalator clause and renewal is authorized only if the contractor maintains the prices, terms, and conditions that applied to the preceding year, the decision date should still precede the anniversary date by at least ninety days. As noted earlier, contracts that require that original prices, terms, and conditions be maintained generally allow the contractor to decline the renewal offer, and time must be allowed for a re-bid in case the contractor decides not to renew.

Changing from private to public service delivery

As noted in the introduction to this chapter, the transition from contracting out to in-house service delivery may be planned or unexpected. An unexpected transition may occur for a number of reasons: the current contractor may default, a re-bid may yield no responses, or the decision to renew may have been delayed and there may not be enough time to re-bid the service. Unless the local government has retained some in-house capacity or can otherwise mobilize other internal resources on short notice, it will likely be very difficult or impossible bring services back in house unexpectedly. If the local government's default contingency plan includes absorbing some of the work of failed contractors, it is necessary to ensure that sufficient in-house capacity exists. Establish the default contingency plan early in the contract term and update it at least every year of the contract term and more frequently if possible.

The next sections address two ways of returning from private delivery of service to public delivery of service: through public-private competition and through planned transition to optimized public service delivery.

Public-private competition[1]

In recent years, dissatisfaction with service contracting has led some local governments to reestablish themselves as the principal deliverers of services formerly contracted out. Among others, Phoenix, Arizona; Indianapolis, Indiana; Philadelphia, Pennsylvania; and Cincinnati, Ohio, have all found that services previously contracted out can be delivered at less cost by establishing more efficient and effective internal service delivery systems.[2]

For local governments to compete successfully with the private sector, they must first acknowledge that the private sector knows something about service delivery that works. If local governments can obtain that knowledge and incorporate it into public service delivery, competitive public service delivery can follow.

Public-private competition (also known as managed competition and in-house bidding) has become an increasingly popular procurement approach. Public-private competition is a formal service procurement method in which public employees compete with the for-profit and nonprofit private sectors to provide services. The goal is to obtain the best value for the public, whether that value is obtained through a public or a private service provider.

Generally, public-private competition focuses on three service delivery objectives: best quality at the lowest cost, performance outcomes that meet or exceed expectations, and increased accountability. In many cases, governmental agencies have successfully competed against private bidders. In other cases, private providers are found to be the best alternative.

According to public-private competition experts, there may be other benefits to a public-private competition than saving money.[3] First, administrators and the municipal staff must determine exactly what work they accomplish on a daily basis. While this may seem easy, service delivery departments often find aspects of the work being completed that they never realized existed or discover employee problems that administrators were unaware of. This information can benefit both the department providing the service and citizens receiving the service.

Second, during a competition, public service employees are encouraged to suggest ways of improving efficiency in their daily work. As the department matches budget dollars to tasks performed and involves employees in the process, the creative ideas of employees can be improve work processes. If employees feel that managing administrators are listening to their ideas, a more cohesive workplace is fostered.

Third, public-private competition can dispel the perception that management salaries will be higher if the managing administrator has a larger staff and an inflated budget. If management compensation is based on performance and not on the dollars allocated to a departmental budget, then the public-private competition process encourages management to compete with the private sector without fear of losing influence or compensation as costs are reduced.

Fourth, public-private competition motivates employees to participate and contribute with increased energy and incentive to enhance the overall functioning of the municipality. Increased feedback on performance, clearer goals, and a sense of pride in the local government are part of the process.

Fifth, if the public entity competes and wins, it may be able to share cost savings with employees. Gain-sharing (profit-sharing) dollars can be a large part of an employee's compensation.

Public-private competition can encounter the same obstacles to implementation that privatization of service delivery encounters, including employee resistance to change, fear of layoffs, and lack of technical expertise to fully allocate costs for services in order to establish a credible evaluation, auditing, and monitoring process. In addition, the department that is bidding to provide a service may have trouble finding time to establish a competitive proposal that has a realistic chance of success.

Getting started

Success in a public-private competition depends heavily on the cooperation and commitment of the public employees ultimately responsible for delivering the service.

Consultants can also be a valuable resource in helping public service delivery organizations improve cost and task management so that they can compete successfully with the private sector. If there is no in-house expertise available, a professional cost management expert may be required to analyze the costs of private sector and public sector service delivery. It may also be helpful to hire a consulting firm with proven experience in private and public sector cost management. A consultant who understands the inner workings of private sector delivery systems may also be helpful. Several national accounting firms offer this type of assistance to local governments. Professional associations such as the Government Finance Officers Association (GFOA) and the International City/County Management Association (ICMA) may also be of assistance.

To ensure a credible and sound process, it is important that procedures be in place for each specific proposal to provide a level playing field, one that neither favors nor disadvantages any offeror, including the public entity. When the public sector advantages of not having to make a profit and not having to pay taxes are considered in the context of providing a level playing field, debate often ensues. Both the public and private sectors have inherent advantages that should be considered apart from the process issues that constitute a valid level playing field. The "Leveling the playing field" sidebar highlights these issues.[4]

It is important to determine at the outset how the process will work. Who within the local government will be responsible for writing specifications and overseeing the bid process? Who will serve on the evaluation panel that determines the contract award? A list of steps in the public-private competitive process is provided in the sidebar on page 194.

The public bid

A scope-of-work team should be formed to help develop specifications, conduct prequalification screening, and evaluate all proposals received. Chapter 4 provided

Leveling the playing field

A number of process issues are critical to a sound public-private competition process. Lawrence Martin offers the following checklist:

Process issue	Tends to favor public sector	Competitively neutral	Tends to favor private sector
Sequential process	✓		
Parallel process		✓	
Public sector has access to consultants		✓	
Public sector does not have access to consultants			✓
Bid and proposals from the public sector are independently reviewed		✓	
Bid and proposals from the public sector are not independently reviewed	✓		
Purchaser and provider functions are separated		✓	
Purchaser and provider functions are not separated	✓		

Source: Adapted from Lawrence L. Martin, *Determining a Level Playing Field for Public-Private Competition* (Washington, D.C.: Pricewaterhouse Coopers Endowment for the Business of Government, 1999).

a detailed discussion of the scope of work. Members of the contract administration team should consult this chapter and ensure that all other important considerations are addressed in the scope of work when soliciting public-private competitive bids/proposals.

One thing that is unique to public-private competition is the need to create a "firewall" between the evaluation team and those involved with the development of the public bid to ensure a level playing field.[5] Failure to establish a sound firewall may create an unfair advantage for the public employees in the bid process, which compromises the integrity of the bid process and gives private sector providers a disincentive to bid the next time around. The bid evaluation team may be comprised of local government administrators, but these must be persons whose interests favor getting the best value at the lowest cost. In other words, the bid evaluation team must be clearly separated from the public employees who are bidding on the service. The evaluation team might include the following:

1. A management-level staff person from the department that would ordinarily provide the service
2. Members of the contract administration team overseeing the current contract
3. Representatives of other departments that may be affected by the transfer of the service in house
4. A representative of the internal auditing department
5. When needed, the services of a consultant.

The public bid is least likely to come under criticism if the finance or auditing department is heavily involved in preparing the bid response. Under this method, the department submitting the bid prepares staffing and equipment plans and presents them to the reviewing department (auditing or finance), which then verifies the calculation of the costs necessary to cover in-house provision of the service. If funds are available, an outside accounting or auditing firm can cost out the service. Using an outside accounting or auditing firm may help reduce errors in cost estimation that public bidders sometimes make.

Alternatively, the audit or finance department can draft the entire bid response, involving the service delivery department that knows the service the best in order to develop a sound bid. Whatever the approach to preparation of the bid document, the local government bid must be supported by documentation showing all direct and indirect costs expected to be incurred during the contract term. The local government should also distinguish fixed from variable costs and not consider the costs included by the public bidder that are ongoing expenses for the local government regardless of whether the public or private bidder wins the contract.

Prior actual expenses should serve as the primary guide for preparation of a competitive bid. The previous year's budget is of interest, but expenses from a recent

---

Steps in the public-private competition process

Public-private competition is a formal service procurement method in which public employees compete with the private for-profit and nonprofit sectors to provide services. The following describe the basic steps taken by local government administrators when allowing the local government workforce to compete with the private sector to provide a service.

Step 1: Determine the scope of service

A. Determine that a service should be subjected to competition.

B. Discuss the service with customers to determine their expectations and possible concerns.

C. Decide if all or only a portion of the service should be included in the proposal.

D. Determine the contract period.

E. Define the current service level.

F. Modify, re-engineer, or retain the existing service delivery method.

Step 2: Provide internal notification of decision to compete

A. Discuss with employees who are currently delivering the service of the local government's decision to compete and get their input.

B. Clearly define policy issues.

C. Notify any applicable citizen or advisory committee and city manager or county manager of the local government's decision to compete.

Step 3: Develop a draft RFP

A. Identify who will be responsible for preparing specifications.

B. Decide whether the proposal will be drafted by an interdisciplinary team, existing staff, or a consultant or some combination of these three.

C. Collect sample RFPs from other cities. Identify and benchmark the service with other comparable cities and private providers.

D. Ensure that all competition guidelines are followed.

E. Ensure that other local government policies are followed.

F. Define performance criteria and ensure that the local government can meet the same criteria.

G. Identify, reference, and attach all applicable ordinances, charter provisions, interlocal agreements, and federal, state, and local laws pertinent to the service to be proposed.

Step 4: Prepare for transition

A. Prepare a transition plan for changing service provider(s) and begin to identify the costs of changing service providers.

B. Determine how the service and the service contract will be administered and monitored.

C. Develop a contingency plan for service delivery if the local government loses the bid and the private sector contractor subsequently defaults.

(continued on page 195)

period are a better indication of future expenses than estimates that were prepared eighteen to twenty-four months earlier. Audited results are preferred but may not be as timely.

If the bid relies on actual local government expenditures, budget reconciliation (recent actual expenses compared to the proposed budget) is required to explain increases or decreases in each significant line item. Small items need not be explained, but generally differences greater than 10 percent or $10,000 need at least a brief comment. It may be helpful to include one or more prior years of actual expense data to better understand expenditure trends.

Supplies (and some services) that are purchased in quantity or under contract may require special documentation. When possible, bids should be based on long-term contracts that will fix the price of items such as chemicals or asphalt (or the specific service). The lack of a contract should be explained, and projections will

---

(continued from page 194)

D. Determine employee impact should the service be awarded to the private sector and begin to develop a plan to address it.

Step 5: Finalize the RFP

A. Decide whether or not to prequalify bidders.

B. Take the draft RFP to committees, as applicable, with any outstanding issues.

C. Develop and conduct the prequalification process. The internal audit department may assist in determining prequalification criteria.

D. Finalize the RFP.

Step 6: Develop a schedule for implementation

Develop a schedule/timetable that carries the process from completion of the RFP through the day of contract implementation.

Step 7: Complete the requests for proposals process

A. Issue the final RFP. If prequalification was used, issue the RFP to qualified vendors only.

B. Conduct the proposal process.

Step 8: Make a local government proposal

A. Finalize total local government costs per competition guidelines.

B. Finalize the transition plan and costs per competition guidelines.

C. Finalize the monitoring plan and costs per competition guidelines.

D. Finalize the employee impact statement and costs per competition guidelines.

E. Obtain review and approval of public proposal/proposal at the appropriate level (internal audit, etc.) and negotiate changes as necessary.

F. Finalize the proposal.

G. Sign and seal proposal and submit the sealed proposal to the agency receiving proposals prior to the deadline. Include information on total public entity costs, transition costs, employee impact costs, and monitoring costs.

Step 9: Appoint an evaluation team

Appoint an evaluation team to evaluate proposals.

Step 10: Receive and open proposals

Step 11: Evaluate proposals

Step 12: Make recommendations

Evaluation team makes recommendations to the citizen or advisory committee, as applicable.

Step 13: Award the contract

Step 14: Begin the contract period

A. Begin monitoring and administering the contract.

B. Prepare reports as appropriate, including reports on actual costs, contractor performance, customer satisfaction, and so forth, to departments, the governing board, and committees, as applicable.

Cost accounting

Steps in the development of a cost accounting system that can support public bidding on service delivery include:

A. Define/determine variable costs (costs that go away), semi-variable costs (costs that may go away if additional services are outsourced), fixed costs, and standard billing rates.

B. Determine what costs to track and include (avoidable costs).

C. Develop a cost control system.

D. Track budget to actual performance.

E. Define a process for tracking actual costs after the proposal is won or lost.

F. Use information on the next proposal process.

G. Include costs of managing/inspecting in-house or contracted service.

H. Make sure that management has all cost information as a tool for refinements.

I. Give each department an opportunity to use their own cost accounting system. Verify that the system is adequate.

J. Present cost may include:
   a. Employees
      1. Wages (per hour)
      2. Benefit costs (per hour)
   b. Equipment, tools, and vehicles
      1. Original cost and expected life (determine cost per /hour)
      2. Maintenance cost (per hour)
      3. Fuel cost
   c. Facilities
      1. Rent/depreciation
      2. Utilities
   d. Materials
      1. Identify materials/costs

K. Develop appropriate interdepartmental chargeback systems when necessary for allocation of the service cost, cost of contract, cost of contract administration, conversion costs, and asset loss or gain.

L. Have a schedule of standard billing rates for personnel and equipment to be used in preparing estimates.

M. Make sure that all data is current information and is entered only once in the system. Tie payroll time reporting and cost accounting into one system.

N. Report to employees on a timely basis what their actual costs have been and the target costs of the contract.

need to be based on industry and trend analysis and/or economic forecasts from reliable sources rather than on an arbitrary percentage increase.

Monitoring costs must also be considered. Whether the public entity or an outside contractor performs the service, the public entity will need to monitor the performance. The impact of public-private competition on internal monitoring costs (administration) should be considered during the process that is used to determine whether competition is a viable alternative. This determination may need to include consultation with the internal audit or finance departments to reach an understanding of what documentation will be required to meet verification requirements.[6]

If the local government is the lowest bidder, the other bidders will probably want proof that the department's offer includes all the costs of providing the service and may request copies of the department's bid response and supporting documentation. Department bids that do not include all costs are quickly challenged. Typical costs to consider when preparing the local government bid response are listed in the sidebar on the opposite page. Once the department's price is established, it is sealed and is to be opened simultaneously with the responses from private contractors. The department price, whether it is prepared in house or by an outside consulting firm, is confidential and is not disclosed to anyone—including department employees—until the bid opening.

Cost items for government services

Salaries and wages	Safety equipment
Direct labor (labor used in direct delivery of service, including full-time, part-time, and seasonal employees)	Uniforms
	Travel to meetings
Other labor (clerical support, the cost of providing contract and department management)	Recruitment costs
	Office equipment
Overtime	Equipment purchases and maintenance
Outside assistance (e.g., consultants)	Computer hardware and software
Expected salary increases during contract term	Fleet operations
Fringe benefits	Operation, repair, and maintenance
Paid holidays, sick leave, vacation	Vehicle depreciation
Pension contributions	Vehicle rental charges
Longevity pay, incentives, bonuses, awards	Vehicle insurance
Social Security	Interdepartmental charges
Workers' compensation insurance	Personnel
Health and life insurance	Finance
Unemployment insurance	Data processing
Expected benefits increases during contract term	Purchasing
Materials, supplies, utilities	Custodial
Rent	Liability insurance
Utilities	Capital expenses
Operating materials and supplies	Facility construction
Printing and related costs	Major renovations
Postage	Fleet purchases, including finance charges

Source: The cost components listed are drawn in part from John Tepper Marlin, *Contracting Municipal Services: A Guide for Purchase for the Private Sector* (New York: John Wiley & Sons, 1984); and Joseph T. Kelley, *Costing Government Services: A Guide for Decision Making* (Washington, D.C.: Government Finance Research Center, 1989).

Optimization

Methods of service delivery evolve over time. Local governments such as Charlotte, North Carolina, have learned through experience that service contracting can ebb and flow. Work previously let through competition may be transitioned back in house through a process of optimization, which returns public service delivery to the local government without consideration of private sector bids. Optimization involves using lessons learned from competing with the private sector and applying them to similar service areas in order to gain increased internal efficiencies.

Optimization is similar to public-private competition in a number of ways. Employees and management are working together to find the best way to perform the required service, and employees are working toward a common well-defined goal. Optimization provides an opportunity for managers to closely evaluate the work being done and re-engineer processes and personnel to do the required work in the most efficient manner. As with public-private competition, an internal audit provides timely feedback on job performance. This creates an atmosphere of entrepreneurship and an incentive for employees and managers to find new ways of work. The sidebar on page 198 highlights the process of optimization and the ways it differs from public-private competition.

Optimization versus public-private competition in Charlotte, North Carolina

Items for Consideration	Competition	Optimization
Employee risk	The employee's job is at risk to be eliminated to a private sector company.	The employee's job is not at risk to be outsourced, although efficiency gains may eliminate some positions.
The marketplace	The marketplace is tested each time for new companies, more aggressive pricing, and changes in the marketplace or in how services are delivered through new technology or work processes.	A current picture of market forces, available providers, technology improvements, and current costs is not available.
Budgeting for equipment	New equipment and personnel changes are planned and allocated in the budget process.	New equipment and personnel are not guaranteed.
Setting the bar for employee performance	The marketplace and the winning proposal set the benchmark for employee performance and the cost of services.	The benchmark for employee performance and the cost of providing services is estimated.
Gain-sharing	When the cost of services is less than the internal contract amount, employees can receive up to 50% of the difference.	When the cost of services is less than the internal contract amount, employees can receive up to 33% of the difference.

Transitioning between public and private service provision involves matters of equipment and staffing levels and therefore it requires significant planning. It is often difficult, especially in smaller local governments, to retain operating resources to bring a contracted service back in house. For this reason, it is critical that a strategic policy discussion be held about which services to contract and in what amounts.

Competitive services policies: Arlington, Texas

In 2002, the city of Arlington, Texas, adopted a competitive services policy to reduce costs and improve services. The policy requires that all city departments periodically review their services to determine ways to increase service quality, efficiency, and cost effectiveness. For each service, the department must determine which course of action to pursue:

• *Eliminate:* Discontinue provision of the service.

• *Retain:* Continue the program as it is currently operating if it is found to be efficient.

• *Reengineer:* Improve processes to reduce costs and retain the program or service.

• *Divest:* Transfer the program to an outside vendor or third party. The city no longer retains control of the program or service.

• *Outsource:* Let the work to an outside vendor while the city retains ultimate control of the program or service.

• *Enter managed competition:* Government employees compete with private sector vendors to win specific government service work. Under managed competition, the government providers and private firms compete to determine who is the most economic and efficient service provider for a municipality.

The department presents its findings to the competitive service steering committee, which includes the deputy city manager, finance manager, and human resources manager. If a service is designated for managed competition, city staff submit a proposal that is reviewed for price and quality along with proposals from outside contractors. If an outside contractor is selected, the contractor must agree to develop a plan for existing employees.

Source: *Ideas in Action* 10, no. 3 (Summer 2004).

Local governments may find it helpful to view transitions in service delivery as a dynamic process. Service delivery methods and providers can be changed if another approach is determined to be more efficient and be transitioned yet again to another method if the need arises over time. Recognizing this, some local governments are adopting "competitive services policies" that require city departments to periodically evaluate their services to detect ways to increase service quality, efficiency, and cost effectiveness. Ultimately, service delivery choices will depend on the specific needs and preferences of the local governments, its citizens, and the governing body, all of which inevitably change. It is important that the local government manager be aware of the various tools available for reducing service costs and improving quality; then the local government is able to select the approach to service delivery that best matches the local context and service delivery environment.

Endnotes

1 The editor wishes to thank Kim Eagle, evaluation manager, Charlotte, North Carolina, for substantial contributions to this chapter. Dr. Eagle is to be credited for providing much of the content on public-private competition and optimization and for the sidebars on pages 193-198.

2 Emmanuel S. Savas, *Privatization in the City: Successes, Failures, and Lessons* (Washington, D.C.: CQ Press, 2005).

3 City of Charlotte, *The Charlotte Story: Public Service Is Our Business* (Charlotte, N.C.: City of Charlotte, 2000), 57-71.

4 Lawrence L. Martin, *Determining a Level Playing Field for Public-Private Competition* (Arlington, Va.: PricewaterhouseCoopers Endowment for the Business of Government, 1999).

5 City of Charlotte, *The Charlotte Story,* 57-71.

6 "City of Charlotte Internal Audit: Guide to Competitive Bidding and Optimization," Charlotte, N.C., July 2006.

Appendix A

Clauses for service contracting documents

Appendix A includes alphabetically by title the complete texts of the service contracting clauses referenced throughout the book, particularly in Chapter 5. Unless otherwise noted, the clauses are designed to be used under competitive sealed bidding procedures. To alter a clause so that it can be used under competitive negotiation procedures, change the terms bid and bidder to offer and offeror, bid form to proposal form, invitation to bid to request for proposals, and so forth.

Many clauses require the inclusion of additional information. A word or phrase in square brackets indicates that the information identified is to be inserted (e.g., [time], [date], [name of local government]). Clarifications of clauses are in parentheses at the end of the clause.

Remember that no clause should be used until it has been reviewed by legal counsel for conformity with local laws and regulations.

Acknowledgment of amendments

Bidders shall acknowledge receipt of any amendment to the solicitation by signing and returning the amendment with the bid, by identifying the amendment number and date in the space provided for this purpose on the bid form, or by letter. The acknowledgment must be received by the [local government] by the time and at the place specified for receipt of bids.

Additional information

Questions about the contract portions of the bid document must be submitted in writing to [name of contact person] at [address/fax machine number]. Questions concerning the technical portions of the bid document should be directed to [name of contact person] at [address/fax machine number]. Bidders are cautioned that any statements made by the contract or the technical contact person that materially change any portion of the bid document shall not be relied upon unless subsequently ratified by a formal written amendment to the bid document. To find out whether the local government intends to issue an amendment reflecting a statement made by the contract or technical contact person, contact [name of person responsible for issuing amendments] at [telephone number]. No contract or technical questions will be accepted after seven (7) days prior to the date set for bid opening.

Alternative bids

Bidders offering service delivery methods other than those permitted by the scope of work may submit a separate envelope clearly marked "Alternative Bid." Alternative bids will be deemed nonresponsive and will not be considered for award. All such responses will, however, be examined prior to award. Such examination may result in cancellation of all bids received to permit rewriting the scope of work to include the alternative method, or the alternative method may be considered for future requirements of the [local government].

Antitrust

By entering into a contract, the contractor conveys, sells, assigns, and transfers to the [local government] all rights, titles, and interest it may now have or hereafter acquire under the antitrust laws of the United States and the [state] that relate to the particular goods or services purchased or acquired by the [local government] under said contract.

Applicable law

The contract shall be governed in all respects by the laws of the [state], and any litigation with respect thereto shall be brought in the courts of the [state]. The contractor shall comply with applicable federal, state, and local laws and regulations.

(Many legal departments require any law or regulation known to apply specifically to the contract to be identified in full in this clause.)

Assignment

The contractor shall not assign, transfer, convey, sublet, or otherwise dispose of any award or any or all of its rights, title, or interest therein, without the prior written consent of the [local government].

Bid acceptance period

Any bid submitted as a result of the solicitation shall be binding on the bidder for [number] calendar days following the bid opening date. Any bid for which the bidder specifies a shorter acceptance period may be rejected.

Bid form submission

The original and [number] copies of the bid form, [number] copies total, shall be signed and submitted in a sealed envelope or package to [place for receipt of bids] no later than the time and date specified for receipt of bids. Timely submission of the bid form is the responsibility of the bidder. Bids received after the specified time shall be rejected and returned to the bidder unopened. The envelope or package shall be marked with the bid opening date and time and the number of the invitation to bid. The time and date of receipt shall be indicated on the envelope or package by [department receiving bids]. Each page of the bid form and all attachments shall be identified with the name of the bidder.

Failure to submit a bid on the bid form provided shall be considered just cause for rejection of the bid. Modifications or additions to any portion of the bid document may be cause for rejection of the bid. The [local government] reserves the right to decide, on a case-by-case basis, whether to reject a bid with modifications or additions as nonresponsive. As a precondition to bid acceptance, the [local government] may request the bidder to withdraw or modify those portions of the bid deemed nonresponsive that do not affect quality, quantity, price, or delivery of the service.

(Nonresponsive portions of the bid that do not affect service quality, quantity, price, or delivery may be, for example, clauses that specify the state in which litigation is to be brought or that provide for high interest charges for late payment.)

Bid withdrawal

If the price bid is substantially lower than those of other bidders, a mistake may have been made. A bidder may withdraw its bid from consideration if certain conditions are met:

1. The bid is submitted in good faith.
2. The price bid is substantially lower than those of other bidders because of a mistake.
3. The mistake is a clerical error, not an error of judgment.
4. Objective evidence drawn from original work papers, documents, and other materials used in the preparation of the bid demonstrates clearly that the mistake was an unintentional error in arithmetic or an unintentional omission of a quantity of labor or material.

To withdraw a bid that includes a clerical error after bid opening, the bidder must give notice in writing to the [local government] of claim of right to withdraw a bid. Within two business days after the bid opening, the bidder requesting withdrawal must provide to the [local government] all original work papers, documents, and other materials used in the preparation of the bid.

A bidder may also withdraw a bid prior to the time set for the opening of bids by simply making a request in writing to the [local government]; no explanation is required.

A bidder may also withdraw a bid if the [local government] fails to award or issue a notice of intent to award the bid within [time period] after the date fixed for the opening of bids.

No bidder who is permitted to withdraw a bid shall, for compensation, supply any material or labor to or perform any subcontract or other work for the person to whom the contract is awarded or otherwise benefit from the contract.

No partial withdrawals of a bid are permitted after the time and date set for the bid opening; only complete withdrawals are permitted.

Bidder certification

The bidder agrees that submission of a signed bid form is certification that the bidder will accept an award made to it as a result of the submission.

Bidder investigations

Before submitting a bid, each bidder shall make all investigations and examinations necessary to ascertain all site conditions and requirements affecting the full performance of the contract and to verify any representations made by the [local government] upon which the bidder will rely. If the bidder receives an award as a result of its bid submission, failure to have made such investigations and examinations will in no way relieve the bidder from its obligation to comply in every detail with all provisions and requirements of the contract documents, nor will a plea of ignorance of such conditions and requirements be accepted as a basis for any claim whatsoever by the contractor for additional compensation.

Certificates and licenses

The contractor shall provide notarized copies of all valid licenses and certificates required for performance of the work. The notarized copies shall be delivered to the [local government] no later than ten days after the contractor receives the notice of award from the [local government]. Current notarized copies of licenses and certificates shall be provided to the [local government] within twenty-four hours of demand at any time during the contract term. Licenses and certificates required for this contract include, by way of illustration and not limitation, the following:

1. A business license valid in [local government]

2. A professional license or certificate in the field of [specialty area]

3. [Any additional licenses that may be required to be held by architects, health professionals, pesticide or herbicide application technicians, asbestos removal contractors, etc.]

Certification of independent price determination

The bidder certifies that the prices submitted in response to the solicitation have been arrived at independently and without—for the purpose of restricting competition—any consultation, communication, or agreement with any other bidder or competitor relating to those prices, the intention to submit a bid, or the methods or factors used to calculate the prices bid.

Change in scope of work

The [local government] may order changes in the work consisting of additions, deletions, or other revisions within the general scope of the contract. No claims may be made by the contractor that the scope of the project or of the contractor's services has been changed, requiring changes to the amount of compensation to the contractor or other adjustments to the contract, unless such changes or adjustments have been made by written amendment to the contract signed by the [local government] and the contractor.

If the contractor believes that any particular work is not within the scope of the project, is a material change, or will otherwise require more compensation to the contractor, the contractor must immediately notify the [local government] in writing of this belief. If the [local government] believes that the particular work is within the scope of the contract as written, the contractor will be ordered to and shall continue with the work as changed and at the cost stated for the work within the scope.

(A contractor ordered to proceed with the work is not prohibited from filing a claim against the local government under state or local contract dispute procedures. This clause requires only that work under the contract proceed while any dispute is being settled).

Collusion among bidders

Each bidder, by submitting a bid, certifies that it is not a party to any collusive action or any action that may be in violation of the Sherman Antitrust Act. Any or all bids shall be rejected if there is any reason for believing that collusion exists among the bidders. The local government may or may not, at its discretion, accept future bids for the same work from participants in such collusion.

More than one bid from an individual, firm, partnership, corporation, or association under the same or different names may be rejected. Reasonable grounds for believing that a bidder has interest in more than one bid for the work being bid may result in rejection of all bids in which the bidder is believed to have interest.

Nothing in this clause shall preclude a firm acting as a subcontractor to be included as a subcontractor for two or more primary contractors submitting a bid for the work.

The phrase "may be rejected" in the second paragraph permits the local government to retain some discretion in considering two bids from the same corporation. For example, if bids are submitted by two divisions of the same manufacturer or distributor that operate completely independently of one another, the bids may be accepted. The legal department must rule on any questionable responses.

Competitive negotiation solicitation

The [local government] will receive proposals from firms having specific experience and qualifications in the area identified in the solicitation. For consideration, proposals for the project must contain evidence of the firm's experience and abilities in the specified area and other disciplines directly related to the proposed service. Other information required by the [local government] may be included elsewhere in the solicitation. Unless otherwise stated, all offerors shall provide profiles and resumes of the staff to be assigned to the project, references, illustrative examples of similar work performed, and any other information that clearly demonstrates the offerors' expertise in the area of the solicitation.

A selection committee shall review and evaluate all replies and identify the firms that will be invited to submit more detailed proposals, make oral presentations, or both. The selection committee will have only the response to the solicitation to review for selection of finalists. It is therefore important that respondents emphasize specific information pertinent to the work. Evaluation of the responses will be based on the following criteria:

1. The methodology proposed
2. Qualifications and experience of assigned staff members
3. Understanding of the project and its objectives
4. The degree of completeness of response to the specific requirements of the solicitation
5. Experience and history of the firm in the disciplines covered by the solicitation
6. Availability of personnel and whatever else is necessary for the performance of the work
7. The cost of the services to be provided
8. Other evaluation criteria described or included by reference in the solicitation

Contractor personnel

The [local government] shall, throughout the life of the contract, have the right of reasonable rejection and approval of staff or subcontractors assigned to the work by the contractor. If the [local government] reasonably rejects staff or subcontractors, the contractor must provide replacement staff or subcontractors satisfactory to the [local government] in a timely manner and at no additional cost to the [local government]. The day-to-day supervision and control of the contractor's employees and subcontractors is the responsibility solely of the contractor.

Cost reimbursement

The contractor agrees that payment by the [local government] to the contractor for materials used in the performance of any work under the contract on a cost plus a percentage of cost basis is specifically prohibited. The cost of all materials provided in the performance of the work is to be reimbursed to the contractor in the following manner: The [local government] shall reimburse the contractor,

on completion and acceptance of each assigned job, only for those materials actually used in the performance of the work that are supported by invoices issued by the suppliers of the contractor describing the quantity and cost of the materials purchased. No surcharge shall be added to the suppliers' invoices or included in the contractor's invoice submitted to the [local government] that would increase the dollar amount indicated on the suppliers' invoices for the materials purchased for the assigned job.

All incidental costs, including allowances for profit and tools of the trade, must be included in the contract hourly labor rates.

Debarment

By submitting a bid, the bidder certifies that it is not currently debarred from submitting bids for contracts issued by any political subdivision or agency of the [state] and that it is not an agent of a person or entity that is currently debarred from submitting bids for contracts issued by any political subdivision or agency of the [state].

Economic price adjustment

Any reference in the solicitation to economic price adjustment or price escalation shall be considered to mean price decreases as well as increases, unless otherwise stipulated.

When the solicitation does not contain a price escalation formula insert the following paragraph:

> Bids that contain a provision for price escalation with a ceiling will be evaluated at the maximum possible escalation of the bid price. Bids that contain a provision for price escalation without a ceiling will be rejected unless, in the judgment solely of the [local government], a clear basis exists for comparative evaluation with other bids received. Bids that provide for price escalation based upon a method other than a percentage factor will be

rejected unless, in the judgment solely of the [local government], there is a clear basis for comparative evaluation.

When the solicitation contains a price escalation formula insert the following paragraph:

> Bids will be evaluated on the basis of the prices bid without consideration of the allowable escalation. If a bidder increases the ceiling stipulated in the invitation for bid (IFB) or places limits on the provisions of the IFB that allow prices to drop in accordance with the movement of the escalator, the bid will be rejected as nonresponsive.

If a bidder deletes the price escalation clause from its bid, the bid will be rejected as nonresponsive. If a bidder lowers the ceiling stipulated in the IFB, the bid will be evaluated at the base price in the same manner as those bids that do not reduce the stipulated ceiling. If the bidder offering a lower ceiling ultimately receives the award, that ceiling will be incorporated into the contract documents.

Employment discrimination

During the performance of the contract, the contractor agrees to the following:

1. The contractor shall not discriminate against any employee or applicant for employment because of race, religion, color, sex, age, handicap, or national origin except when such condition is a bona fide occupational qualification reasonably necessary for the normal operations of the contractor. The contractor agrees to post in conspicuous places, visible to employees and applicants for employment, notices setting forth the provisions of this nondiscrimination clause.

2. The contractor, in all solicitations or advertisements for employees placed by or on behalf of the contractor, shall state that such contractor is an Equal Opportunity Employer.

3. Notices, advertisements, and solicitations placed in accordance with federal law, rule, or regulation shall be deemed sufficient for the purpose of meeting the requirements of this section.

4. The contractor shall include the provisions of the foregoing paragraphs 1, 2, and 3 in every subcontract or purchase order of more than $10,000 so that the provisions will be binding upon each subcontractor or vendor.

This clause is offered as a guide only. The language of discrimination clauses for local and state governments varies considerably.

Errors in extension

If the unit price and the extension price are at variance, the unit price shall prevail.

Ethics in public contracting

The contract shall incorporate by reference but shall not be limited to the provisions of law contained in [applicable conflict of interest and ethics statutes]. The bidder certifies that its bid was made without collusion or fraud; that it has not offered or received any kickbacks or inducements from any other bidder, supplier, manufacturer, or subcontractor in connection with the bid; and that it has not conferred on any public employee having official responsibility for this procurement transaction any payment, loan, subscription, advance, deposit of money, services, or anything of more than nominal value.

Nominal value is defined by local or state regulations and may vary from a market value of $1.00 to $25.00. Items may include cash or pens, desk accessories, or gifts with or without a company logo.

Exceptions

Bidders taking exception to any part or section of the solicitation shall indicate such exceptions on the bid form. Failure to indicate any exception will be interpreted as the bidder's intent to comply fully with the requirements as written. Conditional or qualified bids, unless specifically allowed, shall be subject to rejection in whole or in part.

Expenses incurred in preparing bid

The [local government] accepts no responsibility for any expense incurred by the bidder in the preparation and presentation of a bid. Such expenses shall be borne exclusively by the bidder.

Failure to deliver

In the event of failure of the contractor to deliver services in accordance with the contract terms and conditions, the [local government], after due oral or written notice, may procure the services from other sources and hold the contractor responsible for any resulting additional purchase and administrative costs. This remedy shall be in addition to any other remedies that the [local government] may have.

Failure to enforce

Failure by the [local government] at any time to enforce the provisions of the contract shall not be construed as a waiver of any such provisions. Such failure to enforce shall not affect the validity of the contract or any part thereof or the right of the [local government] to enforce any provision at any time in accordance with its terms.

Force majeure

The contractor shall not be held responsible for failure to perform the duties and responsibilities imposed by the contract due to legal strikes, fires, riots, rebellions, and acts of God beyond the control of the contractor, unless otherwise specified in the contract.

(Force majeure is a French term meaning "superior power," used to refer to unexpected or uncontrollable events that can interrupt performance of the contract.)

Immigration Reform and Control Act of 1986

The contractor certifies that it does not and will not during the performance of the contract employ illegal alien workers or otherwise violate the provisions of the federal Immigration Reform and Control Act of 1986.

Indemnification

The contractor covenants to save, defend, keep harmless, and indemnify the [local government] and all of its officers, departments, agencies, agents, and employees from and against all claims, loss, damage, injury, fines, penalties, and cost-including court costs and attorney's fees, charges, liability, and exposure, however, caused - resulting from, arising out of, or in any way connected with the contractor's negligent performance or nonperformance of the terms of the contract.

Independent contractor

The contractor shall be legally considered an independent contractor and neither the contractor nor its employees shall, under any circumstances, be considered servants or agents of the [local government]; and the [local government] shall be at no time legally responsible for any negligence or other wrongdoing by the contractor, its servants, or agents. The [local government] shall not withhold from the contract payments to the contractor any federal or state unemployment taxes, federal or state income taxes, Social Security tax, or any other amounts for benefits to the contractor. Further, the [local government] shall not provide to the contractor any insurance coverage or other benefits, including workers' compensation, normally provided by the [local government] for its employees.

Informalities and irregularities

The [local government] has the right to waive minor defects or variations of a bid from the exact requirements of the specifications that do not affect the price, quality, quantity, delivery, or performance time of the services being procured. If insufficient information is submitted by a bidder with the bid for the [local government] to properly evaluate the bid, the [local government] has the right to require such additional information as it may deem necessary after the time set for receipt of bids, provided that the information requested does not change the price, quality, quantity, delivery, or performance time of the services being procured.

Information requested may include, for example, a copy of business or professional licenses or a work schedule.

Insurance requirements

(Insurance requirements for local governments vary considerably. The risk manager of each local government should draft bid clauses describing the coverages required. Do not use the same insurance insert for every solicitation: the insurance must address the risks that apply to the service being purchased.)

Late submissions

A bid received at the place designated in the solicitation for receipt of bids after the exact time specified for receipt will not be considered unless it is the only bid received or it is received before award is made and was sent by registered or certified mail not later than the fifth calendar day before the date specified for receipt of bids. It must be determined by the [local government] that the late receipt was due solely to mishandling by the [local government] after receipt at the specified address.

The only acceptable evidence to establish the date of mailing of a late bid is the U.S. Postal Service postmark on the wrapper or on the original receipt from the U.S. Postal Service. If the postmark does not show a legible date, the contents of the envelope or package shall be processed as if mailed late. Postmark means a printed, stamped, or otherwise placed impression, exclusive of a postage meter impression, that is readily identifiable without further action as having been supplied and affixed by the U.S. Postal Service on the date of mailing. Bidders should request postal clerks to place a hand cancellation postmark on both the receipt and the envelope or wrapper.

The only acceptable evidence to establish the time of receipt at the office identified for bid opening is the time and date stamp of that office on the bid wrapper or other documentary evidence of receipt used by that office.

Limitation of cost

The contractor agrees to perform the work specified and complete all obligations under the contract within the stated amount. The contractor agrees to notify the [local government] in writing no later than when the amounts billable under the contract reach 75 percent of the contract amount. The contractor will include in such notice an estimate of funds required to complete the work. The [local government] will not be obligated to reimburse the contractor for billing in excess of the amount set forth in the contract documents unless such increased costs are (1) due to a change in the scope of work identified prior to performance of the work or (2) identified after initiation of the work and prior to expenditure and covered by a contract amendment that increases the contract amount.

Nonappropriation

All funds for payment by the [local government] under this contract are subject to the availability of an annual appropriation for this purpose by the [governing body]. In the event of nonappropriation of funds by the [governing body] for the services provided under the contract, the [local government] will terminate the contract, without termination charge or other liability, on the last day of the then-current fiscal year or when the appropriation made for the then-current year for the services covered by this contract is spent, whichever event occurs first. If at any time funds are not appropriated for the continuance of this contract, cancellation shall be accepted by the contractor on thirty days' prior written notice, but failure to give such notice shall be of no effect and the [local government] shall not be obligated under this contract beyond the date of termination.

Nonconforming terms and conditions

A bid response that includes terms and conditions that do not conform to the terms and conditions in the bid document is subject to rejection as nonresponsive. The [local government] reserves the right to permit the bidder to withdraw nonconforming terms and conditions from its bid response prior to a determination by the [local government] of nonresponsiveness based on the submission of nonconforming terms and conditions.

Oral statements

No oral statement of any person shall modify or otherwise affect the terms, conditions, or specifications stated in this contract. All modifications to the contract must be made in writing by the [local government].

Patents and royalties

The contractor covenants to save, defend, keep harmless, and indemnify the [local government] and all of its officers, departments, agencies, agents, and employees from and against all claims, loss, damage, injury, fines, penalties, and cost—including court costs and attorney's fees, charges, liability, and exposure, however caused—for or on account of any copyright or patented or unpatented invention, process, or article manufactured or used in the performance of the contract, including its use by the [local government]. If the contractor uses any design, device, or materials covered by patent or copyright, it is mutually agreed and understood without exception that the contract price includes all royalties or costs arising from the use of such design, device, or materials in any way in the work.

Payment terms and discounts (net 20- or 30-day)

Unless otherwise indicated in the bid form, payment terms will be net [twenty or thirty] days. The [local government] will pay the contractor within [twenty or thirty] days after the receipt of a correct invoice for reasonable work allocable to the contract or after the date of acceptance of work that meets contract requirements, whichever event occurs later.

Payment terms and discounts (2 percent 20- or 30-day)

Unless otherwise indicated in the bid form, payment terms will be 2 percent [twenty or thirty] days. A 2 percent discount will be deducted from the contractor's invoice for payment by the [local government] within [twenty or thirty] days after the receipt of a correct invoice for reasonable work allocable to the contract or after the date of acceptance of work that meets contract requirements, whichever event occurs later.

Discounts for prompt payment requiring payment by the [local government] within a stipulated number of days will be interpreted as applying within the stipulated number of calendar days after the date of receipt by the [local government] of a correct invoice describing reasonable work allocable to the contract or after the date of acceptance of work that meets contract requirements, whichever event occurs later.

Discounts for payment in less than twenty days [may/will not] be considered.

(Most local governments cannot meet terms that require payment in less than twenty days and will therefore choose not to consider such terms. However, for contracts with large periodic payments ($50,000 or more), if the finance department can, through special handling, process a payment in less than twenty days, the language of the clause should note that discounts for payment in less than twenty days may be considered.)

Pre-bid conference (mandatory)

A mandatory pre-bid conference will be held at [time] on [date] at [location]. All interested parties are required to attend. The purpose of the pre-bid conference is to allow potential bidders an opportunity to present questions to staff and obtain clarification of the requirements of the bid documents. Because the [local government] considers the conference to be critical to understanding the bid requirements, attendance is mandatory in order to qualify as a bidder. Minutes of the conference [will/will not] be published.

Pre-bid conference (optional)

An optional pre-bid conference will be held at [time] on [date] at [location]. All interested parties are urged to attend. The purpose of the pre-bid conference is to allow potential bidders an opportunity to present questions to staff and obtain clarification of the requirements of the bid documents. Minutes of the conference [will/will not] be published.

Price adjustments based on the Consumer Price Index

The contract unit prices shall remain firm for the first twelve months of the contract term. The unit prices for ensuing contract years shall be based on the movement of the unadjusted figures of the U.S. Department of Labor Consumer Price Index (CPI) for [population group]. The contract unit prices shall be changed by the [local government] in an amount equal to the percentage of movement of the CPI for the twelve-month period ending in the month of [name of month] of each contract year. The contract unit prices changed as a result of this formula shall automatically become effective on each anniversary of the contract and shall be binding on the contractor for the subsequent contract year.

The CPI is calculated monthly for two population groups: Urban Wage Earners and Clerical Workers (CPI-W) and All Urban Consumers (CPI-U). The second group is generally used for escalator clauses. Although the CPI is published on a seasonally adjusted basis, the adjusted figures are rarely used in an escalator clause. For more information, refer to U.S. Department of Labor, Bureau of Labor Statistics, *Using the Consumer Price Index for Escalation,* Report 761 (Washington, D.C.: U.S. Bureau of Labor Statistics, 1989).

Escalator clauses using other benchmarks such as indexes published in regional or national trade papers, local or regional tipping fees (often used in refuse disposal contracts), or the posted fuel prices at regional fuel terminals are constructed using the same elements: length of the firm price period; identification of the publication or reference used; month or date of the publication used; dates used to calculate the price adjustment.

Procurement regulations

The contract shall be governed by the applicable provisions of the [local government regulations], a copy of which is available at [location] for inspection.

Purchase order requirement

Purchases of the [local government] are authorized only if a signed purchase order is issued in advance of the transaction, showing that the ordering agency has sufficient funds available to pay for the service. Contractors providing services without a signed purchase order do so at their own risk. The [local government] will not be liable for payment for any services provided under the contract unless a valid purchase order has been issued to the contractor.

Qualifications of bidders

The bidder may be required before the award of any contract to show to the complete satisfaction of the [local government] that it has the necessary facilities, ability, and financial resources to provide the service specified therein in a satisfactory manner. The bidder may also be required to give a past history and references in order to satisfy the [local government] in regard to the bidder's qualifications. The [local government] may make reasonable investigations deemed necessary and proper to determine the ability of the bidder to perform the work, and the bidder shall furnish to the [local government] all information for this purpose that may be requested. The [local government] reserves the right to reject any bid if the evidence submitted by, or investigation of, the bidder fails to satisfy the [local government] that the bidder is properly qualified to carry out the obligations of the contract and to complete the work described therein. Evaluation of the bidder's qualifications shall include the following:

1. The ability, capacity, skill, and financial resources to perform the work or provide the service required

2. The ability of the bidder to perform the work or provide the service promptly or within the time specified, without delay or interference

3. The character, integrity, reputation, judgment, experience, and efficiency of the bidder

4. The quality of performance of previous contracts or services.

Quality control

The contractor shall institute and maintain throughout the contract period a properly documented quality control program designed to ensure that the services are provided at all times and in all respects in accordance with the contract.

The program shall include providing daily supervision and conducting frequent inspections of the contractor's staff and ensuring that accurate records are maintained describing the disposition of all complaints. The records so created shall be open to inspection by the [local government].

Recovery of money

Whenever, under the contract, any sum of money shall be recoverable from or payable by the contractor to the [local government], the same amount may be deducted from any sum due to the contractor under the contract or under any other contract between the contractor and the [local government]. The rights of the [local government] are in addition and without prejudice to any other right the [local government] may have to claim the amount of any loss or damage suffered by the [local government] on account of the acts or omissions of the contractor.

Renewal of contract

Use this clause when the contractor cannot decline a renewal:

> The contract may be renewed at the discretion of the local government upon written notice to the contractor at least [number] days prior to each contract anniversary date for a period of [number] successive one year periods under the same prices, terms, and conditions as in the original contract. The total number of renewal years permitted shall not exceed [number].

Use this clause when the contractor has the right to decline the renewal:

> Upon written agreement of both parties at least [number] days prior to each contract anniversary date, the

contract may be renewed by the [local government] for a period of [number] successive one-year period(s) under the same prices, terms, and conditions as in the original contract. The total number of renewal years permitted shall not exceed [number].

Requirements contract

During the period of the contract, the contractor shall provide all the services described in the contract. The contractor understands and agrees that this is a requirements contract and that the [local government] shall have no obligation to the contractor if no services are required. Any quantities that are included in the scope of work reflect the current expectations of the [local government] for the period of the contract. The amount is only an estimate and the contractor understands and agrees that the [local government] is under no obligation to the contractor to buy any amount of the services as a result of having provided this estimate or of having any typical or measurable requirement in the past. The contractor further understands and agrees that the [local government] may require services in an amount less than or in excess of the estimated annual contract amount and that the quantity actually used, whether in excess of the estimate or less than the estimate, shall not give rise to any claim for compensation other than the total of the unit prices in the contract for the quantity actually used.

Right of first refusal of employment

The contractor shall give [local government] employees displaced as a result of the conversion to contract performance the right of first refusal for employment openings under the contract for positions for which they are reasonably qualified.

Right to audit

The contractor shall maintain such financial records and other records as may be prescribed by the [local government] or by applicable federal and state laws, rules, and regulations. The contractor shall retain these records for a period of five years after final payment, or until they are audited by the [local government], whichever event occurs first. These records shall be made available during the term of the contract and the subsequent five-year period for examination, transcription, and audit by the [local government], its designees, or other authorized bodies.

Solicitation for information or planning purposes

The [local government] does not intend to award a contract on the basis of the solicitation or otherwise pay for the information solicited. The solicitation is issued solely for the purpose of [description of purpose].

Surety required

1. Bid surety: A bid bond, cashier's check, or certified check in the amount of [percentage] of the amount of the bid made payable to the [local government] shall accompany each bid. The bid surety of all bidders shall be retained until after the award of the contract is made. The bid surety of the successful bidder shall be retained until the posting of a performance bond. The failure of the bidder to accept an award and file acceptable performance and payment bonds within fifteen days after award shall be just cause for cancellation of the award and the forfeiture of the bid surety to the [local government] as liquidated damages. Award may then be made to the next lowest responsive and responsible bidder.

2. Performance surety: A performance bond in the amount of 100 percent of the bid shall be required of the successful bidder to ensure satisfactory

completion of the work. The bond shall be a corporate surety bond issued by a surety company authorized to do business in the [state].

3. Payment surety: A payment bond in the amount of 100 percent of the bid shall be required of the successful bidder to guarantee payment of all persons who have and fulfill contracts with the contractor for performing labor or providing equipment or material in the performance of the work provided for in the contract. The bond shall be a corporate surety bond issued by a surety company authorized to do business in the [state].

4. Alternative surety: A certified check for cash escrow deposit in the face amount of the contract such as a personal bond, property bond, or a bank or savings and loan association letter of credit may be tendered in lieu of a bid, payment, or performance bond subject to approval by the [local government's] attorney.

Termination for convenience

The performance of work under the contract may be terminated by the [local government] in whole or in part whenever the [local government] determines that termination is in the [local government's] best interest. Any such termination shall be effected by the delivery to the contractor of a written notice of termination at least fifteen (15) days before the date of termination, specifying the extent to which performance of the work under the contract is terminated and the date upon which such termination becomes effective.

After receipt of a notice of termination, except as otherwise directed, the contractor shall stop work on the date of receipt of the notice of termination or other date specified in the notice; place no further orders or subcontracts for materials, services, or facilities except as necessary for completion of such portion of the work not terminated; terminate all vendors and subcontracts; and settle all outstanding liabilities and claims.

Termination for default

The contract shall remain in force for the full period specified and until the [local government] determines that all requirements and conditions have been satisfactorily met and the [local government] has accepted the work. Thereafter, applicable provisions of the contract shall remain in force until the [local government] has determined that the contractor has met all requirements and conditions such as guarantees and warranties that relate to the work following the contract term. The [local government] shall have the right to terminate the contract sooner if the [local government] determines that the contractor has failed to perform satisfactorily the work required, as determined by the [local government]. In the event the [local government] decides to terminate the contract for failure to perform satisfactorily, the [local government] shall give to the contractor at least fifteen (15) days' written notice before the termination takes effect. The fifteen-day period will begin upon the mailing of notice by the [local government].

If the contractor fails to cure the default within the fifteen (15) days specified in the notice and the contract is terminated for failure to provide satisfactory performance, the contractor shall be entitled to receive compensation for all reasonable, allocable, and allowable contract services satisfactorily performed by the contractor up to the date of termination that were accepted by the [local government] prior to termination. In the event the [local government] terminates the contract because of the default of the contractor, the contractor shall be liable for all excess costs that the [local government] is required to expend to complete the work covered by the contract.

After receipt of a notice of termination, except as otherwise directed, the contractor shall stop work on the date of receipt of the notice of termination or other date specified in the notice; place no further orders or subcontracts for materials, services, or facilities except as necessary for completion of such portion of the work not terminated; terminate all vendors and subcontracts; and settle all outstanding liabilities and claims.

Traffic control

The contractor shall conduct its operations in a manner that will not interrupt pedestrian or vehicle traffic except as approved by the [local government]. The work area shall be confined to the smallest area possible to allow maximum use of the street or sidewalk and to reduce any hazard to traffic or pedestrians to a minimum.

At all times, the contractor shall use workers and traffic control signs and devices necessary to comply with Part VI of U.S. Department of Labor, Federal Highway Administration, *Manual on Uniform Traffic Control Devices for Streets and Highways* (Washington, D.C.: Government Printing Office, 2001). In addition to signs and devices, when the street is obstructed to any extent by contract operations, special workers equipped with flags shall be designated by the contractor to direct vehicle and pedestrian traffic. The workers so designated shall not be assigned to any other duties while engaged in directing traffic. All personnel, signs, barricades, and any other items or devices necessary for the maintenance of traffic and safety shall be provided by the contractor. No separate payment shall be made by the [local government] for this work. All costs of this work are included by the contractor as part of the contract price.

The plan for traffic control for the contract shall be as directed by the [local government].

Unnecessarily elaborate responses

Unnecessarily elaborate brochures or other presentations beyond those sufficient to present a complete and effective response to the solicitation are not desired and may be construed as an indication of the bidder's lack of cost consciousness. Elaborate artwork, expensive paper and bindings, and expensive visual and other presentations are neither necessary nor desired.

Unsatisfactory work

If, at any time during the contract term, the service performed or work done by the contractor is considered by the [local government] to create a condition that threatens the health, safety, or welfare of the community, the contractor shall, on being notified by the [local government], immediately correct such deficient service or work.

In the event the contractor fails, after notice, to correct the deficient service or work immediately, the [local government] shall have the right to order the correction of the deficiency by separate contract or with its own resources at the expense of the contractor.

Vehicle and equipment buyback

In the event of termination in whole or in part of the contract as a result of contractor default, the contractor shall upon demand made in writing by the local government.

1. Sell and transfer to the [local government] the vehicles and equipment specified in the notice that have been or are being used to perform the work under the contract.

2. Assign to the [local government] the benefit of any guarantee or

warranty that may apply to the specified vehicles and equipment.

3. Deliver possession to the [local government] of the specified vehicles and equipment.

4. Permit the [local government] to enter into any premises occupied by the contractor to remove the specified vehicles and equipment therefrom.

The price to be paid for the listed vehicles and equipment shall be agreed upon by the contractor and the [local government] within seven (7) days of the issuance of the notice of termination. In the event of failure to agree upon a price within the seven (7) days, the price shall be the open market value of the listed vehicles as determined by an independent appraiser hired by the [local government].

Appendix B

Preparing various types of service contracts

Appendix B provides guidelines for preparing contracts for various categories of services. Suggestions for evaluating the contractor's performance in each category are included in Appendix C. For each category, Appendix B lists the services that fall within it and provides information on the bidding method usually used, the contract term and pricing method, and recommendations for preparing the scope of work and establishing contract unit prices.

Architectural and engineering services

Architectural and engineering (A/E) services are unique because in a number of states, statutes prohibit discussing price until A/E offerors have been ranked in order of their qualifications.

Services provided under A/E contracts include architectural and engineering design, value engineering, property surveys, engineering testing, construction engineering and inspection (CE&I), and general consulting. Some firms that undertake A/E contracts design and prepare construction documents for public buildings and infrastructure. Some firms specialize in value engineering, a field in which they analyze drawings and specifications prepared by another architectural or engineering firm and advise on methods to reduce costs (see "Value engineering" in this appendix). Property surveyors inventory public buildings and their electrical, structural, and mechanical systems to determine their condition, schedule maintenance, and forecast funds needed for rehabilitation. Testing

engineers provide services that include testing of soil and concrete for construction projects. Services provided by general consultants in the fields of architecture and engineering include traffic and feasibility studies, space planning, and construction management.

Bidding method   State or local law determines whether competitive sealed bidding or competitive negotiation is used to procure A/E services. Competitive negotiation is preferable. Negotiations are generally limited to the number of hours by skill classification, which is then loaded for approved overhead and other audited and approved rates.

Contract term and pricing   Contracts for A/E design services can remain in effect for several years, from the initial design concept through construction. Contracts for other than design services (value engineering, testing services, etc.) range in length from a few months to several years, depending on the project.

Contract pricing methods include lump-sum, cost plus a fixed fee, or cost reimbursement with a not-to-exceed price limit. The range of contract pricing methods and their combinations is broad. The most important factor in pricing A/E contracts is not the pricing method used but the local government's vigilance in controlling costs by monitoring the contractor.

Recommendations

1. Require five or more references for similar work. Reference information

should contain, at a minimum, full identification of the project, its total construction cost, the A/E firm's role in the design of the project (whether principal contractor or a subcontractor), the amount paid to the A/E firm, and a statement of whether the project was completed within budget. For each reference, also obtain the names of the project manager.

2. Select from the projects offered as references those that most nearly match the local government's current project and require copies of the specifications with all amendments and the drawings that were prepared for them. Examination of the drawings may reveal poor drafting and lack of attention to detail; amendments may indicate that the architect or engineer left necessary information out of the specifications, requiring clarification to enable bidders to calculate construction costs accurately.

3. Require that the key personnel assigned to the contract be the same personnel that worked on the projects of the same size and scope described in the references. Require approval of any substitutions of key personnel should substitutions be required.

4. For a large project, require hands-on involvement of the firm's principals. If permitted by state and local laws and regulations, require the firm to specify the number of hours of the principals' time that will be dedicated to the contract. Some caution must be used to ensure that the firm's most expensive employees are not being inappropriately billed to this project. Some state and local government regulations state that only the contractor's qualifications can be requested in the first stage of competitive negotiation; requests for other information are prohibited.

Examples of information typically prohibited are the estimated number of hours to be worked by members of the design team, a cost estimate for the work, and any information that the local government could use to estimate the cost that the contractor may propose for the services. If allowed, the firm's estimate of hours is a good check to ensure the firm understands the scope of services as envisioned. This is especially true for less defined projects such as studies or concept reports.

5. Although many states prohibit requests for costs in the original request for proposals (RFP), require at least that A/E firms identify in their initial response the contract pricing method they prefer. Alternatively, the local government can specify the method it prefers and ask for the firm's comments on its preference. Some states that prohibit soliciting costs in the initial RFP do not specifically prohibit the local government from requiring that the contractor agree to negotiate a fee for basic design services that will not exceed a predetermined percentage of expected construction cost, for example, 6 to 8 percent.

6. If the A/E firm is not locally based, require it to establish a subcontracting or joint venture relationship with a local firm and to relocate some home office staff to ensure that any problems arising during the project will receive an immediate, local response.

7. Require firm hourly rates for all categories of personnel, not a salary plus overhead cost formula. Hourly rates proposed for contractor's staff or subcontractors are to be firm for the contract term; firm rates simplify auditing and invoicing. If the contract will run for more than one year, include a Consumer Price

Index (CPI) escalator clause to apply to the original hourly labor rates.

8. Specify allowable contract reimbursables with a provision for reimbursement at contractor cost only; prohibit any markup over cost.

9. Require progress reports at least once a month during the project.

10. Establish firm dates for deliverables with liquidated damages to apply if the contractor is late meeting obligations. An alternative to liquidated damages is to establish a percentage of retainage for each invoice submitted. Retainage may be released as major phases are completed; however, some retainage should be released only at the successful conclusion of the project.

11. Require that designs, specifications, and plans be submitted at predetermined stages for review and comment by the local government before the work proceeds to the next stage. These reviews usually occur when the work is 25 percent complete, 50 percent complete, and 90 percent complete; exact dates for the reviews are established during contract negotiations.

12. To keep the final construction cost within the projected budget, require the estimated construction cost when 25 percent of the design is complete to be equal to or less than the estimated cost when 90 percent of the design is complete. If the later estimate exceeds the earlier, require the contractor to redesign the project to meet the targeted construction cost at no additional expense to the local government. This approach prevents the cost of the project from creeping upward during the design phase and compels the contractor to focus on construction costs throughout the design process.

13. Contracts for A/E services require special insurance coverage. Require liability insurance to protect the local government against errors or omissions made by the architect or engineer (professional errors and omissions coverage) in addition to basic general liability coverage. The risk manager determines appropriate limits of coverage.

Architectural and engineering: Major construction contracts

Contracting for multimillion dollar projects requires a great deal of thought and effort to ensure that the best delivery method is selected and the government receives the best product. These types of contracts and the development of the scopes of work are well suited for consultants who have the required expertise. Generally major projects will require multiple contracts that include construction and several types of architectural and engineering services contracts. In some cases, several functions can be combined into one contract where the contractor is responsible for the design, construction, and quality assurance, and in the case of public private partnerships these contractor roles can be expanded even further to include operation, maintenance, or even financing.

Bidding method   Either competitive sealed bidding or competitive negotiations are used for large infrastructure projects. Generally, the more complex the project the more likely it is that competitive negotiations will be used. If the scope of work is less specific or less technical and/or innovation or alternative ways to deliver the product are available to the contractor, then competitive negotiations again is more suited. If a full set of plans have been developed, then competitive sealed bidding is suitable. As described in Chapter 3, there are hybrids of these methods. One must understand that the more uncertainty or risk assumed by the contractor, the more contingency he or she will include in the bid to cover these risks.

Contract term and pricing   Methods include lump-sum, cost plus a fixed fee, or cost reimbursement with a not-to-exceed price limit. In some cases, as with contract management at risk, the pricing can change at certain milestone events. The pricing method needs to be one that facilitates the contract and ensures that fiduciary responsibilities are satisfied.

Recommendations

1. It is most common for a consultant contract to be used as part of these projects.

2. Generally some type of multistep contract is preferred. In this process, the prequalification of the offerors ensures a level of confidence that the successful bidder is a high-quality firm and the final product will be high-quality as well.

3. In the prequalification phase, use data and reports produced by other government agencies to ensure you have a good picture of the firm and its capabilities and history. Some governmental departments grade each contractor on each contract. This information is invaluable in making these selections. Ensure that each potential bidder provides the needed references for similar work and ensure that they are relatively current (within the last five years).

4. Require the potential bidders to provide a draft organization with a list of subcontractors that they intend to include in their team. Include language in your procurement document to ensure that you retain the authority to approve any substitution of these organizations.

5. Require the potential bidders to identify key managers to be used on

the projects, especially the project manager. Ensure that you protect yourself from "bait and switch" with key managers.

6. Once you have selected a contractor and (assuming you are using competitive negotiations), ensure that your project is not being loaded with a large number of expensive corporate staff. Be willing to pay for the best, but don't be overloaded.

7. Ensure that your contract management requirements are included in the contract. This should include periodic reports and or presentations. Manage cost carefully; ensure that you track cost closely according to the percentage of completion of the project. Likewise, ensure that you define the role of your CE&I if one is being used.

8. Establish a realistic schedule as part of the contract. Ensure that you allow for bad weather days or make it a "no excuse" contract with an incentive for finishing by a given date or earlier.

9. If a full design is not provided as part of the RFP, then require periodic design reviews at 30 percent, 60 percent, and 90 percent or at similar milestones.

10. Get your risk manager to assist you with insurance requirements.

11. Make sure that your attorney reviews the contract to ensure that the contractor protects you from liability during construction.

12. Frequently a disputes review board is established for very large contracts. Generally this is a three-person panel: one represents the contractor and is selected by the contractor, one is selected by and represents the issuing agency, and one is jointly selected. This panel monitors the project and acts as the first level of review in any claims

or other contract disputes. Their recommendations are not binding, but they are less expensive than attorneys and courts.

13. In some cases the contractor may be willing to put all his or her internal bid documents in an escrow account. In the event that there is a claim, then and only then could these documents be used to determine the viability of a claim.

14. Establish a formal method for correspondence to include reviews, invoices, and general correspondence.

15. Establish a budget contingency. Large contracts almost always require contract supplements or amendments.

16. Consider liquidated damages and/or retainage to provide leverage over the contractor.

Computer services

Local governments may contract for a wide variety of computer services, including hardware and software installations, moves, changes, and general maintenance; help desk support and logging of problems; one-on-one technology support for staff, provided by telephone or in person; file server and network configuration and maintenance; training for end-user and technical staff; design and maintenance of custom Web sites; pre-programmed Web site services and hosting of Web sites and e-mail; and application software development and maintenance.

Larger governments will tend to rely more on their own employees to provide computer services support, whereas smaller governments are more likely to contract for support. But some larger governments that otherwise would have a full-time information technology (IT) staff may choose to contract this complete function to a single contractor.

Bidding   Contracted computer services can be structured in a variety of ways;

hourly "time and materials" basis; fixed price for a block of hours to be used over a time period; set commitment of time (e.g., one day per week); fixed price for a specified project (e.g., "install new server"); fixed price for a specified service (e.g., "maintain all servers for one year"); and one-time and ongoing fixed fees (e.g., for Web site hosting).

As with many types of contract services, the ultimate effectiveness of computer services is dependent on the skill levels of the people doing the work, so the contractor with the lowest price may not necessarily be the most effective. Therefore, most types of computer services lend themselves to purchase through a request for proposal (RFP) process in which the award is based on a variety of factors that include but are not limited to price.

Conventional bidding may not work well for computer services if the size of the engagement is small; a job that is too small may simply fail to attract the attention of the potential contractors. Two ways to increase the size of the award include offering more work over a longer time frame (e.g., rather than installing a single file server, installing all file servers needed over a period of time) or collaborating with neighboring governments. Local governments may also be able to provide references regarding state purchasing contracts, especially for services such as PC installation and support.

Contracting for services such as application software development specialists can also run into problems involving timing. Contract firms strive to keep their employees busy and are at a disadvantage when asked to specify particular individuals with required skills who will be available weeks in the future because of uncertainty about when those individuals will come off their current assignments.

A successful practice is to use the bidding process to identify several preferred provider contract firms and establish the hourly rates for particular skill sets but not to identify specific individuals. Then, when a project actually starts, the local government can select among available staff from the participating firms.

Contract term and pricing   Although some computer services are onetime events, in many cases local governments would be wise to designate preferred provider contractors who would serve for a contract term. The length of the contract might be a minimum of one year with the ability to extend the contract for a second and third year for contractors that are performing well.

Some services or projects such as the installation of PCs may lend themselves to fixed costs. Hourly rates for computer services can vary considerably according to local markets. Expect to pay lower rates for technicians who install new PCs, develop Web sites, and provide help desk services and higher rates for application software development and more sophisticated technical tasks, such as file server maintenance.

If the contractor is also providing overall management of a project, the local government should require a commitment of a not-to-exceed amount of hours required to complete the project.

Rates for Web site hosting and the use of preprogrammed Web site services usually include a onetime start-up fee and an ongoing monthly fee. The start-up fee might be linked to the volume of data involved in the initial setup. Ongoing fees for government-oriented Web site services are often tied to the population of the local government, so they may vary considerably.

Note that Web site services should offer content management ability to allow government staffers to directly post and maintain the Web site content. Use of content management increases the effectiveness of the government staff and reduces the work of the contractor, so it results in lower costs. Conversely, contracting for a custom Web site without content management can lead to greater costs if the contractor must be involved in ongoing maintenance.

Governments that develop their own Web sites may still contract the *hosting* of the site. The most likely hosting contractor would be the Internet service provider (ISP) that provides the government's Internet access. ISPs will in addition often host e-mail services (e.g., e-mail to jsmith@townoflincoln.gov), and this service can be surprisingly low in cost.

The rates for training classes provided by commercial providers are generally determined by the market in your area. Local colleges will often be able to provide training to governments at lower rates than commercial providers. Buying a block of classes will generally reduce costs.

Recommendations

1. Take advantage of opportunities to contract out technology work, but stop short of contracting out the higher-level management of the government's use of technology. Instead, assign the management oversight to a government employee. In addition, establish IT coordinators at the department level, partly to help direct contractors when they are working within departments. The part-time IT manager and coordinators would not need to be career technology specialists.

2. Limit the ability of contractors to identify their own work; instead, have government employees maintain the list of things to do and assign the work.

3. An exception would be for larger governments that contract out the complete IT function, including the role of what otherwise would be a full-time IT manager. But even in

that case it is important to have a government employee who oversees this function and acts as the contact for the contract IT manager.

4. Consider contracting out the operation of the help desk and the related logging of problems. But in any event, ensure that problems are being logged, possibly as a part-time duty of a government employee, and use the data on logged problems to help oversee the work of contractors and their resolution of problems.

5. Strive to bundle the service of the installation and configuration of hardware and software with the purchase, avoiding having to seek a separate contractor for this service.

6. Rather than contracting for development and maintenance of custom application software (e.g., tax systems), use commercial off-the-shelf software, especially for smaller governments.

7. Avoid the development of a custom Web site, especially for smaller governments, and instead consider contracting with a government-oriented Web site service (e.g., GovOffice. com) that will provide the programming for the site and also host it on their Web server.

8. Especially for smaller governments, consider collaborating with neighboring local governments and sharing common contracted services, such as PC and network server maintenance.

Concessions

A concession is a revenue-generating service that is usually operated on public property. The category includes food stands (discussed separately in the section entitled "Food services"); vending machines; the operation of facilities such as swimming pools, tennis courts, and golf courses; and the rental of sailboats, beach chairs, and other recreation-related equipment.

Bidding method   Prequalification followed by competitive sealed bidding or multistep sealed bidding is an effective method. Competitive negotiation is used primarily when establishing a new service area. The principal qualification criteria for a concession operator are the quality of the management staff, the firm's experience in the specific field, and financial stability.

Contract term and pricing   Concession contract terms range from two to more than ten years. The length of the contract frequently depends on the amount of capital the contractor is required to spend for leasehold improvements required by the local government, such as new equipment, walls, floors, or ceilings. Because these improvements revert to the local government at the end of the contract term, the contractor needs adequate time to amortize the capital outlay; consequently, the higher the investment by the contractor, the longer the contract term. If a local government does not want a long contract term but still wants substantial leasehold improvements, it must expect to receive lower revenues from the contract as a trade-off for the shortened amortization period.

Percentage of revenue is the principal method of payment in the concession industry. The usual contract calls for payment to the local government of a fixed or sliding percentage of gross sales. Most concession stands in small sports fields, general recreation areas, or beachfronts are poor revenue producers, and it is not unusual for a local government to accept a small bid for smaller concession contracts. A token payment for a seasonal concession contract is usually a better option than operating the concession with public employees. Even a dollar per year revenue from a concession contract can be considered profitable if the facility is not supported by the local government budget except for general maintenance of the structure or grounds.

Recommendations

1. When preparing concession contracts, research all available sources for sample contracts for the same service. Other local governments will have incorporated the lessons they learned into their contracts, and referring to these contracts should prevent many problems associated with writing a scope of work for the service.

2. The contract should state specifically who is responsible for payment of the utility bills.

3. To control what is presented to the public, require advance approval by the local government of the contractor's advertising and all items to be sold or equipment to be rented. Identify all prohibited sale items such as alcoholic beverages and tobacco products.

4. Concession operations are often located near public rest rooms. It is common practice to have the concession operator responsible for cleaning the rest rooms and performing minor maintenance. (Major maintenance of the structure, the roof, and heating, ventilating, and air conditioning systems is usually performed by local government maintenance staff and is not included as part of the contractor's duties and responsibilities.)

Consulting services

The most common types of consulting contracts are often grouped together under the term management consulting; they cover organizational development, management training and development, and professional assistance. Organizational development deals with issues such as integration of new technologies, organizational change, and organizational values. Management training and development includes team building, participatory management, decision making, and conflict management. Professional assistance includes the services of experts in particular fields such as urban planning and computer hardware or software.

Bidding method   Competitive negotiation is preferred for consulting services. Though cost should always be a consideration, the consultant's qualifications are usually more pertinent to the success of the contract.

Contract term and pricing   Contracts are usually short term for projects such as providing advice and assistance to departments but may last one year or more for projects involving organizational development or other specialized areas. Training contracts that run for more than one year can be priced either with a CPI escalator or on a fixed price basis for the entire project. Fixed-price contracts for more than one year are common.

Usual arrangements include lump-sum pricing for a specific consulting project, lump-sum pricing for the complete term of the contract, or a unit price for each training presentation. The cost plus a fixed fee method and the cost reimbursement with a not-to-exceed price limit method are used occasionally.

Recommendations

1. Specify allowable contract reimbursables (copy and print charges, class materials, computer time, travel, lodging, etc.), and provide for reimbursement at the contractor's cost with no markup. The contractor's price should include all the profit or overhead costs applicable to the contract.

2. Be sure that the scope of work for organizational development or management training and development

contracts provides the contractor with a thorough understanding of the problem that generated the need for the contract.

3. Require progress reports at least once a month during the project. If the contract calls for a formal report as a contract deliverable, require a draft of the formal report to be submitted for review and comment by the local government about thirty days prior to the date scheduled for its completion to make sure that the report covers all contract requirements.

4. Require candidates for management training and development contracts to provide sample training outlines, handouts, and examples of other materials provided to students. Management consultants should provide one or two samples of previous work products or reports.

Custodial services

Custodial services contracts are one of the oldest types of contracts in local government; they are used for cleaning facilities of every description from maintenance shops to museums. Because different building uses require different levels of cleanliness, each contract must carefully define the level needed for the individual facility.

The custodial services industry usually classifies cleanliness standards into three categories. The first two can be used to identify for a contractor the level of cleanliness expected for various areas of public buildings. The prestige level of cleanliness may not be necessary for every area of every public building; the higher the standard, the higher the cost to the local government.

Prestige cleaning A standard of cleaning that prompts unsolicited compliments from tenants, occupants, employees, and visitors. Complaints are rare.

Adequate cleaning A standard of cleaning that elicits neither compliments nor serious criticism. Some occupants may complain from time to time.

Minimal cleaning A standard of cleaning that provokes frequent criticism from tenants, occupants, employees, and visitors. Special cleanups are often needed.

Bidding method Competitive sealed bidding is used most often when contracting for custodial services. Competitive negotiation or multistep bidding, if allowed, should be used when a high quality of service is needed for museums, historic buildings, heavily used public facilities, court facilities, and so forth. However, because competitive negotiation often favors larger, more experienced firms, it may eliminate small, minority-owned, disability-owned, and other disadvantaged firms from competition.

Contract term and pricing Contracts run for two to three years on a fixed price or fixed price with escalator basis. A two-year term is usually the maximum for a fixed price bid in a metropolitan area. In areas where competition is not as extensive, an escalator can be used to price a third or fourth year after the two-year fixed-price base contract term.

Bids are submitted for a lump sum to be paid each year for each facility plus an hourly rate for day laborers.

Recommendations

1. Unless there is a professional custodial service contractor on the local government payroll responsible for taking measurements, the scope of work should not include a statement of the square feet of space to be cleaned. Errors in calculating the size of the cleaning area can give rise to claims for additional compensation from a contractor who relies on measurements provided

by the local government. Make the bidders responsible for taking the measurements or estimates. Require a mandatory walkthrough at the pre-bid conference and permit bidders to return to the site to take measurements at their convenience.

2. The scope of work must include only necessary services; requiring an unnecessarily high level of service will simply increase service costs.

3. Separate custodial service requirements into individual tasks (dusting, mopping, waxing, etc.), specify how often each task should be done, and establish performance standards for each task.

4. To simplify performance evaluation, define the terms used in the scope of work. The following are examples of definitions adapted from standards established by the custodial services industry.

   Dusted surface   A surface free of dirt, dust streaks, lint, and cobwebs.

   Swept or vacuumed surface   A floor or stairway free of dust, dirt, and debris in corners, behind doors, and under desks, tables, radiators, and other furniture standing off the floor on legs.

   Mopped surface   A floor free of dirt, dust, debris, streaks, or standing water and without splash marks or water stains on baseboards.

   Waxed surface   A thin, even coating of approved nonslip wax. Floors are clean and bright in the entire area, including corners and under furniture.

5. Custodial workers may be unfamiliar with the duties specified in the contract; not being fluent in English can compound this problem. If applicable, require the contractor to provide (or the local government can provide) translations of the building cleaning specifications into the native languages of the workers and supervisors.

6. Require the contractor's supervisor to maintain a nightly log showing deviations from the assigned work schedule, needed building repairs, when work assignments are not completed, and so forth.

7. A performance bond requirement can restrict bidding to the larger and possibly more expensive firms. Unless a performance bond is required by local laws or regulations, an effective alternative is a provision in the scope of work allowing the local government to deduct a specified amount or percentage from the contractor's monthly payments for documented instances of substandard workmanship. The deduction is taken from the payment for the month in which the substandard work was done.

8. Require fidelity bonding of contractor employees. This is a form of insurance that covers dishonesty or mysterious disappearance of public or personal property during cleaning hours.

9. Require the contractor to pay for rekeying locks if the contractor loses any keys.

10. Require uniforms—at least a smock or T-shirt with the corporate logo—and name tags for all contractor employees.

11. If cleaning is done at night, consider requiring one or more part- or full-time day workers on an hourly basis to handle cleaning problems that occur during business hours and to clean rest rooms during the day.

12. Many local governments require that the contractor provide all paper products and rest room and cleaning supplies. With this approach, the contract is easier to manage, but costs for these supplies are higher

than they would be if the local government purchased them. Moreover, a contractor who is having cash flow problems may try to cut costs by keeping fewer supplies on hand or providing a lower quality of supplies.

13. Include a clause in the scope of work that permits the local government to use any or all of the contractor's cleaning equipment and supplies in the event of a labor action by the contractor's employees.

14. When evaluating the contractor's qualifications, consider the bidder's reputation in the industry, general stability, management quality and depth of management experience, supervisory control, and technical proficiency.

Food services

The food service category includes snack bars in recreational facilities, restaurants in convention centers or at tourist attractions, food services in detention facilities, and meals delivered to elderly, indigent, or homebound citizens. Refer to the discussion of concessions in this chapter for information on food service contracts that produce little revenue.

Bidding method   If the needs are well defined, competitive sealed bidding is most frequently used in contracting for food services. If the service is specialized or new, competitive negotiation may be more appropriate.

Contract term and pricing   For delivered meal or institutional food service contracts, the term is usually two to four years, with a unit price per meal or per person per day subject to an annual escalator. For concessions, terms of ten or more years are common if the contractor is required to make a substantial capital investment for equipment or to construct the concession facility. Pricing is generally on the basis of a fixed or sliding percentage of revenue. For a sliding percentage of revenue, the bid form is typically structured as in the following example, with the bidder entering the proposed percentage:

Gross revenue received by contractor ($)	Percentage of gross revenue paid to local government
0-20,000	_____
20,001-40,000	_____
40,001-60,000	_____
More than 60,000	_____

Recommendations

Institutional and delivered meals:

1. The scope of work must clearly define dietary needs of the recipients of delivered meals. Use standards established by state or federal legislation, the public health department, or program dieticians. Include a provision for separate menus for clients with special needs—for example, diabetic, low-salt, low-fat, or kosher diets.

2. Require the contractor to provide varied menus every week, frequently changing vegetables, side dishes, and entrees and the method of cooking them to avoid client boredom with the food. Require holiday meals that include foods traditionally associated with the holiday. If the clients are predominantly of one ethnic group, require that their culturally preferred foods to be prepared.

3. Require bidders to submit sample menus with the bid response. As part of the evaluation process, an independent dietician should analyze the menu for food value (calories, fats, carbohydrates, cholesterol, salt, etc.) and acceptability under applicable regulations.

4. Specify in the scope of work that the contractor is responsible for meeting all health regulations except those

that apply to areas of responsibility retained by the local government, such as maintenance and repair of equipment or facilities.

5. Require a detailed description of the bidder's method of delivering food, including methods of protecting against external contamination and spoilage.

6. If the facility is eligible for donations of U.S. Department of Agriculture (USDA) products, require the contractor to use USDA foods when available and provide a rebate to the local government equal to the fair market value of the products established by USDA.

7. Consider providing part or all of the labor, either directly or indirectly, and contracting for management only. A labor pool can be assembled from the recipients of the service, clients of programs for handicapped citizens, local government employees placed on light service because of a job injury, or inmates, a common source for food service workers in detention facilities. Under such a program, the contractor provides the skilled labor and hires, trains, and supervises the employees in the labor pool. If permitted by local government regulations, this arrangement can cut the cost of the service considerably and provide valuable training and experience to the members of the labor pool.

Recommendations

Food concessions:

1. Require the concession operator to provide complete details of revenues, customer counts, and other operational data on a regular—monthly or quarterly—basis. This information is valuable for a re-bid or if the local government decides to move the operation in house in the future.

2. If the concession is a free-standing facility on public property, consider requiring that the contractor pay the cost of utilities, minor repairs, exterminating services, equipment maintenance, and public rest room cleaning. This can reduce the workload of the local government custodial staff. If a concession's high sales make it very attractive to contractors, the contractor's responsibilities could include some maintenance of the adjacent grounds as well.

Landscape maintenance

Landscape maintenance includes maintenance of traffic medians, parks, athletic fields, and the areas surrounding public buildings. Maintenance may also be bid as part of the scope of work for the installation of landscaping, in which case a one- or two-year maintenance contract should start immediately after installation is complete.

Bidding method   Competitive sealed bidding is most likely to be used for contracting landscape maintenance services.

Contract term and pricing   A lump-sum fixed price for each year of the maintenance contract or for a two-year term is the usual pricing method; an escalator is recommended for pricing contracts lasting more than two years.

Recommendations

1. Use a standard industry reference for maintenance of plants such as that published by the American Association of Nurserymen.

2. The scope of work must distinguish precisely between damage to plants caused by poor maintenance (e.g., lack of water, poor drainage, uncontrolled weed growth) and damage to plants caused by factors beyond the control of the contractor (e.g., preexisting soil conditions, severe weather).

3. Assign to the contractor responsibility for:
   - Spraying regularly for insect and plant diseases; specify safety measures and the application rates of the chemicals permitted.
   - Cleanup of trash in the landscaped areas once a week.
   - Repair of damages to sprinkler systems discovered during maintenance operations. This service requires the inclusion of time and materials pricing for the contractor's employees or subcontractors responsible for the repairs.

4. Require the contractor to direct vehicle and pedestrian traffic safely around the contractor's area of operations.

5. The quality of landscape maintenance services varies greatly. Start the contract during the months that plants require only limited maintenance so that the work can be evaluated before the plants require more careful maintenance. If performance is unsatisfactory, the contract can be terminated before plants are damaged by an inexperienced or substandard contractor.

6. A performance bond in the full amount of the contract guaranteeing the survival of the plants can help ensure satisfactory performance by the contractor, though it may limit bidding to larger contractors and may also be difficult to enforce. Because an untended landscaped area can suffer irreparable damage during the time required to obtain satisfaction from a bonding company, performance bonds are not always the best guarantee of performance for services such as landscape maintenance. A warranty period for plants is another alternative.

Medical services: Residential, correctional, and detention facilities

This category covers the on-site delivery of medical services to the population residing in residential, correctional or detention facilities. The contractor pays for all medical services, including those provided at the contractor's request by outside medical providers and hospitals, up to the dollar limit per patient specified in the contract.

Bidding method   Medical services can be obtained through competitive sealed bidding when they can be accurately and completely described or through competitive negotiation when the definition of the service is not as precise.

Contract term and pricing   The term is usually three to five years. Cost is usually based on cost per client per day. The monthly payment is calculated by multiplying the average facility population for the preceding month by the contract unit price per day.

Recommendations

1. List all medical care that will be provided (e.g., dental, psychiatric, surgical, gynecological, cardiology services).

2. Require bidders to submit a manual of operating procedures, copies of all reporting forms used, a medical team organization chart, and staff resumes.

3. Require bidders to submit a staffing chart to demonstrate how medical staff coverage will be provided twenty-four hours per day. If, on the basis of prior experience with the service, a particular staffing plan or coverage pattern is preferred, require it in the scope of work.

4. Describe the minimum qualifications for each medical staff member.

5. Require the contractor to maintain in effect any necessary certifications

and to obtain any desired by the local government.

6. Include a requirement for a quarterly or semiannual peer review by the local medical association or other regulatory body such as a county, state, or regional health department.

7. Medical services contracts require special insurance coverage. Require liability insurance to cover the rendering of or failure to render medical professional services (medical professional liability coverage, commonly called malpractice insurance) in addition to basic general liability insurance. The risk manager determines appropriate limits of coverage.

8. Define the limits of the contractor's liability for outbreaks of contagious disease in the facility; injuries resulting from riot or disturbances within the facility, prolonged illness or serious injury affecting one patient, and, for detention center services, injuries that occur before an inmate is booked. For example, the contractor may be held liable only for costs under $200 for an inmate who is injured before booking or for the first $5,000 spent for the prolonged illness of a patient. Charges incurred above these limits would be reimbursed by the local government at the contractor's cost with no markup. This arrangement protects the contractor from unforeseen and catastrophic losses that could result in default. It also helps to keep down a contractor's base price because the contractor does not have to establish a fund for catastrophic expenses.

9. Include a medical professional on the local government evaluation team. Contact the local medical association for candidates.

Medical services: General physical and mental health care

This category covers services provided by individual members of the health care profession such as general practitioners, specialists, dentists, nurses, psychiatrists, psychotherapists, and physical therapists who contract at an hourly rate to work in local government health care facilities, clinics, or other programs. Services may be offered full-time or part-time during days, weekends, or evenings. This type of contract is also used to provide replacement or backup staff for local government medical services providers.

Bidding method   Medical professional services are usually purchased through competitive negotiation.

Contract term and pricing   The term is typically one year. Obtain firm hourly rates from the providers; if they are part-time, establish the minimum number of hours per day that they will work. Services are typically reimbursed on an hourly rate. If purchasing on-call services, be sure to specify this in the bid so the contractor can submit a separate rate for these services in their bid.

Recommendations

1. Medical services providers must purchase medical professional liability insurance. Some health care providers, particularly those without an established practice, may not have professional liability coverage or have less than the risk manager considers adequate. Adequate insurance should be the first evaluation criterion to be met by respondents.

2. Some private health care providers may not adapt easily to the delivery of health care services in a public health setting. The scope of work should include a description of problems that may be encountered in treating indigent, elderly,

or disabled citizens as well as other recipients of public health care. If possible, require experience in treating these types of patients.

3. Depending on the anticipated volume of work, the contract can be awarded to one primary provider or multiple providers. A list of qualified backup candidates should be maintained in the event that that turnover becomes a problem.

4. When several providers are available, the contract should include a clause that permits immediate cancellation by either party at its convenience. This clause allows the local government to cancel if a problem of any nature concerning a provider occurs during the contract term, and it may help to avoid the expense of legal or default actions against a medical professional.

Mowing services

Mowing services contracts can be divided into separate contracts according to the type of mower required (flail or reel mowers for rough mowing in fields and open spaces; small power or tractor-operated finish mowers for parks, landscaped areas, or golf courses); the nature of the area being mowed (park, traffic median, open field, roadside, sports field, or golf course); or the geographical district (north, south, east, or west). The type of mowing required and geographical locations can also be combined: bidding individual geographical areas by type of mowing can create more active competition among smaller, more specialized contractors, providing additional business opportunities for small, minority-owned, or other disadvantaged businesses. A drawback of multiple contracts is that they increase the workload of the contract administration personnel.

Bidding method   Competitive sealed bidding is generally used for mowing services. Because the service is easy to describe accurately and completely, negotiation is seldom used.

Contract term and pricing   Mowing contracts are usually established for one or two years at a fixed price. If an escalator clause is incorporated into a mowing contract, the price increases may be higher than the prices that can be obtained through competitive bidding every one or two years. Prices in this highly competitive field tend to fluctuate, seldom tracking an escalator index.

In many mowing contracts, bidders submit a single price for all locations for an entire mowing season. This method does not take into account extra mowing during an especially wet season or less mowing than usual during an especially dry season, An alternative is to establish unit prices for one mowing of each area included in the contract. Under this method, the contractor is paid each time a location is mowed.

If the local government opts to accept a single price for an entire mowing season at all locations, it is still desirable to obtain a lump-sum price from the bidders for a onetime mowing of the entire area and unit prices for individual locations within that area. The unit prices can be used if it is necessary, for example, to prepare a location for a special event that occurs between scheduled mowings.

A per-acre price can be used to price areas that are added to the contract during the contract term or to calculate a new contract amount if an area is dropped from the contract. Obtaining an hourly rate for a complete crew (supervisor, laborers, and all equipment) is also useful, in case problems develop with another mowing contractor. If trash removal is included as part of the contract, request a separate hourly rate for trash removal and disposal. This rate can be applied when the contractor's employees prepare for and clean up after special events at a park or sports facility.

Recommendations

1. If the number of acres to be mowed is included in the scope of work, be sure it is accurate or disclaim responsibility for the accuracy of the measurements. Errors in local government calculations could result in a contractor's claim for additional compensation once work has begun. Preferably, require bidders to make their own estimates.

2. Specify in inches the height after mowing and the frequency of mowing. Specify where and how clippings will be disposed of.

3. To eliminate the expense of hand trimming along walls or fences, require the application of specified herbicides by qualified contractor technicians, if permitted by local ordinances or regulations.

4. Require the contractor to file a detailed schedule for areas to be mowed each week. The schedule will enable the contract administration team to inspect the areas and evaluate performance during or immediately after mowing.

5. Require the contractor to redo immediately, at the contractor's expense, any work that is unsatisfactorily completed.

6. Include in the scope of work a requirement for the removal of trash or debris. For example, if the contractor discovers an unusual amount of trash (over ten cubic feet, for example), the contractor is responsible for removing it or at least for notifying the local government so that it can be removed by public employees. Responsibility for emptying litter receptacles in parks can also be incorporated into a mowing contract.

7. Require safety hazards, dead animals, or landscaping damage to be reported to the local government on the day of discovery.

Recycling wastepaper

Contracts for recycling wastepaper are slightly different from other contracts in that they are contracts to sell rather than to buy. Instead of paying for the service, the local government is receiving revenue for something it once threw away at a landfill or burned in an incinerator.

Contracts for the sale of wastepaper cover two primary paper types, newspapers disposed of by households and wastepaper from public offices (both white paper and computer printout paper). Newspapers are either left at central drop-off points by citizens or picked up by residential refuse collection crews. Office paper is collected and brought to the contractor's containers at a central point in a public building, usually by in-house staff.

Bidding method   Competitive sealed bidding is used for recycling wastepaper contracts.

Contract term and pricing   Fixed price with escalator contracts with terms of one to three years are generally used for recycling services. The indexes most commonly used are those listed in trade publications of the recycling industry.

Establish a guaranteed minimum price per ton, to be adjusted when the escalator index shows an increase in wholesale prices. The following is an example of a price escalator provision tied to the changes in wholesale prices:

For every $5.00 increase in the wholesale price for [type of paper], the local government will receive the same increase in the price paid per ton over the initial bid by the contractor. Increases will become effective on the date that the wholesale price reaches a level $5.00 above the price currently in effect.

Decreases in the wholesale price will be calculated in the same manner, reducing the price per ton paid to the local government in $5.00 increments. The local government reserves the right to cancel the contract without notice or to renegotiate its terms if referenced wholesale prices drop so that application of the above formula requires the local government to pay the contractor for wastepaper pickup.

In a depressed newspaper market, the local government may be forced to pay for newspaper pickup. The bid form acknowledges this possibility as follows:

Contractor will complete applicable entries:

Contractor will pay local government	$_____ per ton for newspaper
Local government will pay contractor	$_____ per ton for newspaper
Contractor will pay local government	$_____ per ton for office paper
Local government will pay contractor	$_____ per ton for office paper

Recommendations

1. Because recycling firms may not respond to a solicitation that calls for the purchase of newspaper alone and office paper is much more attractive to a recycling firm than newspaper, keep the two types together and award a contract only for the sale of both. This ensures that the local government can dispose of its newspaper even in a depressed newspaper market.

2. An office paper contract requires an internal system for transferring paper from individual offices to a central collection point. The contractor usually provides containers for both offices and the central pickup point but picks up only from the central collection point.

3. To verify contract payments for newspaper, require the contractor to provide truck weight tickets from the disposal plant or other commercial scales. Payments for office paper are often based on the average weight when full of the contractor's central pickup containers.

Refuse collection

Refuse collection contracts include collection of household refuse, yard waste, appliances, furniture, and emptying of street litter receptacles and dumpsters.

Bidding method   Competitive sealed bidding is used for contracts for refuse collection.

Contract term and pricing   Contracts are usually long term (four years or more) and tied to an index such as the CPI or to multiple indexes, as discussed in Chapter 3. A longer contract allows the contractor to amortize equipment purchased for the contract. It also protects the local government from fluctuations in contract prices associated with changing contractors and with rapid changes in the market.

If multiple indexes are used, the CPI can be the escalator for the collection portion of the unit price and the local disposal facility's tipping fee can be the escalator for the disposal portion of the unit price.

The unit price per household method is used most often for refuse collection contracts. Separate unit prices can be requested for curbside collection, backyard collection at the homes of infirm or elderly citizens, collection of different sizes of containers, and mechanized collection. Where the bid form requests separate unit prices, multiply each unit price by the frequency of collection by the number of pickups for each price category, then use the extended totals to rank the bidders by price.

Recommendations

1. Require a list of equipment and personnel to be dedicated to the contract.

2. Require two-way radio communications capability between collection vehicles and the contractor's central office to permit rapid deployment of crews to assist with problems or to handle missed pickups. It is desirable to require the contractor to provide an extra radio on the contractor's supervisor's frequency for use by the local government field manager.

3. Require payment of liquidated damages if problems such as spilled debris or failure to collect refuse remain uncorrected after a stipulated time.

4. Consider including a vehicle and equipment buy-back clause in the bid document. See "Vehicle and equipment buyback" in Appendix A.

Security services

Security services contracts for public buildings or for special events require extensive evaluation of the bidder's screening and training procedures. Price should always be a secondary factor in obtaining security services. A prequalification process is advisable to eliminate marginal firms.

Bidding method   Competitive sealed bidding, multistep bidding, or competitive negotiation can be used to contract security services. Prequalification procedures are recommended when competitive sealed bidding is used.

Contract term and pricing   The contract term is usually two or three years. If the contract is for more than one year, include an escalator. Security services contracts are usually priced at a fixed price per hour, but some service areas lend themselves to an annual fixed price.

   Obtain separate hourly rates for day, evening, and weekend assignments. Even if no evening or weekend assignments are anticipated, obtain rates in case other departments require guard services for these hours, other needs develop in the department contracting for security services, or guards are needed for special events or emergencies.

Recommendations

1. Obtain the details of the contractor's employee screening process. The contractor must periodically test guards for evidence of substance abuse.

2. In the general terms and conditions, include a clause allowing immediate termination by the local government if the quality of security personnel provided falls below acceptable levels or if the contractor repeatedly fails to provide personnel when needed (e.g., more than three times in a 60-day period). This prevents lengthy default procedures if performance problems develop with the firm.

3. Require the contractor to provide uniforms identifying guards as security officers or specify a dress code and require that each guard wear a name tag with prominent corporate identification.

4. Specify exactly what force, if any, the guard is authorized to use while on assignment, what defensive or offensive equipment is allowed, and what equipment is prohibited.

Social services

Social services that are frequently contracted included child welfare, substance abuse treatment, case management for persons with psychiatric illnesses, occupational skills training, chore services and personal care for persons with disabilities, housing and homeless services, and programs for senior citizens.

Bidding method   Social services contracts are usually awarded through competitive negotiation. Competition is usually limited, and the award may be divided among various providers offering specialized services to particular segments of the client population.

Contract term and pricing   The contract term is two to four years, depending on the program and the type of clients to be served. Fixed price per unit with escalator contracts are commonly used. Unit costs are based on the cost per client served on an hourly, weekly, or monthly basis. Fixed price with incentives are also used, but incentives must be structured cautiously so contractors are not tempted to prematurely terminate services. Several renewal options beyond the original contract term are often included.

The award is usually made as a requirements contract with a limit on local government expenditures per year, usually based on the amount available to the local government from a budget allocation or a federal, state, or local grant. The local government controls the contract amount by limiting clients' use of the services to the amount of available funds. However, some services, such as mental health, may be funded through a federal entitlement program (e.g., Medicaid) in which clients must be served if they meet eligibility criteria. In this case, the local government should ensure the contractor has prior experience providing the service and that their rates realistically reflect the capacity to manage some uncertainty in client load.

The unit prices for subsequent contract years can be tied to a CPI escalator or to client payment limits established by the state or federal agency responsible for issuing or monitoring grants for the social service area under contract. When the responsible department adjusts the amount to be spent per client, the contract price changes with it.

Recommendations

1. In social services contracts, a structured response from the offeror is essential because of the amount of information required. Indicate the order of the topics to be covered and the maximum length in pages of the response to each part. One way to structure the response format is as follows:

Part 1: Knowledge and experience with the population served. Offeror must demonstrate an understanding of the needs of the clients to be served and propose means to meet those needs.

Part 2: Technical approach and implementation plan. Offeror must explain how the goals stated in Part 1 will be achieved. Be attuned to any particularly innovative approaches and proposals that intend to incorporate best or evidence-based practices in their implementation.

Part 3: Evaluation plan. Offeror must present a plan for the evaluation of client status and effectiveness of care.

Part 4: Management plan. Offeror must describe administrative and fiscal management of the program, personnel policies, expected use of subcontractors, how client complaints will be resolved, etc. Because staff turnover is often an issue in social service organizations, the offeror must also specify (per the scope of work) how staffing transitions will be handled and a backup plan (that involves management if necessary) for ensuring no disruption in services.

Part 5: Capability statement. Offeror must describe experience and disclose any citations received within the past five years for violations of contracts, grants, safety regulations, employment practices, building codes, and so forth and state their disposition. Offeror must also list prior and existing contracts with other local governments and provide related financial data and the names of references associated with these contracts.

Part 6: Personnel. Offeror must provide job descriptions, resumes of staff and outside consultants, letters of agreement with any outside consultants proposed for use in the contract, a training plan, an organizational chart describing the chain of command, and a description of staff assignments.

Part 7: Pricing. Offeror must list all costs associated with the provision of service on the basis of the cost per day per client (or another basis to be specified by the local government) and specify the minimum and maximum number of clients to be served at the unit price proposed, unless the contractor is involved in making eligibility determinations for service funded by federal entitlements. Offeror must describe any additional costs that would apply, such as transportation for clients. Offeror must also propose a complete budget indicating administrative and overhead costs, operating costs, equipment costs, start-up costs, and any other costs associated with service delivery. For programs in which participants generate revenue, through operating a café or catering business, for example, projections of contract revenue are required. All prices submitted are nonbinding at this stage of the procurement process and are subject to negotiation.

2. In the scope of work, describe the history of service delivery within the community and the local government's philosophy on how services should be administered.

3. List the program objectives clearly and describe all acceptable treatment or service delivery methods. If the contractor is required to use a particular treatment model or evidence-based practice, describe the approach in the scope of work.

4. The scope of work should include the local government's expectations with regard to client service. For example, specify the expectations with regard to clients' nutritional and medical needs, counseling and supervision to be provided to clients, the extent of services to be provided at a central facility on an inpatient or out-patient basis or at clients' homes, the method of reporting to the local government on client progress, and the types of treatment plans and programs that will be used. Describe in detail all required reports (financial reports, quarterly performance reports, audits, and treatment plans, etc.).

5. Pay close attention to organizational capacity and the ability of the offeror to fulfill contract requirements and to comply with any applicable federal regulations and requirements.

Street repair

Street repair includes asphalt work, concrete repair, and other services such as installation of streetlights, traffic poles and foundations, and sidewalk paving blocks, as well as street and parking lot striping. Asphalt work includes asphalt milling and grinding, the partial removal of excess asphalt before new asphalt is laid, the complete removal and replacement of asphalt road surfaces, crack sealing, and application of a liquid asphalt coating (slurry) for streets, bicycle paths, sports courts, and parking lots. Concrete repair includes repair and replacement of curbs and gutters, installing catch basins and short runs of concrete pipe, and other general repair or maintenance of streets and highways. Street repair service contracts are usually established for small- to medium-size repair or maintenance jobs requiring only a day or two of labor and a few truckloads of material. They should not be used for major street construction, which uses higher quantities of materials and requires that the contractor move equipment to the site once for an extended period. These factors create economies of scale that are not possible in street repairs.

Bidding method Competitive sealed bidding is used for street repair contracts.

Contract term and pricing A one-year contract term is standard. Multiyear contracts can be established by using an escalator to determine subsequent years' pricing, but when competition is high, the service should be bid every year.

A street repair bid form may include twenty or more unit prices: unit costs per square yard for installing various depths of asphalt for asphalt milling and grinding and for various types of curb and gutter work; unit prices for installation of street light poles, traffic lights and pedestals, sidewalk paving block; and so forth. Because of the number of items in the average street repair contract, each with its own unit price, it is difficult to identify the lowest bidders. To permit identification of the lowest bidder, annual estimates can be included for each item in the bid form to permit a total price comparison of the bid responses.

Sample jobs or sample invoices are an alternative price evaluation method. For the sample job method, prepare line drawings of one or two typical street repair jobs using as many unit price items as possible. Specify the number of units of each item required for the job (linear feet of curb and gutter, square yards and depth of asphalt, square yards of driveway and handicapped ramps, etc.) Seal the job until the open-

ing of the bid responses, then use the unit prices submitted by the contractors to calculate the cost of the sample jobs. The lowest sample job total identifies the lowest bidder.

Another ranking method consists of assembling representative contractor invoices from the work done in the preceding year representing an average month's billing. Invoices must be selected that show such entries as the units of work, materials purchased, and the number of labor hours billed. The invoice entries must include most of the items for which unit prices are being requested in the bid form. Seal the invoices and open them at bid opening with the bidder responses. After bid opening, apply the unit prices of each bidder to the units shown on the invoices (ignore the prices from the previous year, just use the quantities of each item from the invoice multiplied by the unit prices of each bidder). The totals of the bidders indicate their ranking by price for what has been determined to be a representative month's work under the contract.

Recommendations
1. Specifications are usually based on the standards of the local government public works department or the state transportation department.
2. Payment is based on measurement of actual work performed. To ensure that the request for payment matches the actual number of units provided, require that jobs be physically inspected before payment is made.
3. Assign to the contractor responsibility for directing vehicles and pedestrians through or around the work site.

Street sweeping

Street sweeping includes sweeping of streets, parking lots, and garages.[1]

Bidding method Competitive sealed bidding is used for street sweeping contracts.

Contract term and pricing A three- to four-year term is average under a fixed price with escalator contract. If the contractor is required to provide new equipment, a longer term is necessary to allow the contractor time to amortize the cost.

Unit price per curb mile swept is the usual basis for payment. The service can be priced on a lump-sum basis, but this is not standard. Bad weather may prevent the contractor from providing as many sweeping hours as had been expected, resulting in higher costs than necessary for the work done. Request hourly rates for the cost of the equipment and operator for snow removal and emergency cleanup.

Recommendations

1. Include in the scope of work a map showing the areas covered by the contract; a definition of the portion of the street to be cleaned (curb lane only, curb to curb) and areas to be excluded from the contract and a schedule indicating how frequently streets are to be swept and specifying the times of the day or night that sweeping is permitted. Provide a detailed description of conditions that permit exceptions to the schedule (e.g., inclement weather, Sundays, holidays, special events).

2. Require the contractor to be responsible for removing and disposing of rocks, tree limbs, and debris not picked up by the sweeper. So that debris that would have been picked up by a heavier sweeper will not be left behind, require a specific level of efficiency of the equipment to be used.

3. Require the contractor to provide extra services such as special cleaning for parades or festivals and, if applicable, snow removal.

Temporary help

Temporary help contracts for on-site personnel can include not only clerical employees but also computer programmers, light and heavy laborers, specialized repair technicians, and architects and engineers working on small projects.

Bidding method Competitive sealed bidding is used most often to purchase services from agencies that provide clerical employees or laborers. The contractor provides temporary employees from a labor or clerical pool and the hourly rates bid for each category of employee apply to any member of the pool within the category, such as receptionist, heavy laborer, word processor. Categories may also be broken down by different levels of skill—for example, "proficiency with Microsoft Excel."

When establishing a personal services contract with individuals who will directly provide specialized or professional services on an as-needed basis, competitive negotiation is the preferred bidding method because it permits the individuals to be evaluated on the basis of their qualifications with price as a secondary factor. Specialized or professional services may be provided by an individual or a firm specializing in this type of temporary help. The difference between hiring from a firm that provides a pool of employees and issuing an RFP for specialized or professional services is that with the RFP, only selected individuals who meet specific qualification criteria provide the service.

Contract term and pricing Temporary help contracts are usually for one year at a fixed price per hour for each employee classification, whether labor, clerical, professional, or technical. A renewal option at the same price can be included if the parties agree. Because the labor market is highly volatile, escalator clauses are rarely used.

For clerical contracts, simplify contract administration, purchase order preparation, and payment processing by awarding the contract to the overall lowest bidder for all clerical classifications (typists, word processor operators, receptionists, file clerks, data entry clerks, etc.).

Recommendations

1. Backup contractors should be designated for times when the primary contractor cannot provide the requested personnel. The second lowest responsible bidder is usually the backup source.

2. Include a clause that permits termination for convenience of the local government. This avoids prolonged default proceedings if a contractor fails to provide acceptable workers, and it allows immediate use of the backup contractor.

3. For temporary laborers and clerical workers, use generic task descriptions rather than governmental position classification titles, which are seldom applicable to the private sector. Keep the requirements to a minimum (words typed per minute, familiarity with a specific type of word processor or software application, etc.). Divide each classification into at least two experience levels, such as under two years or over two years.

4. Require the contractor to waive all charges if an assigned employee is unacceptable and the contractor is notified within four hours after the employee reports to work.

5. When contracting for professional or technical temporary help, list the specific qualification and experience criteria to be met and require resumes of the individuals.

6. In the private sector, temporary help firms often charge a fee if a client hires a temporary employee who has worked for that client. In the case of local government service contracting, the client is a public body that is required to use competitive hiring procedures to fill job openings. The temporary help contractor therefore does not obtain a fee if the employee applies to the local government and is successful in obtaining work through its competitive process. Temporary help contractors are generally willing to comply with a clause that prohibits requiring a fee if employees are hired through the competitive employment procedures of the local government and not hired directly by the department in which they worked as a temporary employee.

7. Temporary services contracts require special insurance coverage. Require liability insurance to protect the local government against loss to the local government of money or property caused by dishonest acts of the contractor's employees (employee dishonesty coverage, commonly called a blanket bond) in addition to basic general liability insurance. The risk manager determines appropriate limits of coverage.

Towing services

Towing contracts are primarily for towing disabled vehicles away from accident scenes at the request of the police department, but towing disabled public vehicles and illegally parked cars is often included as part of the service. Competition is usually high because of the revenue potential from both towing and storage charges.

Bidding method   Competitive sealed bidding is used to contract towing services. Make an award to one contractor or to several contractors in different geographical zones if the size of the jurisdiction warrants it.

Contract term and pricing The contract term is commonly two years with a one- or two-year renewal option at the discretion of the local government. If a business has to expand its fleet to compete for a large towing contract, a longer contract term enables it to amortize the cost of new equipment purchased for the contract. Towing contracts are established with unit prices that are bid firm for the two-year term. Escalators are seldom used in this highly competitive market.

Unit prices to be submitted by the bidder include day and night towing charges for passenger and light vehicles, winch fees, dolly charges, charges for towing heavy equipment, and daily storage charges. All charges are paid by the vehicle owner. Request unit prices for towing local government fleet vehicles of various sizes (from sedans to refuse trucks) in the event the local government requires towing services.

The unit price for towing should include all storage charges up to midnight of the day of the tow so that owners receive a single combined charge if the vehicle is picked up the same day it was towed. Charging a separate full day's storage fee for two hours of storage (if a vehicle is towed at 10:00 p.m.) can generate complaints.

To rank bidders by price, always include in the bid form estimates of activity for the key unit price items. Not every unit price has to be accompanied by an estimate, just the unit prices of activities that, when added together, represent 90 percent or more of annual contract activity. If the local government can estimate the average number of night tows and day tows (night and day towing charges usually differ) and the average number of days that each vehicle is stored, these three figures—which represent about 90 percent of the dollar volume of an average towing contract—should be enough to rank the bidders by price. Police departments usually maintain records of towing and storage. Records for a current contract (available under the right to audit provision of the contract) can also provide information about average annual activity.

Recommendations

1. The scope of work must cover all the contractor's duties and responsibilities required under state and local laws and regulations. A member of the police department familiar with the state and local motor vehicle and towing laws and regulations should be a member of the scope-of-work and evaluation teams.

2. Monitoring contractor performance and resolving conflicts between the contractor and vehicle owners is usually a function of the police department.

3. If the contractor is responsible for storing towed vehicles, require adequate insurance to protect the vehicles and their contents from theft or vandalism while in the custody of the contractor.

Trades services

Trades services contracts are generally time and materials contracts for trades personnel to back up in-house maintenance staff. Examples are contracts for electrical work, air conditioning service, boiler maintenance and repair, painting, plumbing repairs, heating system maintenance, roof repair, and carpentry.

Bidding method Competitive sealed bidding is used for trades services contracts.

Contract term and pricing Trades services contracts are time and materials requirements contracts usually established for a one-year term. Hourly rates for labor are fixed, and material used is charged at contractor cost or assigned a fixed discount from list price. Labor rates for renewal years are based on an escalator, with the provision that the labor rate may not exceed general market labor rates in effect when the decision to renew is made.

The contract unit prices are the cost per hour for labor for a supervisor (journeyman plumber or electrician) and separate rates for apprentices, helpers, or laborers. A cost per hour for a crew consisting of a specified number and type of workers can also be used. It is better to specify time and a half for overtime and double time for weekend and holiday work than to request separate prices from the contractor. Each contractor may have a different corporate overtime policy. Some may charge double time for Saturdays and triple time for Sundays, others may charge time and a half for Saturdays and double time for Sundays. Some may not charge time and a half until 6:00 p.m., others may charge it beginning at 4:00 p.m. Always try to keep as few price variables as possible in the bid form. With fewer price entries, the lowest bidder is much easier to identify.

Require that all material be provided at the contractor's cost or at a specified discount from list price. Do not permit cost plus a percentage of cost pricing for material.

Consider requesting unit prices for major tasks and include in the bid form an estimate of the number of times the tasks are performed each year. For example, request a unit price for providing and installing drinking water fountains; a unit price for painting standard offices (using a cost per square foot or square yard of surface or a cost for standard room sizes); and a unit price per linear foot of interior partition, per door, and per square foot of suspended ceiling installed.

To allow the contractor to cover other costs, include a contract unit price for a mobilization and demobilization charge (the expense incurred by the contractor to move personnel, equipment, tools, and vehicles to and from the job site).

Specify that the mobilization charge will be charged only once per job, whether the job lasts one day or several days.

Specify that the cost of trade consumables (welding gases, solder, masking tape, paint brushes, thinners, drop cloths, etc.) be included as overhead in the labor rate or as part of the mobilization charge for each job assignment rather than as material. Only paint, lumber, electric switches, and other items that remain as part of the repair, installation, or work provided should be included in material charges.

In electrical, air conditioning, or heating contracts, require a separate annual lump-sum price for preventive maintenance inspections and seasonal checks. Require status and condition reports on all equipment checked or serviced. Request unit prices (hourly or daily rental rates) for specialized equipment such as backhoes, tractors, power drain cleaners, scaffolding, or other special equipment that the contractor may occasionally need, but do not include these prices when determining the lowest bid, because it is uncertain how often this equipment may be required.

Recommendations

1. Consider excluding from the contract items that are frequently used, and state in the scope of work that the local government may provide certain items to the contractor. Examples include freon for air conditioners, major plumbing fixtures (commodes, water fountains), and other materials that the local government can purchase at less cost under other contracts or may stock in its central warehouse. Insert a cost reimbursement clause in the contract to aid in controlling costs (see Appendix A).

2. Specify that payment will be made for work performed on site only. Do not accept portal-to-portal pricing, which allows labor charges from the

time the workers leave their shop to the time they return. The farther the distance of the shop from the work site, the higher the charge for non-productive employee travel time.

3. Require that for work that is expected to exceed a specified dollar amount—$2,000, for example—the contractor provide written estimates to the department requesting the service. This allows the department to decide whether to use the contractor or to bid the job separately and possibly obtain better prices.

4. The time and materials trades services contract is primarily for incidental repairs, replacements, and maintenance. Beyond a low threshold (about $3,000), the cost of a time and materials contract may become prohibitive. Consider limiting the size of an individual job to $3,000. Because of the economy of scale and added competition, separate competitive bids for larger jobs usually result in more saving.

5. Specify the size of an average work crew. A bidder who submits a low price per labor hour may provide a three-person crew when the industry standard is a two-person crew. Require advance approval by the local government for any work that requires a larger crew than that specified in the contract. Specify the makeup of the crew. For example, specify that one supervisor (e.g., journeyman electrician or plumber) will be provided for every two helpers (apprentices or laborers.) Specify experience, qualifications, and any licensing required for key crew members.

6. If competition is extensive, include in the contract a termination for convenience clause to permit rapid release from a contract with an unsatisfactory contractor.

Transportation services

Transportation services include supplemental public transportation and taxi, bus, or van service for social services and recreation programs.

Bidding method   If the specifications for the service are well defined, competitive sealed bidding is usually used. For specialized transportation services (tour vehicles, trams) in which the experience of the contractor is a vital award factor, competitive negotiation is preferable.

Contract term and pricing   Firm fixed price with escalator contracts are established with a term of one to five years, depending on the investment necessary to meet contract requirements.

Contract pricing is based on a firm unit price for each hour, day, week, or month of service provided. Request hourly rates or unit prices for unusual requirements such as operation outside the normal schedule, use of vehicles for local government transportation needs, and temporary extension of routes. Unit prices for unusual requirements are usually not considered when bidders are ranked by price.

Recommendations

1. The scope of work must be as detailed as possible, including schedules, routes, methods of handling revenue received, responsibilities for maintenance of equipment, staffing plans, and so forth.

2. Contracts can be structured so that either the contractor or the local government provides and maintains the vehicles. To minimize disruption of service when a contractor defaults, the local government can purchase the equipment and lease it to the contractor, who is then responsible for operation and maintenance.

3. If publicly owned vehicles are leased to or maintained by the contractor,

require periodic inspection of the equipment at the local government maintenance facility to evaluate the maintenance performed by the contractor. The contractor must also keep complete maintenance records at its repair facility for periodic inspection by the local government.

4. Do not establish insurance coverage minimums without knowing the minimums required by state or local law. For example, some taxicab companies have liability insurance coverage that just meets the statutory minimum, which may not be enough to adequately protect the handicapped, elderly, or mentally disabled clients of the service. The local government risk manager should determine whether the available coverage is acceptable. If higher coverage is available from some companies than from a common carrier (taxi or transportation company), obtain legal advice before eliminating the common carrier from bidding for the work. If acceptable to the legal department, consider restricting the bidders to firms with insurance coverage acceptable to the risk manager.

5. Require bidders to submit a plan describing how service will be maintained during interruptions because of inclement weather, unavailability of vehicles, employee labor actions, and so forth.

Value engineering

Value engineering is the analysis by a professional architectural or engineering firm of plans and specifications for a construction project to determine whether the design can be changed to reduce construction costs, construction time, or postconstruction maintenance costs. Value engineering is particularly valuable in correcting an unclear scope of work, a construction schedule that seems too short or too long, uneco-

nomical or unrealistic material or work requirements, and construction drawings and specifications that seem inadequate.

Bidding method Competitive negotiation is used most often for value engineering contracts.

Contract term and pricing The pricing method may be fixed price, cost plus fixed fee, or any other combination. The prices for value engineering contracts are negotiated. Refer to "Architectural and engineering services" in this appendix.

Recommendations

1. List in the scope of work the specific goals of the contract (e.g., reduced construction costs, construction time, postconstruction maintenance costs) and problem areas to investigate (e.g., unclear scope of work, unworkable construction schedule, unrealistic requirements, unclear plans and drawings.)

2. Do not award a contract unless the firm certifies in writing that it has no business relationships or other ties with the engineer or architect whose work will be reviewed. Objectivity as well as the requisite skills is being purchased under a value engineering contract.

Vehicle repair services

Vehicle repair contracts encompass a wide range of services, including body work; transmission and radiator work; starter, alternator, and air conditioner repair; road service for tires; auto interior maintenance; and car washing.

Bidding method Competitive sealed bidding is used for vehicle repair services.

Contract term and pricing The contract term is usually one year with a renewal option at the same price. Vehicle repair services contracts are usually fixed price contracts and can be priced on a time and materials or unit price basis. Materials are priced at contractor cost or at a discount from an established price list (never on a cost-plus basis).

A unit price can be obtained for specialized repair of each type of automotive component. For example, list all transmission types and the estimated number of each type in the fleet and obtain a preventive maintenance cost, seal replacement cost, and overhaul cost for each type. When services are for general repairs to trucks or passenger vehicles, include separate unit prices for each. Truck repair labor can be more expensive than labor for passenger vehicles.

To compare costs effectively when contractors use different pricing schedules, include sample jobs for the contractor to price on the basis of the contract unit prices and return with the bid response. List a specific type of transmission to be overhauled, a specific type of radiator to be replaced, and so forth. The prices bid for the sample jobs will indicate which bidder's price lists will result in lower material costs to the local government.

Recommendations

1. Establish vehicle repair contracts as requirements contracts and include a clause permitting cancellation at the local government's discretion.

2. Multiple or backup awards should be established for all vehicle repair contracts. Few smaller contractors can handle the volume of work generated by even small local governments.

3. Many vehicle repair contractors use the same regional or national price guides to price their repair jobs. Contact potential bidders to identify price guides in use in the area. Select a price guide used by all or most of the repair firms and name it in the bid document as the pricing standard for the contract. If area contractors use different guides, the bid form should ask for the name of the guide (and a sample copy) and the parts discounts

and hourly labor rates to be used to price repair work. Price guides are used extensively for automotive repairs ranging from body work, automotive glass replacement, radiator recoring, and transmission repair to rebuilding engines.

When a price guide named in the bid document is used to price the work, request in the bid form the discounts to be applied to the parts prices identified in the guide and the hourly labor rate to apply to the number of hours listed for individual repair jobs. For body work, always include an option in the bid document to use less expensive reconditioned or used parts and other components instead of the new parts priced in the guide.

If no single price guide is named, require the bidders to identify the price guide they will use and submit a copy with their bid. Include in the bid form one or more sample repair jobs to be used to identify the lowest bidder. Bidders calculate the price of the sample jobs by using their price guide and the discounts and labor rates they give in the bid form.

4. Vehicle repair facilities require special insurance coverage. Require liability insurance to protect the vehicle while being towed (garage-keeper's legal liability), while being worked on (garage liability), and while in the care, custody, and control of the contractor (garage liability). The risk manager determines appropriate limits of coverage.

5. Obtain a 90-day warranty or guarantee on all parts and labor for the services performed.

Endnotes

1 The section on street sweeping is based on *General Guidelines for Developing Street Sweeping Contracts* (Chicago: American Public Works Association, 1982).

Appendix C

Monitoring various types of service contracts

Appendix C provides suggestions on monitoring and evaluating various categories of services. Descriptions of the services are included in Appendix B. Appendix C does not address all the monitoring procedures and evaluation criteria that may apply to a given contract; instead, it offers general guidelines, some of which may be new to local government staff inexperienced in contract administration.

Architectural and engineering services

Architectural and engineering (A/E) contracts are monitored principally by the follow-up method. Evaluation is based on the quality of reports, specifications, plans, and the final product. Unless the contract manager has an architectural or engineering background, A/E contracts for major construction projects may be difficult to monitor. Public works departments sometimes assign an employee with an architectural or engineering background to monitor A/E contracts, but other demands on staff time may make this impractical.

One option is to hire a professional project management firm to monitor A/E contracts, particularly those with high construction budgets: the function of the firm is to ensure that a construction project is satisfactorily completed at or under the local government's budget for the project. Using a project management firm may be expensive, but it can easily yield savings that more than offset the expense.

It is best to hire a project management firm before the A/E contractor is engaged. A project management firm hired early in the planning stages for the project can help the local government with a number of tasks, including designing the request for proposals (RFP) for the A/E services, prequalifying and selecting A/E and construction contractors, negotiating the final contracts, and monitoring the A/E and construction firms from predesign through completion of construction. Project management firms can also provide value engineering for the A/E firm's designs and cost estimates to check against the A/E firm's estimates.

If a local government decides not to hire a project management firm and the contract manager has little or no background in architecture or engineering, the original solicitation should include more stringent qualification and experience requirements and the investigation of the finalists' experience and qualifications should be especially thorough, with particular focus on each firm's experience with other local governments, its reputation for staying within budget, and its working relationship with staff. A contract manager unfamiliar with the A/E disciplines must rely heavily on the offeror's track record in previous projects as an indication of future performance.

To establish and maintain strict control over the A/E firm's activities, include in the contract document a firm schedule for all deliverables and a provision allowing monetary damages to be assessed for failure to meet the schedule. Require frequent progress meetings, and require all reports and deliverables to be subjected to local government review and comment before being put into final form. Require that narrative progress reports accompany monthly payment requests and that the firm's project manager is available to discuss the contract when requested.

Occasionally, technical problems arise that are beyond the expertise of an in-house monitoring team. To obtain technical advice, establish personal services contracts at hourly rates with outside engineers, architects, value engineers, and cost estimators.

Architecture and engineering: Large infrastructure projects

Large infrastructure construction projects are typically multimillion dollar projects that require constant vigilance to ensure that the requirements and standards established in the contract are complied with. In most cases, the use of a private specialty engineering firm is recommended. These contracts are generally referred to as construction, engineering and inspection (CE&I) contracts. Although expensive, generally between 5 and 10 percent of the construction cost, they are critical to the delivery of a quality product. The CE&I firm becomes the issuing agency's representative to manage and evaluate the contract on a daily basis. The services provided by the CE&I range from actual scientific testing, administration of the contract to include negotiating change orders, verifying invoices, and defending claims. The CE&I essentially becomes an augmentation to the issuing agency's staff. CE&I staff are generally a mix of professional engineers and contract administrators. These firms are selected based on qualifications, as are other professional services.

In addition to the CE&I, the issuing agency will require periodic reports and schedule updates; production meetings are common. These meetings cause the contractor to make a periodic presentation on the status of the project. With millions or billions of public funds involved in these major projects, the monitoring and oversight of the contractor is a major requirement and should never be underestimated.

Computer services

Monitoring of services such as PC installations might include quick testing of each unit by a government employee or collection of feedback from end users on the quality of the installations. Services such as file server configuration might require more extensive testing by a government employee.

Services such as help desk support lend themselves well to the use of metrics in evaluation. Typical metrics for help desk–related support would include percentage of problems resolved on the original call, percentage of problems resolved within 24 hours, etc. Monitoring of services such as one-on-one support and training is more challenging and might require measures such as end-user satisfaction surveys.

As with other types of contracting, the contract relationship for computer services will work best when the management oversight of the contractor is assigned to a specific government employee.

Monitoring is easier when the contractor has been designated as a preferred provider and granted a longer-term contract. The contractor will then be more motivated to perform well in the hope of having the contract extended for additional years.

Concession services

Evaluation of concession services is primarily through direct observation and focuses on the courtesy and personal appearance of staff, the skill and expertise of staff and management, the cleanliness and general condition of the concession area, adherence to health and safety requirements, and the quality of the products served.

Because customer satisfaction is the prime indicator of the success or failure of a concessionnaire, periodic customer surveys and analysis of the type and quantity of complaints are helpful monitoring tools.

Consulting services

Evaluation of consulting services contracts focuses on ensuring the quality of deliverables. Monitoring may take a number of forms—for example, examining draft and final reports, surveying students to determine the quality of training received, interviewing participants in a management consulting project to determine whether the contractor is effectively communicating with them, and conducting periodic surveys to gauge the effectiveness of the work performed. Whatever the monitoring technique, however, it is essential to monitor throughout the planning and performance stages of the project, not simply to evaluate the product (report, training, software program, etc.) after the project is complete.

Meet frequently with the consultant to review progress, survey staff members either personally or through questionnaires, require that draft reports be submitted for local government review before being put into final form, and require advance outlines and briefings on the service to be delivered. Close monitoring during the planning and preparation stages of the consultant's work allows the local government considerably more control over the quality of the final product.

Contracts for consulting services should include a clause permitting termination at the convenience of the local government. It is not unusual to misjudge completely the potential of a consultant; this clause permits quick termination of an unsatisfactory contractor without initiating a default action.

Custodial services

Monitoring custodial contracts is time consuming, but not difficult. Follow-up monitoring of work done the previous night is the monitoring method used most often, but unannounced site visits during cleaning hours should also be conducted periodically. If performance problems develop, increase the frequency of unannounced inspections.

Use the definitions of cleanliness in the contract as the evaluation standard (see Appendix B). During inspections, check to be sure that only approved cleaning materials, disinfectants, and floor finishes are used and that specific cleaning procedures are followed. Rating systems for custodial contractors can take many forms; the point evaluation systems described in Chapter 4 work well with custodial contracts.

To ensure strict adherence to contract obligations, enforce liquidated damages provisions quickly. Schedule weekly or monthly meetings with the contractor to review complaints and the actions taken by the contractor to prevent their recurrence.

Comments from local government clients should be encouraged and complaints followed up on quickly; the contractor should be required to correct deficient work immediately. Periodic surveys of client departments are helpful in determining the quality of contractor performance.

Food services

A food services contract should include descriptions of acceptable, poor, and unacceptable performance and specify the liquidated damages to be assessed for each violation. Examples of standards include timeliness; the freshness, appearance, and temperature of the food at delivery; and the cleanliness of the food preparation facilities. With other services, liquidated damages are seldom enforced for the first violation of performance standards. However, violations of standards in food services contracts may put clients' health at stake, and liquidated damages should therefore be assessed immediately.

Conduct periodic tours of the food preparation facilities and require copies of all relevant health department reports. Conduct user surveys and evaluate the type and number of user complaints.

Landscape maintenance

Landscape maintenance contracts are monitored in three ways: through frequent follow-up inspection of the sites, comparison of conditions at the sites to photographic standards, and strict enforcement of maintenance schedules. The frequency of inspections depends on the season, weather conditions, and the level of investment in plant materials at the contracted sites. Direct observation is rarely used unless service problems develop.

Failure to correct performance problems quickly can result in irreparable damage to plants, trees, or grass. If the field manager does not have professional experience in assessing the health of plants, professional advice should be obtained as needed to monitor the quality of the work. To obtain assistance as needed, establish a personal services contract at an hourly rate with a landscape architect or other qualified professional.

Medical services: residential, correctional and detention facilities

The professional performance of the medical services contractor must be periodically reviewed by one or more qualified medical professionals or health service providers in addition to the contract administration staff. These peer reviews may be conducted by medical professionals employed by the local government or, if this is not possible, by a committee of nongovernmental medical professionals. The local government may request a local medical association either to establish a peer review committee within its organization or to assist the local government in assembling its own committee of one or more medical professionals and hospital or health service administrators.

A peer review committee assists the contract administration staff by evaluating contractor effectiveness in maintaining an acceptable quality of medical care on a monthly, bimonthly, or quarterly basis, depending on the size and complexity of the contract. The committee may also monitor the contractor's adherence to contract performance requirements through random, on-site observation of service delivery, and it may function as a panel to review patient complaints and report its findings and recommendations to the local government. Surveys or interviews of patients conducted by contract administration staff also may be used to help evaluate the contractor; however, the responses of nonvoluntary patients (e.g., the inmates of correctional facilities) may not be reliable.

Medical services: General health care

A peer review committee can help evaluate the performance of medical services contractors. The peer review committee would function in the same manner as described above for a residential facility medical services contract. To avoid having to claim professional incompetence as a reason for termination, be sure that medical services contracts include a provision for termination at the convenience of the local government. If problems develop with the quality of service delivery, the best solution may be to terminate the contract immediately and award it to the next-ranked service provider or to rebid the contract.

Mowing services

Even when several field managers are assigned to different geographic sections of a mowing services contract, the overall contract area is often so large that it is impossible to monitor every mowing. A citizen hotline is a valuable aid in monitoring any contract in which operations are spread over a geographic area too large for effective follow-up or direct monitoring. If a hotline is used, however, citizens will lose faith in the system unless complaints are acted upon quickly.

Recycling

For recycling contracts, the principal areas of monitoring and evaluation are adherence to pickup schedule, the accuracy of the weight information provided with payments, prompt payment of contract revenue, and the condition of the pickup area after collection.

Refuse collection

Refuse collection contracts require intensive monitoring to keep customer complaints to a minimum. Evaluation criteria include the number and type of complaints received, the number of collections missed, cleanliness of the area immediately after collection (often compared with previously established photographic standards), safety record (accidents per mile), and adherence to assigned schedules. Customer surveys and hotlines are also valuable monitoring tools.

Security services

Monitoring security services once the contract has begun is almost secondary in importance to screening the contractor before award. Always thoroughly evaluate the contractor's recruitment and training procedures and the qualifications of the guards to be provided.

Direct observation by the user department is the most common monitoring method. The department should have the right to remove any guard who does not meet contract standards for performance or personal conduct: for example, poor communication skills are unaccept-

able in a guard who handles inquiries from the public; intoxication cannot be tolerated; the use of force, threats, or intimidation is not permitted in public buildings.

Liquidated damages are assessed for poor performance and to cover any charges incurred by the local government if a guard fails to report for an assignment and local government personnel are required to fill in.

Social services

Areas to be evaluated should include the number of units of service delivered, adherence to program schedules, adherence to the program budget, adherence to local, state or federal service guidelines, compliance with regulatory requirements, condition of the service delivery facility, and client satisfaction with services. In addition, standards must be developed to measure the effectiveness of the program, which is not an easy task. The following are examples of standards used to evaluate the effectiveness of a case management program for persons with severe and persistent mental illness.

Standards for a case management program for adults with mental illness:

1. Access: 95 percent of persons deemed eligible for services will begin ongoing treatment services within 14 days of nonemergent intake/assessment.

2. Recidivism: 15 percent or fewer persons discharged from an inpatient hospital or unit be will readmitted within 30 days.

3. Continuity of care: 95 percent of persons will be seen for follow-up care within seven days of discharge from an inpatient psychiatric unit.

4. Recovery: 75 percent of persons deemed capable of competitive employment (by a certified occupational therapist) will attain a job.

5. Quality of life: 95 percent of clients will report satisfaction with living arrangement.

Standards for a family preservation program:

1. Timeliness of services: A treatment/crisis plan will be developed for each family served within 3 days of initial intake.
2. Effectiveness: Out of home placement (foster care, residential setting, etc.) will be prevented for 85 percent of children served.
3. Client satisfaction: 95 percent of parents and children participating in the program will report a high level of satisfaction with the service process.

Standards for a welfare-to-work job training program:

1. All participants will complete a two-week "work-readiness" workshop. Ninety-eight percent of participants will successfully graduate to the occupation skills training program.
2. Ninety percent of participants will successfully complete the 16-week occupational skills training program for the employment track of their choice.
3. Upon completion of the job training program, 75 percent of participants will secure competitive employment.
4. 60 percent of those who become employed will remain employees for a minimum of three months.

Street repair

For street repair contracts, contract administration and quality assurance are usually assigned to inspectors from the departments responsible for the services (e.g., highway, public works, utilities). The team assists the inspectors in resolving contract disputes or interpreting contract issues and may use surveys and hotlines to evaluate the satisfaction of both public and private clients.

Evaluation criteria include time required to complete the work, number of complaints received about problems with traffic control, and response time for emergency work. The quality of the work is monitored by direct or follow-up observation.

Street sweeping

Evaluation of street sweeping services is based on the level of cleanliness after sweeping, adherence to schedules, driver and equipment safety, courtesy of operators, and number of complaints received. Photographs may be used to establish various levels of cleanliness.

Temporary help

The principal indicator of the quality of temporary help provided by the contractor is an evaluation form completed by the user department for each temporary employee. The form should be as simple and straightforward as possible. It is completed and forwarded to the contract administration team after one or two days' work by the temporary employee or at the completion of the work assignment.

Overall evaluation criteria include the number of employees determined to be unacceptable and discharged on their first day of work, the number of times the contractor was unable to provide an employee when requested to do so, and the overall skill level of assigned employees.

Contracts should require the contractor to replace an unacceptable employee by the following workday and should specify that no payment will be due for employees rejected within the first four hours of the assignment.

Temporary help contracts usually include a termination for convenience clause (see Appendix A). A backup award is generally made to the next-ranked bidder to ensure that employees are available if the lowest bidder cannot satisfy the temporary help needs of the local government.

Towing services

Monitoring the towing contractor at the scene of an accident is usually done by the police officers in charge. There is seldom room for variation from contract procedures, many of which are based on law and police department rules and regulations regarding safety practices at accident scenes (for example, determining the ownership of towed vehicles and correctly preparing towing documents, using the correct equipment and ensuring that the towing hookup does not further damage vehicles, preventing fire, cleaning glass from the street, and assisting in traffic control).

Because field monitoring is performed by the police department, liquidated damages, suspension, or cancellation provisions are enforced quickly if legal or procedural requirements are violated.

Although field performance is important, do not neglect to monitor the paper side of towing contracts: obtain samples of customer invoices at least monthly and compare the invoice charges with the contract unit prices.

Follow-up questionnaires mailed to recipients of the service are also a valuable means of assessing the quality of the towing service.

Trades services

Evaluation of trade services is straightforward: Is the work acceptable or not? The contract should state that the department responsible for payment has the final decision on the acceptability of the finished work. Examine payment requests to check the accuracy of the time billed and the materials used.

Transportation services

For transportation service contracts, evaluate driver and vehicle safety (number of accidents), adherence to schedules, quality of preventive maintenance, frequency of vehicle breakdowns, and number and type of passenger complaints. Criteria such as driver courtesy and vehicle cleanliness can be evaluated through follow-up random interviews or questionnaires.

Value engineering

Value engineering contracts are supervised in the same manner as architectural and engineering contracts. Value engineers analyze specifications and plans to determine where costs can be cut; thus, evaluation focuses primarily on the costs saved through the identification of errors or unnecessarily expensive design options.

Because prompt analysis is essential to obtain cost savings, the value engineering contractor must adhere rigidly to the contract schedule. Delay may cause the design contractor to fall behind schedule, which can result in higher design costs and, ultimately, in higher construction costs.

Vehicle repair services

For vehicle repair services, performance is judged primarily by the quality of the finished work or the number of times a vehicle is returned for correction of a problem. Repeated rejection of repairs because of poor materials or workmanship is grounds for cancellation.

Glossary

Act of God   An unforeseen occurrence beyond human control caused by nature, such as a hurricane, lightning, or a flood, that is not attributable to negligence of the contractor. Compare with "force majeure."

Addendum   A change, addition, alteration, correction, or revision to a bid or contract document. The terms "addendum" and "amendment" are synonymous.

Administrative remedies, exhaustion of   The completion of the process of direct appeal to a local government defined in the local government's administrative regulations. When all procedures for review of the appeal by public officials have been followed and the relief sought by the appealing party still has not been obtained to that party's satisfaction, administrative remedies are considered to be exhausted. The appealing party then may pursue legal action through the courts.

Agreement   In local government service contracting, an understanding, usually in writing, between two or more competent persons under which one person (the contractor) agrees to perform a service in a manner defined in the agreement and the second person (the local government) agrees to compensate that person for the services performed in accordance with the conditions of the agreement. An agreement also can be made whereby the contractor compensates the local government for the contractor's right to perform a service, such as operating a concession or franchise. Synonymous with "contract."

Allocatable costs   Costs that are specifically related to the contract.

Allowable costs   Costs recognized by law, regulation, or the contract.

Alternative bid   A bid response that does not meet the exact requirements of the bid document that is submitted as an alternative to a specified method of service delivery that in the opinion of the bidder achieves the same end as the specified method of service delivery.

Amendment   A change, addition, alteration, correction, or revision to a bid or contract document. The terms "addendum" and "amendment" are synonymous.

Antitrust violations   Violations of federal or state laws that regulate trusts, cartels, or business monopolies by limiting or prohibiting noncompetitive business practices. Violations of antitrust laws include such practices as price fixing, bid rigging, identical bidding, and market division.

Appeal   The resubmission of a protest, contract dispute, or claim to a higher authority with the intent to overturn a decision of a lower authority.

Arbitrary and capricious actions   Actions by whim or caprice. A public official's improper use of discretionary powers.

Arbitration   The resolution of a conflict between two parties by a third disinterested party.

Assignment   The legal transfer of a claim, right, interest, or property.

Best interest of the local government   Whatever is regarded as advantageous to the local government, usually as defined by a public official.

Bid (noun)   The response submitted by a bidder to an invitation for bids (IFB) or a multistep bid. The term is sometimes used to refer to the complete bid document. The response to a request for proposals (RFP) is called a "proposal" or "offer." Synonymous with "bid response."

Bid (verb)　To submit a bid response. By submitting a bid response, one person (the contractor) gives another person (the local government) the legal power to create a contract with the responding contractor in accordance with the bid response.

Bid bond　An agreement issued by an insurance company to a local government on behalf of a bidder—its client—as a guarantee that the client will enter into a contract with the local government if the bid response submitted by the client is accepted. If the bidder fails to enter into a contract, the insurance company pays the local government the difference between the accepted bid and the next acceptable bid plus any additional administrative costs upon receiving evidence of the additional costs and evidence that the bidder qualified for an award but refused or failed to enter into a contract.

Bid deposit　A sum of money, a check, or other acceptable cash alternative—irrevocable letter of credit or the contractor's pledge against owned property (property bond) or against personal assets (personal bond)—deposited with the local government by a bidder as a guarantee that the bidder will enter into a contract if awarded. The difference between the accepted bid and the next lowest acceptable bid plus any additional administrative costs is paid to the local government from the amount of the bid deposit.

Bid opening　The process of opening, reading, and tabulating bid responses at a time and place specified in the solicitation in the presence of any interested observer.

Bid security　Any form of guarantee submitted with a bid to ensure that the bidder will enter into a contract if awarded. Synonymous with "bid bond" and "bid deposit."

Bidder list　A list maintained by a local government of the names and addresses of all potential suppliers of various goods and services who have expressed an interest in doing business with the local government, by category of goods or services offered.

Boilerplate　An informal term for standard clauses used in a bid or contract document, often prepared as a preprinted insert. The general terms and conditions and instructions to bidders are sections of a bid document's boilerplate.

Breach of contract　An action by one party to a contract that violates the terms of that contract, thereby permitting the other party to declare the contract in default.

Buyer's market　A market condition in which supply is greater than demand, buyers have greater control over prices and terms of purchase, or prices tend to be low or falling. The opposite condition is called a seller's market.

Calendar day　Every day of the year including Saturdays, Sundays, and holidays.

Change order　A change, principally to a construction contract, executed by the local government alone (unilateral change order) or by the parties to the contract (bilateral change order) amending the contract. The term relates primarily to changes caused by conditions encountered during construction not covered by the specifications and drawings of the project. The term is synonymous with "amendment" and "addendum."

Change order (bilateral)　A change order agreed to by all parties to a contract.

Change order (unilateral)　A written order of the local government directing the contractor to make changes that the contract authorizes the local government to order without the consent of the contractor.

Claim　A demand by one of the parties to a contract for compensation for or relief from demands or actions of the other party.

Collusion　A secret agreement between two or more persons to accomplish a deceitful or unlawful purpose. The term applies to collusive bidding and some violations of antitrust statutes.

Collusive bidding　A violation of antitrust statutes that consists of a response to a solicitation by two or more persons who have secretly agreed to circumvent laws and rules regarding independent and competitive bidding.

Competitive bidding   The offer of firm bids to supply specified services by individuals or firms competing for a contract.

Competitive negotiation   A method for purchasing services whereby qualified individuals or firms are solicited by means of a request for proposals. Negotiations are carried on with selected offerors, and the offeror who submits the best offer is awarded the contract.

Competitive sealed bid   A bid submitted in a sealed envelope to prevent disclosure of its contents before the deadline for the receipt of all bids.

Consulting services   Administrative or technical services to provide advice or assistance to a local government.

Consumer price index (CPI)   A monthly publication of the Bureau of Labor Statistics of the U.S. Department of Labor that shows the average monthly change in the prices of food, clothing, shelter, fuels, medical services, and other commodities and services for the United States as a whole and for some regional areas. Many contract escalator clauses are based on the CPI.

Contract (noun)   In local government service contracting, a written understanding between two or more competent persons under which one person (the contractor) agrees to perform a service and the second person (the local government) agrees to compensate that person for the service performed. Synonymous with "agreement."

Contract (verb)   In legal terms, to make an agreement for a consideration (something of value given with a promise to make the promise binding; one of the essentials of a legal contract).

Contract administration   The process of managing, monitoring, and administering service contracts to ensure that the contractor's performance meets contract requirements.

Contract dispute   A disagreement between the parties to a contract about the provisions of the contract that deals primarily with interpretation of the contract documents.

Contractor   The party in a contract responsible for performing the service defined in the contract.

Cost plus fixed fee contract   A contract under which the contractor is reimbursed for its actual costs for material and labor that are reasonable, allowable, and allocable to the contract plus a fixed sum (the fee or profit) established in the contract. The fee is subject to adjustment only when there are changes to the scope of work.

Cost plus incentive contract   A contract under which the contractor receives additional compensation for keeping the total amount expended for the contract below the total contract cost agreed to in the base contract or for achieving certain prespecified goals during performance of the contract such as increased productivity or fewer customer complaints.

Cost plus percentage of cost contract   A contract under which the contractor is reimbursed for its actual costs for materials and labor plus a fixed percentage of those costs as a fee. This type of contract is generally prohibited for use by local governments except in emergencies.

Cost reimbursement contract   A contract under which the contractor is reimbursed for work performed on the basis of negotiated unit prices for labor or material (including contractor profit) that are identified in the contract document.

Damages   Compensation, usually monetary, for failure of a contractor to meet contract provisions; also compensation for injury to persons or property. Compare with liquidated damages.

Debarment   An action of a local government, usually after a hearing with a contractor, that prohibits the contractor from submitting bids or offers to the local government for a definite or indefinite period of time, usually more than one year.

Default   Failure by either party to a contract to comply with material requirements of the contract.

Default notice   A written or oral notice that informs the contractor that the contractor is in default and states what the contractor must do to correct (cure) the deficiency. Oral notices must be confirmed in writing.

Disadvantaged business   Small businesses that are owned or controlled by minorities, physically handicapped individuals, or members of other groups who have been deprived of the opportunity to develop and maintain a competitive position in the economy because of their social or handicapped status.

Dispute   A disagreement between the parties to a contract about the provisions of the contract resolved through preestablished administrative procedures; if an acceptable administrative resolution is not achieved, the dispute is resolved through legal action.

Escalator clause   A clause that allows the contract price to be periodically adjusted up or down in direct relationship to an objective market indicator identified in the solicitation and contract (e.g., Consumer Price Index). Synonymous with "price adjustment clause."

Evaluation criteria   Factors relating to management capability, technical capability, method of meeting performance requirements, price, and other material considerations used to select the most qualified offerors.

Fee   A fixed or variable amount of money to be paid to a contractor as profit, as in a cost plus fixed fee contact; compensation for services rendered.

Fidelity bond   A form of insurance that secures an employer up to the amount stated in the bond for losses caused by dishonest acts of its employees.

Fixed price contract   A contract under which the contractor is reimbursed at a fixed price for services provided regardless of the costs incurred by the contractor.

Fixed price with escalator contract   A contract under which the contractor is reimbursed at a fixed price for all provided services that allows for periodic price increases or decreases at one or more stated intervals during the contract term (usually annually). The amount of increase or decrease is based on the movement of an independent price index (the escalator) for goods, service, or labor.

Force majeure   A French term that refers to unexpected or uncontrollable events, including those caused by nature, that can interrupt performance of the contract; these events are not attributable to contractor negligence and excuse the contractor from performance during the events and under certain conditions caused by them.

General terms and conditions   The section of a solicitation that contains clauses that deal primarily with the contractual obligations of the parties to a contract; a part of the boilerplate of a bid or contract document.

Gross negligence   Flagrant failure to take reasonable or prudent actions or precautions; the want of even slight care.

Hold harmless clause   A clause that requires the contractor to assume liability for damages resulting from an action taken by the contractor and absolves the local government from any responsibility for the consequences of the action. Synonymous with "save harmless clause."

Incentive contract   Any contract, whether payment to the contractor is based on reimbursing the contractor for costs incurred or on a fixed price for the work, that includes a means to reward the contractor for reaching certain prespecified goals to reduce costs, reach a level of performance above the level contracted for, or otherwise produce results beneficial to the local government that exceed contract requirements.

Independent contractor   A supplier of services who must exercise independent judgment as to the means used to achieve results. The supplier must be free from the control or orders of others and responsible for the results obtained.

Indirect costs   Costs that do not relate directly to performance, including employee benefits, equipment maintenance, administrative costs, or other general overhead costs incurred by the contractor in the normal course of business; the costs incurred by a local government that are not directly related to service delivery such as employee benefits, interdepartmental charges, and insurance.

Ineligible bidder A bidder who does not meet the stated qualifications for submitting a bid response or who has been suspended or debarred.

Informalities and irregularities Minor defects or variations of a bid from the exact requirements of the solicitation that do not affect the price, quality, quantity, or delivery schedule of the services being procured.

Instructions to bidders The section of a solicitation that contains clauses that provide primarily information on bid opening, general contractor qualifications, and conditions for bid submission as well as information relating to the process of preparing and submitting bids. These clauses are seldom related directly to the scope of the services to be performed under the contract and are usually omitted from the final contract document. Part of the boilerplate of a bid document.

Intergovernmental contract An agreement in which one government contracts with another for the delivery of a service.

Invitation for bids (IFB) and **invitation to bid (ITB)** Documents, attached or incorporated by reference in the bid document, used to solicit competitive sealed bids, which request from bidders firm fixed prices that are not negotiable. The terms "competitive bid" and "bid" are used interchangeably. The response is called a bid or bid response. In general use, "invitation for bids (IFB)," "invitation to bid (ITB)," and "competitive bid" apply both to the bid document and the method used for a nonnegotiable sealed bid purchase.

Joint venture A joint venture exists when two or more persons combine their resources to submit a single joint bid. The relationship between the persons is created solely to respond to a given solicitation and makes the persons partners for the purposes of the contract.

Letters of interest Similar to "request for qualifications" used to identify qualified firms.

Lien The right one person has to take or keep possession of or to control the property of another for the purpose of satisfying a debt.

Liquidated damages A sum of money agreed by the parties to a contract to be paid as damages by the party who breaches all or part of the contract—usually the contractor—to the other party—usually the local government. The amount may be a percentage of a payment due the contractor or a fixed amount of money to be paid by the contractor for every day that the breach is in effect.

List price The price published in a catalogue or otherwise available at which a seller offers an item for sale.

Lowest responsible bidder A responsive bidder whose bid is lower than those received from other bidders and whose reputation, past performance, and business and financial capabilities have been determined by the local government to satisfy the requirements of a contract.

Lump sum A single price for a group of items or units of service in place of or in addition to unit prices for each. A lot price; an aggregate price.

Mandatory Said of a contract condition or provision that cannot be waived.

Modification A unilateral or bilateral change or alteration to a bid or contract document. The term is synonymous with "addendum," "amendment," and "change order."

Negligence Under a given set of circumstances, failing to do what a reasonable and prudent person would do or doing what a reasonable and prudent person would not do.

Negotiation The interaction between a buyer and seller to achieve an agreement acceptable to both.

Nonresponsive bid A bid that does not conform to the essential requirements of the solicitation.

Offer (noun) The signed document of an offeror submitted in response to a request for proposals. Synonymous with "proposal."

Offer (verb) To submit a response (an offer) to a request for proposals. By submitting a response, one person (the contractor) gives another person (the local government) the legal power to create a contract with the responding contractor in accordance with the response.

Offeror A person making an offer.

Optimization Using lessons learned from competing with the private sector and applying them to similar service areas in order to gain increased internal efficiencies.

Payment bond Insurance issued by an insurance company to a local government on behalf of its client, the bidder, guaranteeing payment of all claimants and subcontractors who have and fulfill contracts to supply labor or materials to the bidder if the bidder is awarded the contract.

Performance bond Insurance issued by an insurance company to a local government on behalf of its client, the bidder, as a guarantee that the bidder will complete the contract to the satisfaction of the local government. It protects the local government from loss due to the bidder's inability or refusal to complete the contract as agreed.

Performance specification A purchase description that emphasizes the end results desired and the performance characteristics sought in a product or service rather than the specific details of how the product will be manufactured or the service delivered; a functional description of the product or service.

Person In business and contract law, any individual or group of individuals or businesses or an organization.

Personal services Services provided by individual independent contractors rather than by a group of individuals, a business, or an organization. These providers—who include, for example, translators, technical editors, and physicians—provide specialized skills or expertise not available within the local government.

Pre-bid or preproposal conference A meeting scheduled prior to the opening of bids, at which attendance by potential bidders may be optional or mandatory, to clarify the solicitation and respond to prospective bidders' inquiries.

Pre-performance conference A meeting between the contractor and the local government convened to review the responsibilities and expectations of the contractor and the local government under the contract.

Prequalification A procedure that limits consideration of bids or proposals to those from vendors who have been evaluated as qualified to perform the service being solicited.

Price adjustment clause Synonymous with "escalator clause."

Professional services The definition of professional services varies among local governments. They are generally defined as services performed by an independent contractor within the scope of practice of accounting, architecture, law, medicine, or engineering.

Prompt payment The timely payment of a correct invoice in accordance with contract payment terms. Usually associated with a discount whereby the local government deducts a fixed percentage specified in the contract documents from the payment if the local government processes the payment within a specified number of days after receipt of a correct invoice.

Proposal An executed offer submitted by an offeror in response to a request for proposals and intended to be used as a basis for negotiations for a contract.

Protest A complaint about an action or decision by the local government regarding the bidding process that a bidder submits with the intention of obtaining remedial action. Not to be confused with "dispute," which refers to a protest of a contract decision by the local government, not a bidding decision. Protests predominantly cover decisions of the local government dealing with the procurement process, the solicitation requirements, and the award of the contract.

Public-private competition A formal service procurement method in which public employees compete with the private for-profit and nonprofit sectors to provide services. Public-private competition is also known as managed competition and in-house bidding.

Public private partnership, or P³   A contractual relationship that is developed between the government and the private sector contractor for major infrastructures projects. In this concept the contractor will design, build, and in some cases operate and/or maintain a major facility for a period of time, after which the facility reverts back to the local government. In other cases the contractor designs and builds the facility, but operation and maintenance is controlled by the local government.

Public record   Information contained in government files that are available for public inspection.

Qualified bidder   A responsive bidder that meets established standards of responsibility for the provision of a specified service, as determined by the local government.

Quality assurance   A contract administration program initiated by the local government to verify that the contractor's delivery of services meets the requirements of the contract.

Quality control   A plan initiated by a contractor to ensure that a service is delivered satisfactorily and an acceptable level of performance is maintained.

Request for information (RFI)   The document used to obtain reactions from contractors before a bid document is issued. Price is not requested. The RFI is used to obtain comments from contractors on a draft specification or scope of work or to solicit information on industry standards and practices and service delivery methods.

Request for proposals (RFP)   The document used to solicit proposals from contractors (offerors). The RFP provides for negotiation of all terms of the proposal before award, including price. The proposal may or may not include an initial price or estimate of cost. The RFP is used with the competitive negotiation bidding method (sometimes called the competitive sealed proposal bidding method). In general use, RFP applies both to the document and the method used for a negotiated purchase.

Request for qualifications (RFQ)   The document used to obtain a statement of qualifications from bidders before the final bid document is issued. After eliminating respondents who do not meet the criteria of the RFQ, the local government issues the bid document to those certified as qualified.

Requirements contract   An indefinite quantity contract under which a local government is obligated to order and a contractor is obligated to supply only the specified services actually required by the local government during the contract term.

Responsible bidder or offeror   A person who has the capability in all respects to perform the contract requirements fully and the moral and business integrity and reliability to assure good faith performance.

Responsive bidder or offeror   A person who has submitted a bid that conforms in all material respects to the invitation for bids or request for proposals.

Restrictive specification   A specification that unnecessarily limits competition by precluding from bidding those capable of fulfilling the intent of a contract.

Retention   The withholding of part of the payment due to a contractor by the local government until final acceptance of the work. The amount to be retained as well as the period of retention is stipulated in the contract.

Rules and regulations   Written policies that have the effect of law that are promulgated by a government to interpret or make a law specific and that contain procedures for implementation consistent with their legislative intent.

Scope of work   A description of services to be purchased as opposed to specification, which is a description of goods. The scope of work is a description of the services to be delivered and the conditions of delivery. Synonymous with "SOW," "statement of work," and "scope of services." In federal government procurement, the scope of work is referred to as "performance work standard."

Sealed bid A response to a solicitation that has been submitted in a sealed envelope to prevent its contents from being revealed before the time and date set for the receipt of responses.

Seller's market A market condition in which demand is greater than supply, sellers have greater control over prices and terms of sale, and prices tend to be high or rising. A market condition in which there are more buyers for a service than there are sellers for the goods or services to be purchased. The opposite condition is called a buyers' market.

Service The furnishing of labor, time, or effort by a contractor.

Service contract A contract that calls for a contractor's labor, time, and effort to perform a service in which the provision of goods is incidental to the main purpose.

Sole source procurement An award for a service to the only known provider of the service because of the unique nature of the requirements.

Solicitation Notification of contractors that the local government is receiving bids or proposals for provision of goods or services. Solicitation is often used interchangeably with "specification," "bid document," "invitation for bid," and "request for proposals" to refer to the complete set of documents sent to a prospective bidder or offeror.

Special provisions Clauses pertaining to a contract that are unique to the service being obtained, which may supplement or (in some cases) supersede one or more of the general terms and conditions that pertain to the same contract. Synonymous with "special terms and conditions."

Specification A description of goods as opposed to a description of services. The term is sometimes used to refer to a complete bid document.

Start-up conference Synonymous with "pre-performance conference."

Subcontractor Any person undertaking part of the work of a contract under the control of the principal contractor.

Surety A pledge or guarantee by an insurance company to a local government on behalf of its client (the bidder) against loss or damage because of the default of the client in performance of its obligations under a bid or contract.

Suspension An action of a local government, which usually does not require a hearing with the contractor, that prohibits a contractor from submitting bids or offers to the local government for a definite or indefinite period of time, usually one year or less. Causes for suspension include a history of poor performance with the local government, lack of business integrity, and past violation of the terms of a contract. Compare with "debarment."

Tabulation of bids A written record of bidders and highlights of their bids, including prices, made for the purpose of recording the names of all bidders and comparing their responses.

Technical proposal An unpriced proposal in response to a solicitation. The proposal describes in detail what a vendor proposes to furnish and the method of delivery.

Termination for convenience Cancellation, at the local government's discretion, of a contract in whole or in part; permitted only if the contract contains a clause permitting such an action.

Termination for default The cancellation, in whole or in part, by the local government of a contract because of the contractor's failure to perform satisfactorily; the cancellation of a contract by a contractor because of the local government's failure to perform in accordance with the contract documents.

Time and materials contract A contract for the provision of services under which the local government pays the contractor for direct labor at fixed hourly rates that include benefits, payroll taxes, overhead, and contractor profit and for the cost of materials and equipment used in the performance of the contract.

Trade standard An understanding between buyer and seller about the meanings of certain words, abbreviations, phrases, and characteristics of a given item or service that are established by agreement or by general usage.

Index

Service Contracting: A Local Government Guide
Second Edition

Text Type
Interstate, Mrs Eaves, ITC Slimbach

Composition
Circle Graphics
Columbia, Maryland

Printing and binding
United Book Press, Inc.
Baltimore, Maryland

Design
Charles E. Mountain
ICMA, Washington, D.C.